Communities of Practice presents a theory of learning that starts with this assumption: engagement in social practice is the fundamental process by which we learn and so become who we are. The primary unit of analysis is neither the individual nor social institutions but rather the informal "communities of practice" that people form as they pursue shared enterprises over time. In order to give a social account of learning, the theory explores in a systematic way the intersection of issues of community, social practice, meaning, and identity. The result is a broad conceptual framework for thinking about learning as a process of social participation. This ambitious but thoroughly accessible framework has relevance for the practitioner as well as the theoretician, and is presented with all the breadth, depth, and rigor necessary to address such a complex and yet profoundly human topic.

Communities of practice

LEARNING IN DOING:
SOCIAL, COGNITIVE, AND COMPUTATIONAL PERSPECTIVES

General Editors
ROY PEA, *SRI International, Center for Technology in Learning*
JOHN SEELY BROWN, *Xerox Palo Alto Research Center*
JAN HAWKINS, *Center for Children and Technology, New York*

Communities of practice
Learning, meaning, and identity

ETIENNE WENGER
Institute for Research on Learning

CAMBRIDGE
UNIVERSITY PRESS

PUBLISHED BY THE PRESS SYNDICATE OF THE UNIVERSITY OF CAMBRIDGE
The Pitt Building, Trumpington Street, Cambridge, United Kingdom

CAMBRIDGE UNIVERSITY PRESS
The Edinburgh Building, Cambridge CB2 2RU, UK   http://www.cup.cam.ac.uk
40 West 20th Street, New York, NY 10011-4211, USA   http://www.cup.org
10 Stamford Road, Oakleigh, Melbourne 3166, Australia

First published 1998
Reprinted 1999
First paperback edition 1999

Printed in the United States of America

Typeset in Ehrhardt

A catalogue record for this book is available from the British Library

Library of Congress Cataloguing-in-Publication Data is available

ISBN 0 521 43017 8 hardback
ISBN 0 521 66363 6 paperback

To Paula, Jad, Sheena, and Kehan

Contents

Series foreword

This series for Cambridge University Press is becoming widely known as an international forum for studies of situated learning and cognition.

Innovative contributions are being made by anthropology, by cognitive, developmental, and cultural psychology, by computer science, by education, and by social theory. These contributions are providing the basis for new ways of understanding the social, historical, and contextual nature of the learning, thinking, and practice that emerges from human activity. The empirical settings of these research inquiries range from the classroom to the workplace, to the high technology office, and to learning in the streets and in other communities of practice.

The situated nature of learning and remembering through activity is a central fact. It may appear obvious that human minds develop in social situations and extend their sphere of activity and communicative competencies. But cognitive theories of knowledge representation and learning alone have not provided sufficient insight into these relationships.

This series was born of the conviction that new and exciting interdisciplinary syntheses are underway as scholars and practitioners from diverse fields seek to develop theory and empirical investigations adequate for characterizing the complex relations of social and mental life, and for understanding successful learning wherever it occurs. The series invites contributions that advance our understanding of these seminal issues.

Roy Pea
John Seely Brown
Jan Hawkins

Acknowledgments

A while ago, I asked my colleague Jean Lave in exactly which publication she had first introduced the term *community of practice*. We had used the term in a book we wrote together, but I wanted to give her proper credit for originating it. To my surprise, she replied: "I thought you were the one who came up with it." Now, whatever she says, I still believe that she was the one. But perhaps there are more important points to make about this anecdote than trying to settle the issue.

The first point is about Jean. Her response is typical of the kind of intellectual generosity that makes her such an outstanding teacher and colleague. It is the gift of great teachers to invite such participation that what they are teaching becomes truly your own. So even if her memory of events were more precise than mine in a technical sense, my version would still reflect a true reality.

The second point is about this book. Regardless of who actually coined the phrase that became its title, it was our collaboration that brought the topic into focus and initiated the inquiry that I am pursuing here. In this sense, this book owes Jean its very existence. Even though she should not be held accountable for everything I say, the spirit of our collaboration clearly lives on in these pages.

The third point is about communities and acknowledgments. Dissecting a creation in order to assign individual credit can easily become counterproductive. To celebrate our efforts and our achievements, we need not become blind to the social fabric that makes them possible. We need not deny each other the recognition of our mutual interdependence. At the very least, we can appreciate those close connections, conversations, and communities in which our participation is obvious, and this is what acknowledgments are about. But this recognition must be an opening, not a closing. If, as complexity theory would have it, a butterfly flapping its wings can trigger monsoons, then how are we to know which butterflies and which flappings of wings to include in the reach of our recognition, and which to exclude?

The idea is not to belittle individual effort or deny the reality of authorship. To produce a book like this one, for instance, is hard work, and I did put my heart in it. I know all too well the daunting loneliness of the encounter between writer and writing. But loneliness is not the right word, because the true threat of loneliness lies in accounting and creating separations and boundaries, not in our personal efforts. Writing is always the production of a community of sorts, and the kind of chicken-and-egg ambiguity of this statement is part of the point: it is not easy to assess whether a book creates a community or the other way around. In my case especially, this book is clearly part of an emerging community. In so many discussions of the concepts I was articulating, I had the humbling yet exhilarating experience that I was giving expression and form to what people already knew, transforming their and my understanding in the process.

It is through the Institute for Research on Learning that I became a participant in the emerging community to which this book is addressed, and it was there − both institutionally and intellectually − that I pursued my inquiry. Few institutions I know would have had the perseverance to see such a project through and the qualities to make it possible. For their steady support I thank the founders, the directors, my fellow researchers and members of the staff, as well as the various partners of IRL with whom I had a chance to work. Their interest, confidence, and understanding have been an essential contribution to this book.

Many people have looked at drafts of my manuscript and offered a range of comments and suggestions, individually or in the context of group discussions. While I cannot possibly thank everyone by name here, I do at least want to acknowledge the contributions of the following people: Bryan Adkins, Thomas Binder, Terry Carter, Debra Cash, Melissa Cefkin, Lone Dirckinck-Holmfeld, Meg Graham, Jim Greeno, Rogers Hall, Peter Henschel, Peter Hillen, Manuel Imaz, Maryalice Jordan-Mash, Tony Kortens, David Little, Brook Manville, Norma Mendoza-Denton, Langdon Morris, Susan Newman, Klaus Nielsen, Geoff Nunberg, John O'Neill, Martin Packer, George Pòr, Kevin Quinlan, George Roth, Williams Rifkin, Judy Rodgers, Craig Rodine, Bill Snyder, Estee Solomon-Gray, Lindy Sullivan, Susan Stucky, Kären Wieckert, and Helga Wild. I also want to thank my editors, Julia Hough and Matt Darnell, for their help and patience.

I owe special thanks to my colleague Penelope Eckert. Her reliable friendship through all this time has made my task considerably more enjoyable, and her intellectual companionship is reflected in this book much more deeply than the few references to her work would suggest. For his part, John Seely Brown has been continuously supportive of my inquiry for many years and in many ways, in particular by using his perspicacity and influence to persuade many people (including me at times) of the importance of this work. Last but not least, Paul Duguid was a very helpful reader of earlier drafts and actually took time away from his own writing projects to do an in-depth editorial review of my first complete draft. His detailed and insightful critique has been invaluable, helping me add much needed clarity and coherence to both the content and the form of the final text.

I gratefully acknowledge the sustained financial support of the Xerox Foundation, without which this project would have simply been impossible. I received additional support from a few corporations: AMR, DEC, Nynex, and Xerox. I thank the individuals whose sponsorship has made this corporate support possible: Jon Abeles, Paul Allaire, Robert Bauer, John Seely Brown, Jim Euchner, David Kearns, Mark Maletz, John McDermott, and Ed Thomas.

I also thank all the employees of Alinsu who have made my fieldwork possible and whose identity I must keep to myself. In particular, I thank the claims processors for opening up their community to my unconventional participation.

I am so indebted to my wife, Paula, and my children, Jad and Sheena (and now Kehan), that I am not quite sure whether to thank them or to apologize to them. It is a miracle, for sure, that they are still as interested as they are in reading books. Whether it is by thanks or apologies that I acknowledge the hardships they endured through the writing of this book, my real debt to them is one of love – transmuting the demands of life into the chance to know, through the resilient closeness of our beings, the sweet pain of too much love. This precious learning does, I think, transpire in subtle ways through these pages.

Prologue
Contexts

Introduction
A social theory of learning

Our institutions, to the extent that they address issues of learning explicitly, are largely based on the assumption that learning is an individual process, that it has a beginning and an end, that it is best separated from the rest of our activities, and that it is the result of teaching. Hence we arrange classrooms where students – free from the distractions of their participation in the outside world – can pay attention to a teacher or focus on exercises. We design computer-based training programs that walk students through individualized sessions covering reams of information and drill practice. To assess learning we use tests with which students struggle in one-on-one combat, where knowledge must be demonstrated out of context, and where collaborating is considered cheating. As a result, much of our institutionalized teaching and training is perceived by would-be learners as irrelevant, and most of us come out of this treatment feeling that learning is boring and arduous, and that we are not really cut out for it.

So, what if we adopted a different perspective, one that placed learning in the context of our lived experience of participation in the world? What if we assumed that learning is as much a part of our human nature as eating or sleeping, that it is both life-sustaining and inevitable, and that – given a chance – we are quite good at it? And what if, in addition, we assumed that learning is, in its essence, a fundamentally social phenomenon, reflecting our own deeply social nature as human beings capable of knowing? What kind of understanding would such a perspective yield on how learning takes place and on what is required to support it? In this book, I will try to develop such a perspective.

A conceptual perspective: theory and practice

There are many different kinds of learning theory. Each emphasizes different aspects of learning, and each is therefore useful for

3

different purposes. To some extent these differences in emphasis reflect a deliberate focus on a slice of the multidimensional problem of learning, and to some extent they reflect more fundamental differences in assumptions about the nature of knowledge, knowing, and knowers, and consequently about what matters in learning. (For those who are interested, the first note lists a number of such theories with a brief description of their focus.[1])

The kind of social theory of learning I propose is not a replacement for other theories of learning that address different aspects of the problem. But it does have its own set of assumptions and its own focus. Within this context, it does constitute a coherent level of analysis; it does yield a conceptual framework from which to derive a consistent set of general principles and recommendations for understanding and enabling learning.

My assumptions as to what matters about learning and as to the nature of knowledge, knowing, and knowers can be succinctly summarized as follows. I start with four premises.

1) We are social beings. Far from being trivially true, this fact is a central aspect of learning.

2) Knowledge is a matter of competence with respect to valued enterprises – such as singing in tune, discovering scientific facts, fixing machines, writing poetry, being convivial, growing up as a boy or a girl, and so forth.

3) Knowing is a matter of participating in the pursuit of such enterprises, that is, of active engagement in the world.

4) Meaning – our ability to experience the world and our engagement with it as meaningful – is ultimately what learning is to produce.

As a reflection of these assumptions, the primary focus of this theory is on learning as social participation. Participation here refers not just to local events of engagement in certain activities with certain people, but to a more encompassing process of being active participants in the *practices* of social communities and constructing *identities* in relation to these communities. Participating in a playground clique or in a work team, for instance, is both a kind of action and a form of belonging. Such participation shapes not only what we do, but also who we are and how we interpret what we do.

A social theory of learning must therefore integrate the components necessary to characterize social participation as a process of learning

Figure 0.1. Components of a social theory of learning: an initial inventory.

and of knowing. These components, shown in Figure 0.1, include the following.

1) *Meaning:* a way of talking about our (changing) ability – individually and collectively – to experience our life and the world as meaningful.

2) *Practice:* a way of talking about the shared historical and social resources, frameworks, and perspectives that can sustain mutual engagement in action.

3) *Community:* a way of talking about the social configurations in which our enterprises are defined as worth pursuing and our participation is recognizable as competence.

4) *Identity:* a way of talking about how learning changes who we are and creates personal histories of becoming in the context of our communities.

Clearly, these elements are deeply interconnected and mutually defining. In fact, looking at Figure 0.1, you could switch any of the four peripheral components with learning, place it in the center as the primary focus, and the figure would still make sense.

Therefore, when I use the concept of "community of practice" in the title of this book, I really use it as a point of entry into a broader conceptual framework of which it is a constitutive element. The analytical power of the concept lies precisely in that it integrates the components of Figure 0.1 while referring to a familiar experience.

Communities of practice are everywhere

We all belong to communities of practice. At home, at work, at school, in our hobbies – we belong to several communities of practice at any given time. And the communities of practice to which we belong change over the course of our lives. In fact, communities of practice are everywhere.

Families struggle to establish an habitable way of life. They develop their own practices, routines, rituals, artifacts, symbols, conventions, stories, and histories. Family members hate each other and they love each other; they agree and they disagree. They do what it takes to keep going. Even when families fall apart, members create ways of dealing with each other. Surviving together is an important enterprise, whether surviving consists in the search for food and shelter or in the quest for a viable identity.

Workers organize their lives with their immediate colleagues and customers to get their jobs done. In doing so, they develop or preserve a sense of themselves they can live with, have some fun, and fulfill the requirements of their employers and clients. No matter what their official job description may be, they create a practice to do what needs to be done. Although workers may be contractually employed by a large institution, in day-to-day practice they work with – and, in a sense, for – a much smaller set of people and communities.

Students go to school and, as they come together to deal in their own fashion with the agenda of the imposing institution and the unsettling mysteries of youth, communities of practice sprout everywhere – in the classroom as well as on the playground, officially or in the cracks. And in spite of curriculum, discipline, and exhortation, the learning that is most personally transformative turns out to be the learning that involves membership in these communities of practice.

In garages, bands rehearse the same songs for yet another wedding gig. In attics, ham radio enthusiasts become part of worldwide clusters of communicators. In the back rooms of churches, recovering alcoholics go to their weekly meetings to find the courage to remain sober. In laboratories, scientists correspond with colleagues, near and far, in order to advance their inquiries. Across a worldwide web of computers, people congregate in virtual spaces and develop shared ways of pursuing their common interests. In offices, computer users count on each other to cope with the intricacies of obscure systems. In neighborhoods, youths gang together to configure their life on the street and their sense of themselves.

Communities of practice are an integral part of our daily lives. They are so informal and so pervasive that they rarely come into explicit focus, but for the same reasons they are also quite familiar. Although the term may be new, the experience is not. Most communities of practice do not have a name and do not issue membership cards. Yet, if we care to consider our own life from that perspective for a moment, we can all construct a fairly good picture of the communities of practice we belong to now, those we belonged to in the past, and those we would like to belong to in the future. We also have a fairly good idea of who belongs to our communities of practice and why, even though membership is rarely made explicit on a roster or a checklist of qualifying criteria. Furthermore, we can probably distinguish a few communities of practice in which we are core members from a larger number of communities in which we have a more peripheral kind of membership.

In all these ways, the concept of community of practice is not unfamiliar. By exploring it more systematically in this book, I mean only to sharpen it, to make it more useful as a thinking tool. Toward this end, its familiarity will serve me well. Articulating a familiar phenomenon is a chance to push our intuitions: to deepen and expand them, to examine and rethink them. The perspective that results is not foreign, yet it can shed new light on our world. In this sense, the concept of community of practice is neither new nor old. It has both the eye-opening character of novelty and the forgotten familiarity of obviousness – but perhaps that is the mark of our most useful insights.

Rethinking learning

As I will argue in more detail throughout this book, placing the focus on participation has broad implications for what it takes to understand and support learning.

- For *individuals*, it means that learning is an issue of engaging in and contributing to the practices of their communities.
- For *communities*, it means that learning is an issue of refining their practice and ensuring new generations of members.

• For *organizations*, it means that learning is an issue of sustaining the interconnected communities of practice through which an organization knows what it knows and thus becomes effective and valuable as an organization.

Learning in this sense is not a separate activity. It is not something we do when we do nothing else or stop doing when we do something else. There are times in our lives when learning is intensified: when situations shake our sense of familiarity, when we are challenged beyond our ability to respond, when we wish to engage in new practices and seek to join new communities. There are also times when society explicitly places us in situations where the issue of learning becomes problematic and requires our focus: we attend classes, memorize, take exams, and receive a diploma. And there are times when learning gels: an infant utters a first word, we have a sudden insight when someone's remark provides a missing link, we are finally recognized as a full member of a community. But situations that bring learning into focus are not necessarily those in which we learn most, or most deeply. The events of learning we can point to are perhaps more like volcanic eruptions whose fiery bursts reveal for one dramatic moment the ongoing labor of the earth. Learning is something we can assume – whether we see it or not, whether we like the way it goes or not, whether what we are learning is to repeat the past or to shake it off. Even failing to learn what is expected in a given situation usually involves learning something else instead.

For many of us, the concept of learning immediately conjures up images of classrooms, training sessions, teachers, textbooks, homework, and exercises. Yet in our experience, learning is an integral part of our everyday lives. It is part of our participation in our communities and organizations. The problem is not that we do not know this, but rather that we do not have very systematic ways of talking about this familiar experience. Even though the topic of this book covers mostly things that everybody knows in some ways, having a systematic vocabulary to talk about it does make a difference. An adequate vocabulary is important because the concepts we use to make sense of the world direct both our perception and our actions. We pay attention to what we expect to see, we hear what we can place in our understanding, and we act according to our world views.

Although learning can be assumed to take place, modern societies have come to see it as a topic of concern – in all sorts of ways and for a host of different reasons. We develop national curriculums, ambitious corporate training programs, complex schooling systems. We wish to cause learning, to take charge of it, direct it, accelerate it, demand it, or even simply stop getting in the way of it. In any case, we want to do something about it. Therefore, our perspectives on learning matter: what we think about learning influences where we recognize learning, as well as what we do when we decide that we must do something about it – as individuals, as communities, and as organizations.

If we proceed without reflecting on our fundamental assumptions about the nature of learning, we run an increasing risk that our conceptions will have misleading ramifications. In a world that is changing and becoming more complexly interconnected at an accelerating pace, concerns about learning are certainly justified. But perhaps more than learning itself, it is our *conception* of learning that needs urgent attention when we choose to meddle with it on the scale on which we do today. Indeed, the more we concern ourselves with any kind of design, the more profound are the effects of our discourses on the topic we want to address. The farther you aim, the more an initial error matters. As we become more ambitious in attempts to organize our lives and our environment, the implications of our perspectives, theories, and beliefs extend further. As we take more responsibility for our future on larger and larger scales, it becomes more imperative that we reflect on the perspectives that inform our enterprises. A key implication of our attempts to organize learning is that we must become reflective with regard to our own discourses of learning and to their effects on the ways we design for learning. By proposing a framework that considers learning in social terms, I hope to contribute to this urgent need for reflection and rethinking.

The practicality of theory

A perspective is not a recipe; it does not tell you just what to do. Rather, it acts as a guide about what to pay attention to, what difficulties to expect, and how to approach problems.

- If we believe, for instance, that knowledge consists of pieces of information explicitly stored in the brain, then it makes sense to package this information in well-designed units, to assemble prospective recipients of this information in a classroom where they are perfectly still and isolated from any distraction, and to deliver this information to them as succinctly and articulately as possible. From that perspective, what has come to stand for the epitome of a learning event makes sense: a teacher lecturing a class, whether in a school, in a corporate training center, or in the back room of a library.

But if we believe that information stored in explicit ways is only a small part of knowing, and that knowing involves primarily active participation in social communities, then the traditional format does not look so productive. What does look promising are inventive ways of engaging students in meaningful practices, of providing access to resources that enhance their participation, of opening their horizons so they can put themselves on learning trajectories they can identify with, and of involving them in actions, discussions, and reflections that make a difference to the communities that they value.

• Similarly, if we believe that productive people in organizations are the diligent implementors of organizational processes and that the key to organizational performance is therefore the definition of increasingly more efficient and detailed processes by which people's actions are prescribed, then it makes sense to engineer and re-engineer these processes in abstract ways and then roll them out for implementation.

But if we believe that people in organizations contribute to organizational goals by participating inventively in practices that can never be fully captured by institutionalized processes, then we will minimize prescription, suspecting that too much of it discourages the very inventiveness that makes practices effective. We will have to make sure that our organizations are contexts within which the communities that develop these practices may prosper. We will have to value the work of community building and make sure that participants have access to the resources necessary to learn what they need to learn in order to take actions and make decisions that fully engage their own knowledgeability.

If all this seems like common sense, then we must ask ourselves why our institutions so often seem, not merely to fail to bring about these outcomes, but to work against them with a relentless zeal. Of course, some of the blame can justifiably be attributed to conflicts of interest, power struggles, and even human wickedness. But that is too simple an answer, and unnecessarily pessimistic. We must also remember that our institutions are designs and that our designs are hostage to our understanding, perspectives, and theories. In this sense, our theories are very practical because they frame not just the ways we act, but also – and perhaps most importantly when design involves social systems – the ways we justify our actions to ourselves and to each other. In an institutional context, it is difficult to act without justifying your actions in the discourse of the institution.

A social theory of learning is therefore not exclusively an academic enterprise. While its perspective can indeed inform our academic investigations, it is also relevant to our daily actions, our policies, and the technical, organizational, and educational systems we design. A new conceptual framework for thinking about learning is thus of value not only to theorists but to all of us – teachers, students, parents, youths, spouses, health practitioners, patients, managers, workers, policy makers, citizens – who in one way or another must take steps to foster learning (our own and that of others) in our relationships, our communities, and our organizations. In this spirit, this book is written with both the theoretician and the practitioner in mind.

Intellectual context

Because I am trying to serve multiple audiences, I will endeavor to propose a synthetic perspective rather than to enter deeply into the arguments, technicalities, and controversies of any one academic community. In fact, whenever I make references to the literature covering such debates, I will do so in the notes. It is still useful, however, to spend a few paragraphs outlining the intellectual traditions that have influenced my thinking, whose influence I have tried to weave together, and to which I hope this work will make some contributions. If you are not interested, skipping this section will not impair your ability to follow my argument.

In an earlier book, anthropologist Jean Lave and I tried to distill – from a number of ethnographic studies of apprenticeship – what such studies might contribute to a general theory of learning. Our purpose was to articulate what it was about apprenticeship that seemed so compelling as a learning process. Toward this end, we used the concept of *legitimate peripheral participation* to characterize learning. We wanted to broaden the traditional connotations of the concept of apprenticeship – from a master/student or mentor/mentee relationship to one of changing participation and identity transformation in a community of practice. The concepts of identity and community of practice were thus

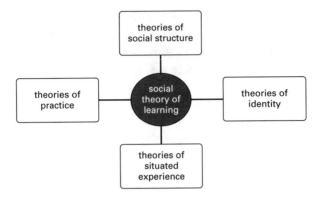

Figure 0.2. Two main axes of relevant traditions.

important to our argument, but they were not given the spotlight and were left largely unanalyzed.[2] In this book I have given these concepts center stage, explored them in detail, and used them as the main entry points into a social theory of learning.

Such a theory of learning is relevant to a number of disciplines, including anthropology, sociology, cognitive and social psychology, philosophy, and organizational and educational theory and practice. But the main tradition to which I think this work belongs – in terms of both influences and contributions – is social theory, a somewhat ill-defined field of conceptual inquiry at the intersection of philosophy, the social sciences, and the humanities.[3] In this context, I see a social theory of learning as being located at the intersection of intellectual traditions along two main axes, as illustrated in Figure 0.2. (In the notes I list, for each of the categories, some of the theories whose influence is reflected in my own work.)

In the tradition of social theory, the vertical axis is a central one. It reflects a tension between theories that give primacy to social structure and those that give primacy to action. A large body of work deals with clashes between these perspectives and attempts to bring them together.

• Theories of *social structure* give primacy mostly to institutions, norms, and rules. They emphasize cultural systems, discourses, and history. They seek underlying explanatory structures that account for social patterns and tend to view action as a mere realization of these structures in specific circumstances. The most extreme of them deny agency or knowledgeability to individual actors.[4]

- Theories of *situated experience* give primacy to the dynamics of everyday existence, improvisation, coordination, and interactional choreography. They emphasize agency and intentions. They mostly address the interactive relations of people with their environment. They focus on the experience and the local construction of individual or interpersonal events such as activities and conversations. The most extreme of them ignore structure writ large altogether.[5]

Learning as participation is certainly caught in the middle. It takes place through our engagement in actions and interactions, but it embeds this engagement in culture and history. Through these local actions and interactions, learning reproduces and transforms the social structure in which it takes place.

The horizontal axis – with which this book is most directly concerned – is set against the backdrop of the vertical one. It provides a set of midlevel categories that mediate between the poles of the vertical axis. Practice and identity constitute forms of social and historical continuity and discontinuity that are neither as broad as sociohistorical structure on a grand scale nor as fleeting as the experience, action, and interaction of the moment.

- Theories of *social practice* address the production and reproduction of specific ways of engaging with the world. They are concerned with everyday activity and real-life settings, but with an emphasis on the social systems of shared resources by which groups organize and coordinate their activities, mutual relationships, and interpretations of the world.[6]
- Theories of *identity* are concerned with the social formation of the person, the cultural interpretation of the body, and the creation and use of markers of membership such as rites of passage and social categories. They address issues of gender, class, ethnicity, age, and other forms of categorization, association, and differentiation in an attempt to understand the person as formed through complex relations of mutual constitution between individuals and groups.[7]

Here again, learning is caught in the middle. It is the vehicle for the evolution of practices and the inclusion of newcomers while also (and through the same process) the vehicle for the development and transformation of identities.

These two axes set the main backdrop for my theory, but it is worth refining the picture one step further with another set of intermediary

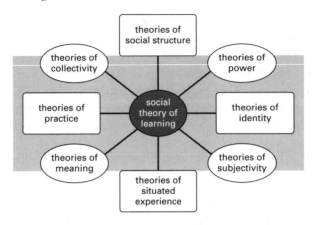

Figure 0.3. Refined intersection of intellectual traditions.

axes (see Figure 0.3). Indeed, while the vertical axis is a backdrop for my work, I shall have little to say about structure in the abstract or the minute choreography of interactions. I have therefore added these intermediary diagonal axes to introduce four additional concerns that are traditional in social theory but not quite as extreme as the poles of the vertical axis. For my purpose, they are as far as I go in the direction of social structure or situated experience. Hence, my domain of inquiry is illustrated by the horizontal shaded band. (Note that the resulting figure is not only an expansion of Figure 0.2 but also a refined version of Figure 0.1, outlining in a more detailed and rigorous fashion what I consider to be the components of a social theory of learning.)

One diagonal axis places social collectivities between social structure and practice, and individual subjectivity between identity and situated experience. Connecting the formation of collectivity and the experience of subjectivity on the same axis highlights the inseparable duality of the social and the individual, which is an underlying theme of this book.

- Theories of *collectivity* address the formation of social configurations of various types, from the local (families, communities, groups, networks) to the global (states, social classes, associations, social movements, organizations). They also seek to describe mechanisms of social cohesion by which these configurations are produced, sustained, and reproduced over time (solidarity, commitments, common interests, affinity).[8]

- Theories of *subjectivity* address the nature of individuality as an experience of agency. Rather than taking for granted a notion of agency associated with the individual subject as a self-standing entity, they seek to explain how the experience of subjectivity arises out of engagement in the social world.[9]

The other diagonal axis places power between social structure and identity, and meaning between practice and experience. As the axis suggests, connecting issues of power with issues of production of meaning is another underlying theme of this book.

- Theories of *power*. The question of power is a central one in social theory. The challenge is to find conceptualizations of power that avoid simply conflictual perspectives (power as domination, oppression, or violence) as well as simply consensual models (power as contractual alignment or as collective agreement conferring authority to, for instance, elected officials).[10]
- Theories of *meaning* attempt to account for the ways people produce meanings of their own. (These are different from theories of meaning in the philosophy of language or in logic, where issues of correspondence between statements and reality are the main concern.) Because this notion of meaning production has to do with our ability to "own" meanings, it involves issues of social participation and relations of power in fundamental ways. Indeed, many theories in this category have been concerned with issues of resistance to institutional or colonial power through local cultural production.[11]

The purpose of this book is not to propose a grandiose synthesis of these intellectual traditions or a resolution of the debates they reflect; my goal is much more modest. Nonetheless, that each of these traditions has something crucial to contribute to what I call a social theory of learning is in itself interesting. It shows that developing such a theory comes close to developing a learning-based theory of the social order. In other words, learning is so fundamental to the social order we live by that theorizing about one is tantamount to theorizing about the other.

Structure of the book

This book is divided into four sections:

1) the Prologue sets some contexts for the book
2) Part I, entitled *Practice,* addresses the left half of Figure 0.1 (and 0.3)

3) Part II, entitled *Identity,* addresses the right half of Figure 0.1 (and 0.3)
4) the Epilogue explores the implications of Parts I and II for design.

Each part includes a brief introduction that presents the topic of the section and outlines its structure with a synopsis of each chapter, as well as a coda – a short essay that wraps up the section by using its content to address a specific topic.

Prologue: vignettes

The rest of this prologue contains two vignettes that describe one community of practice. In 1989–90 I did some ethnographic field-work in a medical claims processing center operated by a large U.S. insurance company, which I will refer to by the pseudonym of Alinsu. The claims processors handled health insurance claims of the kind many of us are familiar with, sent in by people who were covered by a plan purchased by their employer.[12]

- *Vignette I* is a fairly detailed account of one working day in the life of a claims processor. It is meant to provide a view of a community of practice from the standpoint of a participant. Ariel, as I will call her, is representative of the claims processors, but she is a composite character. The day I describe is representative of a real day and is a collection of actual events, although I did not observe them all on the same day.
- *Vignette II* describes the use of one worksheet created by Alinsu to facilitate a calculation. This case illustrates the type of problems that can arise when workers are asked to perform procedural activities without a good understanding of what the activities are about.
- *Coda 0* summarizes the vignettes by introducing a perspective on understanding.

I include these vignettes to give some life to my theoretical development, and will often refer to the claims processors to illustrate what I say. However, these examples are mostly self-explanatory and so reading the vignettes is not an absolute necessity. Vignette II is mostly useful for Chapter 9, and even if you skip the vignettes, you still might want to look at Figure 0.4. I will refer on many occasions to the calculation worksheet it displays.

Part I: Practice

Part I provides a series of characterizations of the concept of community of practice, including:

1) the level of analysis at which the concept of practice is useful
2) the defining characteristics of a community of practice
3) the evolution of communities of practice over time
4) boundaries and relations among communities of practice
5) constellations formed by interrelated communities of practice.

Part I ends with an essay on "knowing in practice."

Part II: Identity

Part II focuses on identity. This shift of focus from practice to identity within the same analytical perspective has the following consequences.

1) It injects the notion of the person into the theory without having to posit an individual subject to start with.
2) It expands the domain of inquiry to social configurations other than those defined by practice and to mechanisms by which these configurations become contexts for identity formation.
3) It requires a theory of power by which to characterize the formation of identity in practice as the ability to negotiate an experience of meaning.

Part II thus complements Part I. It argues for a dual relation between practice and identity, and it addresses some limitations of the concept of community of practice by locating it within a broader framework. Part II ends with an essay on "learning communities."

Epilogue: Design

By way of conclusion, I discuss issues of design and learning. I first use the contents of Parts I and II to describe the dimensions and components of a design oriented to learning. Then I use this framework to discuss two kinds of social design:

1) organizations and their relation to practice
2) education and the formation of identities.

Welcome to claims processing!

Ariel runs down the stairs. She has to be at work at 8:00, and with the traffic, she will need a lot of luck to make it. She should really stop using the snooze button. The fact is, she would rather go to work earlier and come home earlier. But it's people with more seniority who get to choose their hours first: they can take the 7:00 to 3:00 schedule. She had it for a while. It's a bit hard in the morning, but when you get off at 3:00, it's like you still have the day in front of you. Staying there until 4:00 makes a big difference. But now the office needed some people to answer the phones between 3:00 and 4:00, so junior processors have to stay later. Although she has been working in the claims office for well over a year, Ariel is still considered a junior processor. She has recently been promoted to a level 6.

Predictably, it's congested between Ridgewell and Lincoln. As her car comes to a halt, Ariel grabs the rearview mirror to check her makeup. Overall, she takes good care of herself. She makes up, but discreetly, and dresses cleanly but not aggressively. Fortunately, the office is rather informal about appearance. You could spend a fortune otherwise. Of course, she could not go to work in shorts, but even jeans are OK as long as they are not torn. Altogether, there are not too many rules about dress, but it has been intimated on a few occasions that it is better to look somewhat professional and that appearance as well as behavior will influence promotional reviews. Besides, proper clothes make her feel better about her work. Today she made a special effort because some visitors are expected in the office: she is wearing her new woolen skirt and matching high heels.

Judith and Eleanor are already waiting for the elevator. "Hi, how are you?" She glances at the indicator: "L" for lobby and the steel doors slide open. The three co-workers step in hastily. The elevator has the soft, rose carpeting that covers the floors inside the building, and its walls are made of smoked mirrors so you don't feel encased in a small box. The inside is at once dark and well-lit: two rows of indirect spot-lights, built deep into the ceiling, shine softly onto people's heads. Like the lobby, with its large glass entrance, its peach walls, and its marble floor, the elevator seems made for business suits and attaché cases, rather than for Eleanor's jeans jacket, lunch bag and thermos, or for Judith's bright sneakers. She still looks like a high-school girl. The numbers flip above the door. "Second floor," says the synthesized voice of the friendly elevator in the same old tone. Ariel can hear that voice in her head whenever she closes her eyes: "second floor."

The office occupies the entire second floor of the building – plus a large part of the third floor, where the clerical unit, the training class, and the employees' lounge are located. The second floor consists of one large room. Only the two management offices in the corners have walls. But even these have large windows so that visually they are almost part of the main room. All that obstructs the view are the two square structures in the middle of the area: the elevator shaft with the entry hall, and the bathrooms. The two bathrooms on this floor are women's. There was no need to reserve a whole bathroom for the few guys who work here; they can just go upstairs.

The first thing Ariel does is walk toward her supervisor's desk to sign in. Since she is ten minutes late, she promises to make up for the time this very day. She will stay until ten past four. Before going to her desk, Ariel checks her bin: only one referral and nine pieces of mail. She usually receives a lot of mail addressed specifically to her. Ruth told her this happens because she always gives her name on the phone. It seems like the right thing to do, but she came to realize that many processors try to avoid doing so.

Ariel's desk is close to the supervisor's desk. Of course, she has to make sure that she does not chat too much. In fact, she suspects that it's the reason she was told to sit there. Before, she was sitting beside Eric, and he kept talking to her. Now she does not have much privacy, but that's good too. It helps her concentrate. She knows herself, and if she wants to "make production" and get her promotions, it's better that she can't fool around. Also, in this location, she's closer to the center of the unit and she always knows what's happening. On her left sits Joan. She is a level 8, who works very hard and is very dedicated. Joan hopes to be a level 9 soon, but then she will no longer be a claims processor; she will become a claims technician or an assistant supervisor. On Ariel's right sits Annette, a level 5 who is having some difficulty and has been placed on warning for a while. Level 5 is the first level at which you are no longer a trainee. Ariel thinks that Annette will most likely be fired soon because her warning has already been extended and she's still having trouble.

Like every desk around, Ariel's is cluttered with the paraphernalia of claims processors. She has organized her small space into an efficient place for doing her work, but she has been careful to leave some room for enough personal objects to make the space her own, including a plant and a photo of her boyfriend and her dog.

As Ariel walks toward her desk, she ignores the two phone messages standing on her keyboard. She also ignores the pile of claims that some-one has placed beside her keyboard for her to work through. Instead she immediately notes two claims covered with pink batch sheets: two "voids." Shit! Two more voids with only two days left this week. "Here goes my quality!" she exclaims. It will take a lot of luck if she is to make up for them and maintain the weekly percentage of correct claims she needs. She hates voids; they are frustrating and humiliating. Not only do they mean a lower quality rating for the week in which they occur, but they also mean more work because they have to be processed again.

She takes a look at the first void. She reimbursed lab charges at the regular rate of 85%, but the quality reviewer claims that these charges were related to outpatient surgery, which the plan reimburses at 100%, and should therefore have been reimbursed at 100% as well. She must check this up. She sits down, pushes papers aside, and starts logging into the system. "What a way to start the day!" she complains to Annette.

She enters her operator number and her password. They are strict about security. You are even supposed to log out if you are away from your desk for a short time, but no one really does it. Ariel has heard through the grapevine that there have been cases of embezzlement in the past, that some people have been fired, but nobody seems to know the details.

When the initial working screen comes up, she enters the control number of the employer contract and the social security number of the employee. Then she inspects the patient's claim history. Quality re-view was right, the current lab charges were related to a surgery that had been the object of a previous claim. She should have caught that: there is no way out. She will not try to dispute this void. She quickly reprocesses the claim.

Then she takes a look at the second void. What? But the patient was seen for headaches. And neurological exams for headaches are con-sidered medical, even if there is a secondary psychological diagnosis.

Therefore the "psych" maximum does not apply. She had actually discussed this case with Nancy and Sheila. She even talked with Maureen, the back-up trainer, who helps people with difficult cases and had agreed with her conclusion. She goes over to show her the void, gets some comforting grumbling about people in the quality review unit, comes back to her desk, pulls out a dispute form from her drawer, and starts filling it out, explaining in detail how she came to her decision. She states emphatically that the back-up trainer had confirmed her determination. Then she goes to her supervisor, who must sign a dispute form before it is submitted to quality review. The supervisor shakes her head in solidarity. Ariel is now quite confident that she will be able to resolve this one in her favor. What a relief!

Now that she has taken care of her voids, Ariel reads her phone messages, and puts them in a tray on her left. She will take care of that in the afternoon. Then she starts looking through the other claims that were sitting on her desk. Lots of "junk claims," as the complicated claims that will require much work are called. Ariel is well organized. "You have to be, in this job," she always says. What she tries to do is process easy claims fast during the morning and early afternoon and so get her "production" out of the way. Once she has reached her daily quota, she uses the last few hours of the day to take care of "junk" claims and to make phone calls.

Quickly, she flips through her piles of claims and separates the ones she will process this morning. Of course, you never really know just by looking at the claim how involved it is going to be, because there can be surprises when you open the customer's file on the system. But with some experience, you have a pretty good idea at first sight about how difficult a claim is likely to be. Usually, Ariel does this sorting before leaving so that her pile is ready for the next day, but yesterday she was held up by a lady who had gotten divorced and who wanted to know why her claims were no longer being paid. That lady was pretty upset because Ariel was supposed to protect the privacy of Alinsu's customer and thus could not disclose the reason for which her claims were being denied. She could only tell her that she had to talk about this with her ex-husband. After a long struggle, Ariel put the person on hold, just to take a breath. She was so angry, her body was shaking. She ended up transferring the call to her supervisor because the conversation was deteriorating fast.

Ariel starts on her first claim. There is an office visit, a series of tests, and some drug bills. Nothing too complicated. She removes the staples and glues the drug bills on blank sheets to keep them together. Next she goes into the database to check that the employee is on file and that the dates of service on the bills fall after the employee's "effective date" – and before termination, if there is any termination date. There are a number of codes to look for: the branch in the client company, the status code of the employee to make sure that the dependents are covered, and some other codes that, if present, would make this claim complicated. But everything checks out fine: she can start processing.

First, she has to enter the social security number and the name again to select the file for processing. Because a claim has to be paid under the plan governing the period during which the charges were incurred, the computer displays the dates of successive plan changes. She chooses the most recent plan change, since this claim is recent. On the next screen, she has to enter the year the claim is for and the date the claim was received, which was stamped in red by the clerical employee who opened the mail. It is easy to forget to do that because the system enters by default the date of the last claim processed. She ignores a number of caution messages and moves on to the next screen where she checks the address. It is important to make sure the address is correct so the check will reach its destination properly. You will definitely get a void if the address is wrong, even the ZIP code. Next, she selects the customer's son as the patient from a list of dependents. She is careful because it is easy to choose the wrong dependent; she got voided for this last month. She makes sure the son is under the age of 19. He is not, but there is a recent note from Patty on his file that he is a full-time student. Patty must have investigated it. She is reliable. But Ariel is bored and she wants to stand up, so she looks over the partition and asks anyway: "Hey, Patty, if you put a full-time student note on a dependent file, does that mean you investigated it?" "You bet," says Patty. No need to confirm the student status.

She now comes to the "paylines," the screen on which she will enter information about the charges so that benefits can be calculated. She starts with the office visit. She enters first the type of service, then the name of the service provider, which leads her into the providers file: there she makes sure she checks that the provider's address is correct since the insured has "assigned" the benefits to be disbursed directly to the doctor. Then she enters the date of service and the charges. In this case, she must also enter a deduction because the provider happens to have a special contract with Alinsu. She uses a calculation sheet to figure out what the deduction is, looking up the standard charge for this type of office visit in a ring binder, entering the amount on her calculator to compute a reduction of 15%, and choosing the larger amount of the two. It has occurred to her that it would be more advantageous for Alinsu to take the smaller one, but the procedure says to take the larger one.

Oh, no! Not again. She does not want to listen once more to Annette's plans to go to Richland Hot Springs this weekend. What's the big deal with that mud bath? Is she afraid, or what?

Since the patient went to such a "preferred" doctor, Ariel must remember to increase the rate of reimbursement from 80% to 85%. But this means that she will have to split the claim in two since the other charges are to be reimbursed at 80% and cannot be included in this payment. She likes the idea of having this claim generate two "batches" that will count toward her production: after spending all this time on that silly void, she can use a bit of luck. But she quickly checks in the providers file that the lab where the tests were performed does not have a similar contract. You will get in trouble for splitting claims unnecessarily.

The rest of the claim goes fairly fast: enter the code for the diagnosis, for the contract type, skip the coordination section, indicate the assignment of benefits. Remember to include two pattern paragraphs, which are prestored explanations you get the system to include with the check: one for the special deduction and one for the deductible, which the system has automatically taken into account.

Ariel types and writes impressively fast. Her eyes scan computer screens quickly, knowing what to look for. Check everything on this last screen and press enter. Then Ariel gets a new claim for the lab charges and for the drug bills. She has to check that a drug she does not remember having seen before is an acceptable prescription drug. Joan says that it's OK with any circulatory condition. The vitamins, of course, have to be denied. All standard stuff. She collects the papers for the two claims, attaches them with paper clips, places them in her outgoing bin, and circles two numbers on the sheet on which she keeps track of her work.

At half past eight, the supervisor comes around to distribute paychecks: consecrated wafers swallowed into expectant rows of purses. She also reminds everyone of the unit meeting to be held at 9:00, and asks who is going to do overtime this Saturday. Ariel will certainly be there, in the morning at least. She can use the money, and on Saturdays there are no phones; you can catch up on production.

Presently, Ariel's phone is ringing: once, twice. She reluctantly grabs the handset. While she talks, however, she does not interrupt her work immediately, but holds the phone with her shoulder and keeps processing the current claim.

> Thanks for calling Alinsu Insurance Company. Can I help –
> Yes, I would like to know what's happening with my claim.
> When did you submit it?
> I sent it more than a month ago.

Now Ariel realizes that she will need to access information to answer this person's question and that she will not be able to finish the claim she is currently processing before having to do so. She will have to "clear" out of this claim and thus lose all the information she has already entered. This stupid system, you have to lose all your work every time you are interrupted, and that's pretty often. She resigns herself, clears out, and starts typing the access information as her interlocutor gives it to her. The caller does not know the company's control number. "I can look it up for you."

Ariel muffles the phone and turns to Annette. "What's the control number of ZollePro?" she asks. "I don't know, 211 something." Ariel flips through her binder and enters the control number of the company. "It's 21131," she informs Annette. The phone conversation continues for a while, sometimes testing Ariel's patience. There is a backlog; what can she do about it? And it's not her fault if there is no way that clerical can log the receipt of submitted claims into the system. Finally, the caller hangs up. "That guy, he just wouldn't let me go," Ariel complains to Annette. "I know," Annette replies, "as if we had nothing better to do."

At 9:00, the claims processors converge on the supervisor's desk for a unit meeting. They roll their chairs and sit in a semicircle around her desk. Postures vary, ranging from straight backs to leaning over a desk nearby. Most processors sit cross-legged with their notebooks on their laps. Ariel looks at the familiar faces of her colleagues. It has been only a little over a year, and yet so much has happened. So many conversations, so many events. Of course, people get petty around the office. They have nothing better to do. Everybody is here, and it's a matter of interest. You come and you work here eight hours a day. It's your life. People know everything that's going on. They do it out of boredom, she thinks to herself.

There is a mixture of local chat with interjections across the semicircle. The atmosphere is generally relaxed and the talking as well as the configuration convey a sense of familiar conviviality. These meetings are a regular occurrence in the office. They take place at least once a month, but usually at shorter intervals – whenever there is business to discuss. Harriet, the supervisor, checks that everyone is there. Esther is still on the phone. "We'll wait for her." There she comes on her chair: after some shuffling and scooting, everyone is ready.

First Harriet reminds everyone of the visit of some important clients and asks processors to clean their desks and to make sure they do not fool around while the visitors are present. Then she announces that she has the vacation list and that she wants people to fill it out. The list is ordered by seniority. Harriet is at the top, and she has already filled her slot out. The list will go around the office in the order in which it is printed, and nobody can be skipped.

There is a problem with the toll-free 800 number that Alinsu customers can call to get information. Management has a suspicion that this number was given out by some processors to their acquaintances as a way of calling them free of charge. From now on, all phone calls exceeding fifteen minutes will be marked. Harriet senses the tension that her remark has brought into the meeting and is quick to clarify that the marking of these phone calls does not in itself constitute an accusation. It is only if patterns develop that an investigation will result. Still the subject seems delicate, and there is some grumbling and a few defensive remarks.

Then they discuss the idea of creating a phone unit within the unit. The gist is that at all times only a few processors would take all incoming phone calls and that people would take turns handling the phones. They have not yet figured out how to do that. Harriet asks for suggestions and requests that processors think about how they would want to go about implementing such an idea. Ariel, like all the processors she talked to, is not even quite sure that she wants a phone unit at all. She is rather ambivalent about phone calls. She sees them as interruptions, either welcome or unwelcome depending on circumstances. She certainly perceives them as obstacles to production. Sometimes she spends as much as half her time on the phone. They disturb her peace and can be a real pain when customers are nasty. But they also break the routine. And having to answer the phone allows her to receive private calls without drawing attention to herself.

The next item on the agenda is a memo that modifies the codes that processors are supposed to use to indicate the types of service rendered by providers. Harriet goes through the memo with the processors, paraphrasing each item and letting them ask questions. The change is substantial because these codes are used very frequently, but it is received rather casually by everyone: just another change, another "improvement" that will complicate their work only very slightly. The change will take effect on Monday, after the new version of the system has been installed. On this job, if you can't take change, forget it.

Harriet then asks the processors if they have any items of business to bring up. The assistant supervisor complains that there have been too many overpayments lately. She blames it on the fact that processors do not check eligibility carefully enough. Nancy reminds everyone that they cannot keep paying for physical therapy for a long time, even with a new prescription from a doctor. They must have a progress report. And if physical therapy goes on for more than a year, it has to be referred to the technical unit. Finally, Beliza says, "Well, for me, it's just this deductible." Everyone understands what she is talking about. Certain plans stipulate a complicated way of determining when a family deductible is satisfied. An animated discussion ensues with everyone contributing examples and partial explanations until Beliza seems satisfied: "It's easy to explain here, but it's a pain to explain it on the phone," she says. Many processors nod.

Last Sunday was the birthday of Sara, the assistant supervisor. A half-sheet birthday cake is placed on her desk, along with a small present from the unit. Even little events like this make the place more enjoyable, like the potluck on Valentine's Day, or the Christmas party. And on Halloween, it's hard to believe you are in an office, with decorations everywhere, competitions for the best unit and the best costumes, parade, and prizes. But Ariel's favorite remains "Kringeling." For a week before Christmas, people put little presents on each other's desks every day, and you have to guess who is putting them on your desk. People get so elaborate – scheming, misleading, guessing, tricking, faking, trading information. Then you realize how well people know each other. Last year, Ariel was able to eliminate all but four candidates because she got a sophisticated note produced on the computer system, and she knew that only four people could do that.

Now Sara blows the candle and starts cutting the cake, and the whole unit applauds and cheers. She and Trish distribute pieces. These cakes are a nice break from the daily routine, but the frosting is always much too thick. Ariel got a corner piece with close to a half-inch coat of white sugary fat on three sides. Before Ariel can complete her eating duties, however, the supervisor says: "Well, it was nice seeing all your faces again." Ariel complies with this invitation to return to processing, taking her piece of cake with her.

The meeting and the cake-cutting ceremony have lasted 45 minutes and Joan wonders whether the cake-cutting part of the meeting must be considered morning break. There is some discreet talk about the issue, but the question is never posed directly to the supervisor. Along with everyone, Ariel decides to assume that this did not count as a break and to see what happens. At a quarter past ten, she leaves for the lounge with Joan, where they spend most of their ten minutes discussing Trish's use of her sister's driver's license to get into a bar last Saturday and her fright when there was a check-up. Lucky she and her sister look alike. As they come down the spiral stair to return to their desks, Ariel reminisces about her own escapades. At her desk, she logs back into the system and starts processing. After a while she adds, without actually turning to Joan, "One good thing about being over 21 is you don't have to deal with this anymore." Two easy claims, two circles in quick succession. Joan has been thinking about Ariel's remark on being over 21, and says: "But then, you know, there are so many other things to worry about."

A few minutes before eleven, Beliza comes by Ariel's desk and asks what she wants for lunch because she is getting ready to call the deli. It's a bit cheaper and there is less waiting when one orders in advance; and since they have only a half hour for lunch, they do not have much time to spare. Still, thinks Ariel, it's better to have a short lunch break and get out earlier. "A ham sandwich with everything on it."

As she circles the code numbers of her processed claim on her "circle sheet," she does a little calculation on the side to figure out how close she is to her hourly quota. Today is going well, not like yesterday.

Now there is no TIN (taxpayer information number) for this doctor. Why can't they just fill out these forms completely? Ariel has to send a letter requesting the information: this means clearing out of the claim and putting it on the paper tray where she keeps claims awaiting further information. Five or six years ago, she heard, they could simply call the doctor's office, but now it is necessary to have all this in writing. She pulls out a form from her drawer and fills out a request to send a form letter. Annette wants to know if she can assume that the date of emergency room treatment is the date of the accident when the patient did not enter the accident date. Ariel is not sure: accident dates are important because of temporary supplemental benefits for accidents on certain plans. Joan says that she always assumes the dates are the same and that she's never been voided on it.

Ariel is processing a claim for which there is a suspicion of a pre-existing condition. On the computer, she flips through the claim history to get an idea of how this has been handled so far. The plan has a $2,000 waiver limit on expenses for pre-existing conditions, and the expenses related to this condition amount to only $384 so far, so she need

not investigate it. An investigation is started only when the related expenses approach the limit. It is one of those things where it is understood that just nobody does it. Good. Investigating a "pre-exist" can
become quite involved, with numerous letters and phone calls. In this
case, she pays the claim and enters a claim note stating how much has
been paid out of the limit so far. In this office, some people are good
about notes and some are not. For instance, every time you change an
address – something Ariel has already done three times today – you are
supposed to enter a note to that effect, with the date and the source of
the new address, so that if another processor later receives an old claim
dating before the change, that processor will not put the old address
back in. Because not everybody does it, it causes trouble for other people. Ariel is quite diligent about notes herself, but with notes you have
to know whom to trust.

Suddenly, Trish asks behind the partition: "Maureen, do you know
what's 'incompetent cervix'? The insured put this as a justification of
ultrasound." Maureen replies: "I'm pretty sure that it's eligible, but
we should have this from the doctor, not just the insured." Ariel wonders what an incompetent cervix might be. It sounds pretty bad. And
Maureen's reply, if adequate for the present purpose, is not exactly instructive. There is a lot of medical terminology in claims processing.
In training, they had this course on medical terms with all the Greek
roots, but she never learned anything from it. Now that she's been on
the floor for a while, she knows quite a bit. When she goes to the doctor,
she can tell. Of course, she doesn't show it, because her own understanding is not really medical. It is just processing claims. Like this
cervix. That's right, that is what an incompetent cervix is: it's eligible.
She does not ask Maureen.

It's noon. Beliza goes around to gather the lunch group. Ariel looks
at her circle sheet to see how many claims she has processed so far. She
counts twenty-two, not including the void she re-entered since these
do not count as production. She is on schedule, but she might have to
skip her afternoon break. Ariel, Beliza, Sandra, Eric, and Ruth take the
elevator down to the deli on the ground floor. Sandra is worried about
her quality, which has been in the eighties lately. It's supposed to be
above 95%.

The deli's modest furnishings are in sharp contrast with the style
of the building. The first time Ariel left the lush decor of the lobby
through a small door in the corner to the right of the elevator shaft, she
remembers being surprised. She had expected a nice café with a full

array of delicatessen refinements. Instead she had found herself in a small, poorly lit room, with a few homely, dark brown tables and chairs and a TV on in a corner. The counter offered a simple menu of cafeteria food, and the walls were covered with shelves of food items in truck-stop style. But on reflection, she likes it that way now because at least it is affordable. She sometimes smiles at the thought that this deli, cooped in a corner of a building whose style reflects the tastes of cosmopolitan executives and the means of her mammoth employer, is very much like her.

After getting their orders, they all sit around a table. Beliza reassures Sandra that her quality won't affect her pay until she is put on warning. When Sandra expresses her surprise that this has not happened yet, Ariel asks her, "Do you want us to tell them to put you on warning?" They all laugh. "That was a pretty quick morning," Eric comments. Ariel agrees: "Yeah, a unit meeting always helps." They fall silent for a while, enjoying the time perhaps as much as the food.

The conversation resumes. Quality is a problem with the whole unit. That's why the idea of a phone unit has been raised. With all these phone interruptions, it is easy to make careless mistakes. Eric does not know whether he would like to be just on phones for a whole week. And what would they do when there are too many calls at the same time? And now they are going to monitor long calls! Everyone knows that there are business calls that are long. Beliza reminds everyone of that 45-minute phone call that drove her crazy. Surely "they" will recognize that this is unfair.

Ruth mentions the storm that is expected for tonight. So Beliza starts telling a story about her adventure during that terrible flood a few years back. Her husband was sure that the road was safe and that the water was shallow, and he drove on. But suddenly the car started to sink and water started to ooze in from every crack. They had to get out through the windows and climb on the roof. Her husband had to jump into the water and wade through it to get some help. The AAA officer was teasing her husband with mocking skepticism until he saw the car and realized that he was going to have to dive into this water to hook the car up and get it out. Mind you, the car started before the incredulous eyes of all onlookers. Beliza always comes up with these amazing stories. But it is time to go back.

As the group reaches the office, they see a gorgeous flower arrangement on Harriet's desk. Since she is out to lunch, they get the story from Trish that her husband had forgotten their anniversary yesterday and was really sorry about it. To send all these flowers like that, he must have been. Ariel notices that Joan's desk is all clean. She remembers the visitors and gets her desk in some order. In her mail bin she has found a response to an inquiry she had sent to technical. "This guy's gonna yell at me." Joan asks her who that is and she reminds her of the case.

> His wife's deductible is not transferable from one employer
>   to another.
> Make sure you tell him about the three-month carry over.
>   That will make him feel better.
> Good idea.
> This guy's a kid.
> He's twenty-three.
> He can't get too mad.
> He works in the warehouse or something.

When Harriet comes back from lunch, she hands Ariel the response from quality review on her void dispute. Her judgment has been accepted as valid. Good! In spite of her weight concern and the morning cake, Ariel allows herself to take a piece of chocolate from the jar on Harriet's desk. It's hard to resist when that jar is always there, tempting you. And Roberta, a level 8, has taken it upon herself to be the snack provider for the whole unit. She keeps a stock of goods, from candy bars to chewing gum, even Band-Aids®. She says that processors are kids and need to be kept happy.

Back to work. On an ambulance claim, Ariel does not see a diagnosis. She goes over to Nancy, who tells her to find one that would do in the patient's claim history. Just anything that will do? Well, she is right, you've got to keep processing moving, keep the cost per claim down, but this is the kind of shortcut you never get in training. Without them, there is no way the job could be done. Ariel's face must have revealed her thoughts, because Nancy just reassures her with a friendly smirk: "Welcome to claims processing!"

In training, everything looks so strict and black-and-white. But on the floor, everybody learns the shortcuts in order to meet production. For instance, in training, you are taught to start a claim by filling out the forms that will serve as cover sheets for microfilmed records. Yet much of the information on the cover sheet is never used and is redundant with the attached claim record. So experienced processors do not fill out the form completely; they wait until they have completed the entire claim. When they hit the key that indicates they are done, the computer system gives them a batch number. If the number ends with a D, no problem, it will just get paid and archived. If the number ends with a Q, the claim must be sent to quality review, and so you quickly complete the cover sheet. Everyone learns to do that within the first few weeks after moving to the floor.

You are good at claims processing when you can quickly find legitimate ways to get the charges reimbursed to a reasonable extent. You have to choose procedure codes for medical treatment that will allow enough coverage. You have to develop a good sense of how much is reasonable, juggling the whole thing to produce quickly a reasonable story. What makes a story "reasonable" can't be taught during the training class. Even her instructors acknowledged that trainees had to learn it "the right way" for now but that, once they got to the floor, they would learn the shortcuts.

But the shortcuts are not always good for the company or the customer. For instance, Alinsu has a rule that, if a completed claim comes out as a "Q," recalling that claim to make a change will count as a void, that is, as an error on the processor's quality rating. Of course, if you could just recall your Qs, you would process everything super fast, and then quickly recall your Qs to check them carefully. They want you to pay the same attention to every claim. So what people learn to do is that if you notice a mistake on a Q claim after completing it and sending it in, it is better just to let it go, because then there is a chance that the quality reviewer will overlook the error. An error that is discovered outside the internal review process – say, through a complaint by a customer – does not count against you.

Now this claim looks like a duplicate, but Ariel can't tell from the claim history on-line; she needs to check the original bill to see if the services covered are really the same. She goes to the microfilm reader, but the claim was recent and the film has not yet come back from the lab. So Ariel has to fill out a request for clerical to get a copy of the original bill on paper. She clears out of the claim and puts it aside. She'll have to start over when she gets the answer. From across the walkway, Beliza asks, "Transco is 'end of the month' or 'date of termination'?" She wants to know whether a Transco employee who leaves the job is still covered until the end of that month. Some companies do that, some don't. Annette replies, "I think it's 'end of the month'." But Joan corrects her, "No, they just changed it. It was in a memo last week." Ariel overhears the conversation and makes a mental note.

The four visitors announced in the morning have arrived, and they come toward Ariel's unit. Kathryn, the assistant manager, and Roger, from technical, are giving them a tour. There is also someone from the home office, who has been here before to talk with the office manager, but Ariel does not even know who he is. She knows so little about the home office. The visitors are important clients who represent a large case with over 20,000 "lives." The office looks pretty good. Ariel can't hear what the touring group is talking about, and she does not try. She is, for a moment, struck by the way they walk, slowly, with assurance and enduring smiles. She notices their sweeping gazes and their wide gestures as they stroll around the office, discussing, pointing, laughing, nodding. There is a managerial elegance about the way they look at the landscape of her working world. She thinks fleetingly of long distances, of airports and carphones, of meeting rooms and signatures, of statistics and charts. The visitors and their guides pass by Ariel's desk, otherworldly beings gliding through the aisles. Ariel stoops over her work, her knuckles busy with their staccato on her keyboard, her gaze intently scanning characters on her screen, her spirit huddled over the partitioned field of her desk space. Suddenly, the gliding is interrupted. One of the visitors, the benefit representative, has just recognized Beliza's nameplate. They have talked on the phone quite often, but have never met face to face. Beliza stands up politely. "Nice to meet you." They shake hands and exchange a few giggling words; they are colleagues. Then Beliza sits down, and the group glides on.

The afternoon drags on for Ariel. On this job, hours sometimes go by astonishingly fast, in busy chunks between breaks, but sometimes excruciatingly slow, in a trickle of restless minutes. Ariel is a bit tired and wants to go home. The morning moves easier, usually, but the afternoon is always a letdown. After lunch is the hardest time. But it usually builds up after the afternoon break, until it bursts out at 4:00 – to the elevator, to the parking lot, and back in your very own car. Today, Ariel will not take her afternoon break and will stay until ten past four. She looks up. Round and white, above the supervisor's desk, the flat, eyeless face of the clock presides over the day, supervising even the supervisor. "God, why is it so slow this afternoon," Joan complains. Ariel nods in agreement.

Five more easy claims before she will start processing her "junk" and taking care of other business until it's time for her to leave. What I need is a weekend, thinks Ariel. The weekend is always there. It's not like the clock. It doesn't regulate production demands. But it gives each day of the week a slightly different feel. It animates conversations with its escapades, past and future. Ariel decides that she will definitely work only half the day on Saturday.

"I already made production," Ariel says triumphantly as she draws her thirty-seventh circle. Having reached production early is something worth announcing to your neighbors. As the day wears on, the afternoon can become a racing stretch or a coasting respite. She thinks of asking Roberta for one of those little candy bars. No, she better not. She quickly opens her mail and makes a few phone calls, including one to her boyfriend. "See you tomorrow." Joan gets to leave at 3:00.

Now Ariel turns to her pile of junk claims, but she is interrupted by Ruth, who comes over, "Can you take a look at my screen?" "What did I do?" asks Ariel. "I can't understand your note," explains Ruth. Ariel goes over to her desk, looks at the note and clarifies the information she had entered about an adopted child.

Back at her desk, Ariel processes her first junk claim. It takes about 25 minutes. When she presses the key to send the claim in, it turns out to be a "Q." Ariel does not know the exact system that allocates Qs. She believes that they are allocated on a somewhat random basis but that certain plans have a higher percentage of them. She does not know exactly to what degree the appearance of a Q is determined by the type of claim being processed or by the way that she is processing it, but she heard that her supervisor can manipulate the system to send specific claims to quality review. Ariel has been getting a greater number of Qs than usual. As she gets this one, she complains aloud: "What? Another Q? That's terrible! I just spent 25 minutes on this claim!" No one says anything. She does not like to get Qs. Sara did explain to her that having a large number of claims reviewed is good, since each error then accounts for a smaller percentage. Still, you never like to have your work checked, especially after spending so much time on it. Well, back to some junk.

It is ten to four; Ariel will be leaving in 20 minutes. She decides to stop dealing with her junk and to prepare her work for tomorrow. She goes to Sara, the assistant supervisor, to ask her for some work. When claims arrive at Alinsu, they are opened by the clerical unit and sorted by plans. Large plans result in homogeneous piles and small plans are gathered in mixed piles. Ariel pleads for an easy pile, reminding Sara of the difficult work she did in the beginning of the week. Sara gives her a pile from the City Hall. That's an easy plan. Ariel thanks her: tomorrow she will be able to make production early and then catch up on her junk. She returns to her desk and prepares the pile for the morning. Only a few foreseeable problems.

Five past four: it is time to leave. Ariel has processed 41 claims, 17 of which were completely routine, 20 of which she perceived as involving some difficulty or complication, and 4 of which were junk. She answered 26 phone calls, 7 of which were unpleasant. She initiated 9 calls, 5 of which required follow-up and 2 of which involved an uncooperative interlocutor. She fills out her production report: "How much time can we write off for the meeting today?" "Forty-five minutes." She quickly clears her desk, grabs her purse and her coat. "Don't forget that on-hand reports are due today," Annette reminds her. Oh, right, she had almost forgotten. She sits down and starts counting the numbers of unprocessed claims she has in various piles on her desk. They need to know how old the claims are. It's already twenty past four when she is done. Poor Annette, she will still be here for a while, struggling to make production. Why doesn't she quit? Ariel guesses that it's hard to accept that you can't do something. She rushes to Harriet's desk to sign off.

What a crowd waiting for the elevator at this late hour! Ariel tells Lisa that she was right about that deductible being carried over. Lisa replies that it was just her guess. The conversation continues into the elevator. Is her brother still going out with Shirley? She had heard they broke up. Oh, they are still together. Good for them. The elevator reaches the lobby and the contained crowd gushes out. Did she know that Norma Wong was quitting after ten years? Really? Yes, she had found a new job with Casus Casualties. They had asked her how much she was making. She lied and they offered her even more. Not bad! In the lobby, some processors become quiet and some of them talk until they reach the door. But as they spread through the parking lot, they fall silent on their eager way home.

The freeway is already a bit slow. Toward the city, Ariel looks at the brownish haze of smog hanging over the hills: the sky looks like it has dragged the hem of its bright evening gown in the dust. The thing is, it only seems to be getting worse. Pollution really worries her. What about cancer? There was that old lady whose husband was dying of lung cancer and who called her three times to ask the same question about hospital deductibles. What is going to happen? Ariel would even pay a bit more for gas if she knew it would help. But it would probably go into someone's pocket. As she turns on the radio and starts tapping the beat on her steering wheel, she thinks of the computer system she uses, of the new one to be installed soon that is supposed to do so much more, of the elevator that talks to you. Pollution? "Well, I'm sure they'll figure out something."

Vignette II
The "C, F, and J" thing

In some circumstances, a person is covered by more than one health in-surance plan. For instance, children may be covered under the plans of both parents. Similarly, retired workers may be eligible for Medicare,[1] but may still be on the plan of their former employer. If each plan paid the usual 80% of medical expenses for a given service, a patient would receive benefits in excess of the actual bills. But U.S. insurance com-panies that provide group coverage have signed a nationwide agree-ment to coordinate the benefits received under multiple coverages. Coordination of benefits (COB) is a fairly common task. In the most common case, the primary carrier covers the first 80%, and then the secondary carrier takes care of the remaining 20%. But coordination clauses can become rather complicated, sometimes leaving both cus-tomers and processors confused.

Especially confusing was a new plan for retired employees covered by both Alinsu, through their former employer, and Medicare. This plan is known as coordination of benefit "by reduction" because Alinsu reduces its liability by the amount of Medicare payments. In other words, rather than filling the gap between Medicare payments and the actual bills, as in regular coordination, Alinsu merely fills the gap be-tween Medicare's coverage and its own. So if a treatment is covered by Medicare at 70% and by Alinsu at 80%, Alinsu pays only 10%. If Medicare coverage is equal to or higher than its own, Alinsu pays nothing.

What makes this situation difficult is that Alinsu compares the two coverages, not on a case-by-case basis, but as aggregates for the patient over an entire year. Because earlier claims can influence later claims, the calculation of benefits often appears random. A kind of bill that usu-ally results in a payment can suddenly receive no payment and equally suddenly result in a payment again, depending on what else has hap-pened in between. Customers are usually bewildered and often infuri-ated by this appearance of randomness.

35

```
┌─────────────────────────────────────────────────────────────┐
│                 Benefit Reduction Worksheet                   │
│                                                               │
│   A.  Agg Prev Alinsu Benefit      $ _____  (C Prev. Stmnt.) │
│                                                               │
│   B.  Al Ben Current Claim         + _____              │
│                                                               │
│   C.  Tot Al Agg Benefit           = _____              │
│                                                               │
│   D.  Agg Prev Medicare Benefit      _____  (F Prev. Stmnt.) │
│                                                               │
│   E.  Medicare Ben Current Claim   + _____              │
│                                                               │
│   F.  Total Medicare Agg Ben         _____              │
│                                                               │
│   G.  Al Total Liability (C – F)     _____              │
│                                                               │
│   H.  Al Prev Payments             – _____  (J Prev. Stmnt.) │
│                                                               │
│   I.  Ben Now Due (enter 0 if                                 │
│       negative figure results)     = _____              │
│                                                               │
│   J.  Total Al Paymnts Released                               │
│       (H + I)                      $ _____              │
│                                                               │
│   **C, F, J must be noted in claimant file                    │
│     for future calculations.                                  │
└─────────────────────────────────────────────────────────────┘
```

Figure 0.4. The COB worksheet.

To calculate these benefits, claims processors used the worksheet shown in Figure 0.4. The COB worksheet, as I will call this form here, was briefly introduced to claims processors in the training class. The instructor did not attempt a detailed explanation of the concept of co-ordination, nor did the trainees ask for one. After a brief introduction, the training quickly focused on the use of the worksheet. Ignoring the content of the labels of each line, the class performed the operations line by line with a few sets of fictitious numbers. The instructor showed the class where to find the values to be entered on the various lines of the worksheet and where to store the results of lines C, F, and J. After a few exercises, no one had any trouble getting the correct answers.

The introduction of the training class, however, was not the real thing. The fictitious numbers they used did not require a commitment to the answers. It was "on the floor" that the real learning was to take place. There, the coordination of benefits caused problems. Processors did not like the procedure. Though they were able to perform the cal-culations of the procedure correctly by simply following the instructions on the worksheet, they were usually surprised by the results they obtained:

> It works both ways to where ninety-nine percent of the time they get no benefit. It's a lot of work for nothing. You see, I am so confused on this, and I have to pay these claims.

Because of their inability to ascertain the reasonableness of their results, the less experienced processors usually asked someone for help whenever they had to do such a calculation. They all knew what to do, but they needed the confirmation of someone with experience. And yet even the person who often helped them, a very experienced and knowledgeable old-timer, was not sure herself why certain results were reasonable. Because she had seen enough of those claims go through quality review successfully, she had gathered enough confidence in the calculation as prescribed to trust that whatever numbers she arrived at were somehow correct. However, just why these numbers were correct and why they were reasonable remained obscure to her.

If all claims processors had to do was calculate benefits to be paid, the coordination of benefits by reduction would have just become yet another activity whose broader meanings were outside of their purview. Many of these COB calculations, however, resulted in phone calls from customers who could not understand the brief message that explained why their claims were denied:

> THIS ADJUSTMENT REDUCES OUR BENEFITS BY
> PAYMENT MADE BY MEDICARE IN ACCORDANCE
> WITH THE PROVISION OF THE GROUP PLAN.

Claims processors expected those calls: "You know this is gonna get you a phone call, you just know it. It never fails." Furthermore these phone calls were known to be difficult: "And anger, a lot of anger. I don't blame them for being angry."

Not only were customers usually upset at receiving benefits in a seemingly random fashion, but the processors also felt ill-equipped to explain how benefits were calculated:

> I know my car runs, but I could not tell you how. And that's not good enough when people call and want to know about their money! But it's embarrassing when you call and you say, "Well, I don't know how, but that's how much money you got. Sorry." I mean, it's embarrassing not to have the information.

Even in the meeting that was eventually called to address the problem, the presentation did not engage claims processors with the underlying insurance concepts and with the kind of information that would enable them to talk with customers. They were repeatedly told to explain to callers that benefits were calculated as aggregates in order to ensure "fairness." Now, it is a true and relevant piece of information that some of the confusion is due to the aggregate character of the calculation. The meeting, however, focused on the definition of the term *aggregate* as a term. Through it all, the notion of aggregate remained an abstract one and fairness but a vague ideal. These terms and the daily activity of using the worksheet remained disjoint. There was no discussion of what aggregates did in this case, of what kind of "fairness" they created, or of how precisely the procedure of the worksheet implemented the principle. Neither was there any discussion of what the customers' issues were, of the types of questions they asked, or of the kinds of explanation they expected. Claims processors I spoke to did not find that the meeting had helped them very much.

ETIENNE   So what do you understand about it?

SHEILA   I understand it. I just don't know how to explain it to a caller. I know how to do it on the computer, everything just fine. And I can do, you know, when it's not "C, F, and J," I can explain that just fine. But when it comes to "C, F, and J," it's like you said in the meeting, you can't tell them "I subtracted this line from this line," you can't do that. And I don't know what to tell [them], that's the only thing.

ETIENNE   So you really don't understand the meaning of what Alinsu is trying to do there?

SHEILA   Not really.

ETIENNE   Not really? And the meeting that [the unit] had [with an instructor] did not help?

SHEILA   No, because she did not tell us why we were doing it, she just told us "this is how you do it." And I don't really think she told us why.

MAUREEN   She never went into it, just that it was an aggregate thing for the whole year. So I guess that's all you need to know: there is an aggregate.

The jargon of the office had come to reflect the processors' own "line-by-line" relation to the coordination of benefits by reduction. Instead of referring to it by its official name, they just called it "the C, F, and J thing."

Coda 0

Understanding

As a nickname for the COB worksheet, the claims processors' expression "the C, F, and J thing" is quite telling. It names the activity not by reference to the insurance concepts it implements but by reference to lines in the worksheet. Indeed, the location of the data and the calculation are prescribed in terms of lines within the worksheet itself, to the point where knowing what to do next does not require any interpretation of the worksheet's underlying purpose. If one assumes that the worksheet has been designed correctly, then one need not take any responsibility for the outcome of the calculation and its implementation of actual contractual relations. The worksheet was specifically designed with this assumption in mind. Instead of giving claims processors the capacity to figure out how to do the calculation, the designers of the worksheet decided to prescribe exactly how to do it, step by step. The form removed from the execution of the procedure the need to assume responsibility for its meaning.

This kind of form is very common, not only in claims processing but in all kinds of activities. Many people who fill out U.S. tax returns, for instance, would be hard-pressed to explain the exact meanings of some of the calculations involved in the various forms, tables, and worksheets, as intended by those who designed them. Still, the line-by-line instructions are clear enough that taxpayers can comply, whether or not they would themselves be able to come up with the calculation process or the information requested. Compliance does not require understanding.

Yet, the question of whether Ariel and her colleagues understood the COB worksheet does not have a single answer. For each way in which the worksheet can be argued to be transparent, one can find a way in which it can be argued to be opaque.

- In procedural terms, claims processors all agreed that the worksheet was, as they called it, "self-explanatory." To them, what to do was clear enough. The worksheet was transparent.

39

- In other ways, however, the worksheet provided claims processors with little sense of what Alinsu was trying to do with this procedure. The very technique by which computational steps were made transparent also rendered invisible the reasons that the calculation was the way it was: institutional systems and legal contracts, insurance concepts and economic issues, definitions of fairness and employment relations. With respect to these issues, the worksheet was not transparent at all.[1]

- Explanations provided to claims processors were neither sufficient nor clear enough to give them some grasp on these issues. In fact, beyond a unit meeting and the showing of a video that promoted courtesy in customer relations, there was no major action undertaken to make information more readily available. In the end, the whole COB incident was never resolved. It merely dissolved into the broader experience of marginalization that characterized the processors' relations to the business of the company. They would have preferred to know what the procedure was about, but the benefit of going out of their way to do so was not evident. The phone calls were uncomfortable and embarrassing moments, but they were not too frequent. Instead of spending their energy worrying about the issue, claims processors put their effort into creating a work atmosphere in which that bit of ignorance would not be a liability. In this silent achievement of a local definition of competence, I would say that claims processors understood the worksheet, its introduction in the training class, and its use in the office rather well. They understood what it was telling them about their position within the corporation and the expectations invested in their relations to their work. In this sense, the worksheet was rather transparent, after all.

As an occupation, medical claims processing at Alinsu is very much focused on procedures, on how to follow them, and on how to use such artifacts as forms, worksheets, computer screens, and manuals. This focus starts during training and continues as trainees join their units. What claims processors learn cannot easily be categorized into discrete skills and pieces of information that are useful or harmful, functional or dysfunctional. Learning their jobs, they also learn how much they are to make sense of what they do or encounter. They learn how not to learn and how to live with the ignorance they deem appropriate. They learn to keep their shoulders bent and their fingers busy, to follow the rules and to ignore the rules. They learn how to engage and disengage, accept and resist, as well as how to keep a sense of themselves in spite of the status of their occupation. They learn to weave together their work and their private lives. They learn how to find little joys and how to deal with being depressed. What they learn and don't learn makes sense only as part of an identity, which is as big as the world and as small as their computer screens, and which subsumes the skills they acquire and gives them meaning. They *become* claims processors.

Words like "understanding" require some caution because they can easily reflect an implicit assumption that there is some universal standard of the knowable. In the abstract, anything can be known, and the rest is ignorance. But in a complex world in which we must find a livable identity, ignorance is never simply ignorance, and knowing is not just a matter of information. In practice, understanding is always straddling the known and the unknown in a subtle dance of the self. It is a delicate balance. Whoever we are, understanding in practice is the art of choosing what to know and what to ignore in order to proceed with our lives.

Part I
Practice

Intro I

The concept of practice

Being alive as human beings means that we are constantly engaged in the pursuit of enterprises of all kinds, from ensuring our physical survival to seeking the most lofty pleasures. As we define these enterprises and engage in their pursuit together, we interact with each other and with the world and we tune our relations with each other and with the world accordingly. In other words, we learn.

Over time, this collective learning results in practices that reflect both the pursuit of our enterprises and the attendant social relations. These practices are thus the property of a kind of community created over time by the sustained pursuit of a shared enterprise. It makes sense, therefore, to call these kinds of communities *communities of practice.*

Claims processors: a community of practice

Ariel and her colleagues do not come to Alinsu to form a community of practice; they come to earn a living. Gathered in Alinsu's office by their need for work, they want to fulfill their individual production quota. They want to make money in order to go on with their own lives, which they see taking place mostly outside of the office. They do focus on their work, but they keep glancing at the clock, waiting for the moment they are free to leave. For most of the time they spend at Alinsu, most of them would rather be somewhere else doing something else. Everyone knows this, employees and employer alike.

Yet the very longing to go home that pulls claims processors apart is also something they share, something that brings them together; it is something they take for granted and implicitly assume behind each other's remarks, something they discuss and joke about. It is something they deal with together. Working with others who share the same conditions is thus a central factor in defining the enterprise they engage in. With each other and against each other, with their employer and

45

against their employer, they collectively orchestrate their working lives and their interpersonal relations in order to cope with their job. Colluding and colliding, conspiring and conforming, it is collectively that they make claims processing what it is in practice.

Because the job can, in the abstract, be described in individual terms, it is easy to overlook the degree to which it is the community of practice that sustains the processors' ability to do their work. When I was talking with many senior managers to get permission to do my study, they expressed some surprise that I would want to study social learning in what they called a "paper assembly line." They took an individual, asocial, linear view of the job, which was reflected in policies and metrics, in training programs, and also in the computer system – with its fixed sequences of screens, designed for one person to process one claim at a time, from beginning to end.

These policies, metrics, training programs, and system designs were often at odds with the reality of their work. Indeed, as Vignette I shows, close examination yielded a completely different picture. I found that it is the collective construction of a local practice that, among other things, makes it possible to meet the demands of the institution. As a community of practice, claims processors make the job possible by inventing and maintaining ways of squaring institutional demands with the shifting reality of actual situations. Their practice:

1) provides resolutions to institutionally generated conflicts such as contradictions between measures and work – for instance, processing claims versus time on the phone

2) supports a communal memory that allows individuals to do their work without needing to know everything

3) helps newcomers join the community by participating in its practice

4) generates specific perspectives and terms to enable accomplishing what needs to be done

5) makes the job habitable by creating an atmosphere in which the monotonous and meaningless aspects of the job are woven into the rituals, customs, stories, events, dramas, and rhythms of community life.

Although claims processors may appear to work individually, and though their jobs are primarily defined and organized individually, processors become important to each other. When I asked them what they thought they would remember about this job later in life, the response was almost always: "The people." They are quite aware of their inter-dependence in making the job possible and the atmosphere pleasant. They act as resources to each other, exchanging information, making sense of situations, sharing new tricks and new ideas, as well as keeping each other company and spicing up each other's working days.

Social practice

A *practice* is what these claims processors have developed in order to be able to do their job and have a satisfying experience at work. It is in this sense that they constitute a community of practice. The concept of practice connotes doing, but not just doing in and of itself. It is doing in a historical and social context that gives structure and meaning to what we do. In this sense, practice is always social practice.

Such a concept of practice includes both the explicit and the tacit. It includes what is said and what is left unsaid; what is represented and what is assumed. It includes the language, tools, documents, images, symbols, well-defined roles, specified criteria, codified procedures, regulations, and contracts that various practices make explicit for a variety of purposes. But it also includes all the implicit relations, tacit conventions, subtle cues, untold rules of thumb, recognizable intuitions, specific perceptions, well-tuned sensitivities, embodied understandings, underlying assumptions, and shared world views. Most of these may never be articulated, yet they are unmistakable signs of membership in communities of practice and are crucial to the success of their enterprises.

Of course, the tacit is what we take for granted and so tends to fade into the background. If it is not forgotten, it tends to be relegated to the individual subconscious, to what we all know instinctively, to what comes naturally. But the tacit is no more individual and natural than what we make explicit to each other. Common sense is only common-sensical because it is sense held in common. Communities of practice are the prime context in which we can work out common sense through mutual engagement. Therefore, the concept of practice highlights the social and negotiated character of both the explicit and the tacit in our lives.[1]

More generally, my usage of the concept of practice does *not* fall on one side of traditional dichotomies that divide acting from knowing, manual from mental, concrete from abstract. The process of engaging in practice always involves the whole person, both acting and knowing at once. In practice, so-called manual activity is not thoughtless, and mental activity is not disembodied. And neither is the concrete solidly self-evident, nor the abstract transcendentally general; rather, both gain their meanings within the perspectives of specific practices and can thus obtain a multiplicity of interpretations.

The term *practice* is sometimes used as an antonym for theory, ideas, ideals, or talk. However, my use of the term does not reflect a dichotomy between the practical and the theoretical, ideals and reality, or talking and doing. Communities of practice include all of these, even if there are sometimes discrepancies between what we say and what we do, what we aspire to and what we settle for, what we know and what we can manifest. We all have our own theories and ways of understanding the world, and our communities of practice are places where we develop, negotiate, and share them.

Even when theory is a goal in itself, it is not detached but instead is produced in the context of specific practices. Some communities specialize in the production of theories, but that too is a practice. The distinction between theoretical and practical then refers to distinctions between enterprises rather than fundamental distinctions in qualities of human experience and knowledge.

The relation between practice and theory is always a complex, interactive one. From this perspective, theory is neither useless nor ideal. Practice is not immune to the influence of theory, but neither is it a mere realization of theory or an incomplete approximation of it. In particular, practice is not inherently unreflective.[2] Of course, a given community of practice may be, at various times, more or less reflective on the nature of its own practice. This is a very important characteristic with respect to the kind of learning that a community engages in. But it is a different issue than the existence of a dichotomy between theory and practice. Ethnographic accounts have provided little evidence to suggest that theoreticians are more likely than others to be reflective on the nature of their own practice. In fact, the formal character of their finished products may well hide the practical complexities and everyday processes from which they arise. Certainly, claims processors spend a lot of time in informal reflections, frequently talking about their own practices while at lunch and on breaks. They do not view themselves as theoreticians, but they always seemed to enjoy immensely answering my questions about their work and taking these conversations as opportunities to explore opinions and engage in a process of reflection.

Even when it produces theory, practice is practice. Things have to be done, relationships worked out, processes invented, situations interpreted, artifacts produced, conflicts resolved. We may have different enterprises, which give our practices different characters. Nevertheless, pursuing them always involves the same kind of embodied, delicate, active, social, negotiated, complex process of participation.

Structure of Part I

Part I is a discussion of the concept of practice and of the kind of social communities that practice defines. Each chapter addresses one basic aspect of practice. Note that, for presentation purposes, I start by talking about communities of practice in isolation, characterizing them in terms of their internal dynamics. I then talk about relations among communities of practice in the last two chapters.

- *Practice as meaning.* Chapter 1 sets the stage conceptually by arguing that the social production of meaning is the relevant level of analysis for talking about practice. In making that argument, I will introduce three basic concepts – negotiation of meaning, participation, and reification – that will serve as a foundation, not only for Part I, but for the whole book.
- *Practice as community.* Chapter 2 defines the concept of community of practice by talking about practice as the source of coherence of a community. I will introduce three dimensions of this relationship between practice and community: mutual engagement, a joint enterprise, and a shared repertoire of ways of doing things.
- *Practice as learning.* Chapter 3 addresses the development of communities of practice over time. Building on the themes of Chapter 1, I will discuss the factors of continuity and discontinuity that constitute a community of practice over time. Building on the themes of Chapter 2, I will argue that practice must be understood as a learning process and that a community of practice is therefore an emergent structure, neither inherently stable nor randomly changeable. I will end by talking about the learning by which newcomers can join the community and thus further its practice.
- *Practice as boundary.* Chapter 4 discusses the boundaries that practice creates. Building again first on the themes of Chapters 1 and 2, I will describe the types of connections that create bridges across boundaries and link communities of practice with the rest of the

world. I will end by arguing that boundaries of practice are not simple lines of demarcation between inside and outside, but form a complex social landscape of boundaries and peripheries.

- *Practice as locality.* Chapter 5 addresses the scope and limits of the concept of community of practice. I will discuss when to view a social configuration as one community or as a constellation of communities of practice. I will thus start talking about other levels of social structure, but still in terms of practice. I will leave the discussion of other types of structuring processes for Part II.

- *Knowing in practice.* Coda I ends this discussion of practice with a brief essay on knowing in practice. Echoing the argument of Part I, I will summarize the themes introduced in each chapter by using them to ponder what it means to know in practice. This will result in a definition of learning as an interplay of experience and competence.

Because Coda I gives an overview of Part I, it offers a logical starting point if you like to begin with an overview and are comfortable with terms that are not yet well-defined. You would first see – in a synoptic fashion and in a specific context – how the whole argument fits together, and then be able to obtain details by referring to individual chapters.

Chapter 1

Meaning

Our attempts to understand human life open a vast space of relevant questions – from the origin of the universe to the workings of the brain, from the details of every thought to the purpose of life. In this vast space of questions, the concept of practice is useful for addressing a specific slice: a focus on the experience of meaningfulness. Practice is, first and foremost, a process by which we can experience the world and our engagement with it as meaningful.

Of course, in order to engage in practice, we must be alive in a world in which we can act and interact. We must have a body with a brain that is functioning well enough to participate in social communities. We must have ways to communicate with one another. But a focus on practice is not merely a functional perspective on human activities, even activities involving multiple individuals. It does not address simply the mechanics of getting something done, individually or in groups; it is not a mechanical perspective. It includes not just bodies (or even coordinated bodies) and not just brains (even coordinated ones), but moreover that which gives *meaning* to the motions of bodies and the workings of brains.[1]

Let me illustrate this point by analogy to a work of art. There are all sorts of mechanics involved in producing a painting: a canvas, brushes, color pigments, and sophisticated techniques. The image itself is but a thin veneer. Yet in the end, for the painter and for the viewer, it is the painting as an experience of meaning that counts. Similarly, in the pursuit of our enterprises, we engage in all sorts of activities with complex bodies that are the result of millennia of evolution. Still, in the end, it is the meanings we produce that matter.

This focus on meaningfulness is therefore not primarily on the technicalities of "meaning." It is not on meaning as it sits locked up in dictionaries. It is not just on meaning as a relation between a sign and a reference. But neither is it on meaning as a grand question – on the

51

meaning of life as a philosophical issue. *Practice is about meaning as an experience of everyday life.*

If the kind of meaning I am interested in is an experience, and if it is not the kind we can find in dictionary definitions or in philosophical discussions, then I need to address the questions of where it is located and how it is constituted. In this chapter, I will first argue that:

1) meaning is located in a process I will call the *negotiation of meaning*
2) the negotiation of meaning involves the interaction of two constituent processes, which I will call *participation* and *reification*
3) participation and reification form a duality that is fundamental to the human experience of meaning and thus to the nature of practice.

These concepts are essential to my argument, and I will start by explaining in some detail what I mean by them and just why they are important.

Negotiation of meaning

The experience of meaning is not produced out of thin air, but neither is it simply a mechanical realization of a routine or a procedure. For Ariel, no two claims are the same, even though she has learned to coerce these claims into manageable categories. Indeed, medical claims processing is largely a classificatory activity. Its purpose is to impose standards of sameness and difference in the midst of a flow of change so that claims can be recognized as belonging to categories amenable to well-understood treatment. But for Ariel, this routinization must constantly be achieved anew, claim after claim.

Our engagement in practice may have patterns, but it is the production of such patterns anew that gives rise to an experience of meaning. When we sit down for lunch for the thousandth time with the same colleagues in the same cafeteria, we have seen it all before. We know all the steps. We may even know today's menu by heart; we may love it or we may dread it. And yet we eat again, we taste again. We may know our colleagues very well, and yet we repeatedly engage in conversations. All that we do and say may refer to what has been done and said in the past, and yet we produce again a new situation, an impression, an experience: we produce meanings that extend, redirect, dismiss, reinterpret, modify or confirm – in a word, negotiate anew – the histories of meanings of which they are part. In this sense, living is a constant process of *negotiation of meaning.*

I will use the concept of negotiation of meaning very generally to characterize the process by which we experience the world and our engagement in it as meaningful.[2] Whether we are talking, acting, thinking, solving problems, or daydreaming, we are concerned with meanings. I have argued that even routine activities like claims processing or eating in a cafeteria involve the negotiation of meaning, but it is all the more true when we are involved in activities that we care about or that present us with challenges: when we look in wonder at a beautiful landscape, when we close a delicate deal, when we go on a special date, when we solve a difficult mystery, when we listen to a moving piece of music, when we read a good book, or when we mourn a dear friend. In such cases, the intensity of the process is obvious, but the same process is at work even if what we end up negotiating turns out to be an experience of meaninglessness. Human engagement in the world is first and foremost a process of negotiating meaning.[3]

The negotiation of meaning may involve language, but it is not limited to it. It includes our social relations as factors in the negotiation, but it does not necessarily involve a conversation or even direct interaction with other human beings. The concept of negotiation often denotes reaching an agreement between people, as in "negotiating a price," but it is not limited to that usage. It is also used to suggest an accomplishment that requires sustained attention and readjustment, as in "negotiating a sharp curve." I want to capture both aspects at once, in order to suggest that living meaningfully implies:

1) an active process of producing meaning that is both dynamic and historical
2) a world of both resistance and malleability
3) the mutual ability to affect and to be affected
4) the engagement of a multiplicity of factors and perspectives
5) the production of a new resolution to the convergence of these factors and perspectives
6) the incompleteness of this resolution, which can be partial, tentative, ephemeral, and specific to a situation.

I intend the term *negotiation* to convey a flavor of continuous interaction, of gradual achievement, and of give-and-take. By living in the world we do not just make meanings up independently of the world, but neither does the world simply impose meanings on us. The negotiation of meaning is a productive process, but negotiating meaning is not constructing it from scratch. Meaning is not pre-existing, but neither is it simply made up. Negotiated meaning is at once both historical and dynamic, contextual and unique.

The negotiation of meaning is a process that is shaped by multiple elements and that affects these elements. As a result, this negotiation constantly changes the situations to which it gives meaning and affects all participants. In this process, negotiating meaning entails both interpretation and action. In fact, this perspective does not imply a fundamental distinction between interpreting and acting, doing and thinking, or understanding and responding. All are part of the ongoing process of negotiating meaning. This process always generates new circumstances for further negotiation and further meanings. It constantly produces new relations with and in the world. The meaningfulness of our engagement in the world is not a state of affairs, but a continual process of renewed negotiation.[4]

From this perspective, meaning is always the product of its negotiation, by which I mean that it exists in this process of negotiation. Meaning exists neither in us, nor in the world, but in the dynamic relation of living in the world.

The dynamics of negotiated meaning

The processing of a given claim form by a processor like Ariel is an example of the negotiation of meaning. It takes place in a context that combines a vast array of factors, including the organization of the insurance industry, the official and unofficial training the processor underwent, the way the particular claim looks, past experiences with similar claims, the way the day is going, who else is around, what else is happening, and so on. The contexts that contribute to shaping the experience of a claim reach far and wide in time and space.

When Ariel grabs a new claim, she may not know exactly what to do, but she is in familiar territory. Even if there is a problem, she may be annoyed but she is not surprised; it will be resolved eventually. In fact, she can hardly recall the tentativeness of that first day, the unsettling mysteriousness of those training weeks, the reaching out during her first months on the floor, when just about every claim she was processing presented one problem or another. It had seemed so big then –

claims processing, Alinsu, the medical establishment. But now it is familiar. It is her job, and she is reasonably good at it.

The claim too comes with a history. It started out as a blank form designed by technical specialists at Alinsu. It was approved by various professional associations before it was printed. It was sent to a client company where a benefit representative distributed it to an employee. It was partially filled out by that employee and submitted to medical professionals who completed it. Then it was sent back to Alinsu, where it was first sorted by clerical personnel to be routed in a bundle to Ariel's processing unit. And now it is on her desk, to be coerced somehow into the confines of the processible.

Processing claims requires a very specific way of looking at a claim form. The ability to interpret a claim form reflects the relations that both the claim and Ariel have to particular practices. Ariel contributes to the negotiation of meaning by being a member of a community and bringing to bear her history of participation in its practice. Similarly, the claim contributes to this process by reflecting aspects of practice that have been congealed in it and fixed in its shape. I would say that the processor as a member of a community of practice embodies a long and diverse process of what I will call *participation*. Similarly, the claim as an artifact of certain practices embodies a long and diverse process of what I will call *reification*. It is in the convergence of these two processes in the act of processing the claim that the negotiation of meaning takes place.

As a pair, participation and reification refer to a duality fundamental to the negotiation of meaning. In order to clarify why this is so, I will first discuss each term separately before turning to the duality that their complementarity forms.

Participation

My use of the term *participation* falls within common usage. It is therefore helpful to start with Webster's definition: "To have or take a part or share with others (in some activity, enterprise, etc.)." Participation refers to a process of taking part and also to the relations with others that reflect this process. It suggests both action and connection.

In this book, I will use the term participation to describe the social experience of living in the world in terms of membership in social communities and active involvement in social enterprises. Participation in this sense is both personal and social. It is a complex process that combines doing, talking, thinking, feeling, and belonging. It involves our whole person, including our bodies, minds, emotions, and social relations.

Participation is an active process, but I will reserve the term for actors who are members of social communities. For instance, I will not say that a computer "participates" in a community of practice, even though it may be part of that practice and play an active role in getting certain things done.[5] Neither will I say that a fish in its bowl in the living room participates in a family. But I would be open to considering that a family dog, for instance, participates in some peripheral but real way in that family. In this regard, what I take to characterize participation is the possibility of mutual recognition. When we shave a piece of wood or mold a piece of clay, we do not construe our shaping these objects as contributing to their experience of meaning. But when we engage in a conversation, we somehow recognize in each other something of ourselves, which we address. What we recognize has to do with our mutual ability to negotiate meaning. This mutuality does not, however, entail equality or respect. The relations between parents and children or between workers and their direct supervisor are mutual in the sense that participants shape each other's experiences of meaning. In doing so, they can recognize something of themselves in each other. But these are not relations of equality. In practice, even the meanings of inequality are negotiated in the context of this process of mutual recognition.

In this experience of mutuality, participation is a source of identity. By recognizing the mutuality of our participation, we become part of each other. In fact, the concept of identity is so central that I will postpone more detailed discussion until Part II, where it will be the main topic. Here I will just say that a defining characteristic of participation is the possibility of developing an "identity of participation," that is, an identity constituted through relations of participation.

Before I proceed, it is worth clarifying a few more points about my use of the term participation.

- First, participation as I will use the term is not tantamount to collaboration. It can involve all kinds of relations, conflictual as well as harmonious, intimate as well as political, competitive as well as cooperative.
- Second, participation in social communities shapes our experience, and it also shapes those communities; the transformative potential

goes both ways. Indeed, our ability (or inability) to shape the practice of our communities is an important aspect of our experience of participation.

- Finally, as a constituent of meaning, participation is broader than mere engagement in practice. Claims processors are not claims processors just while they work in the office. Of course, that time of intense engagement with their work and with one another is especially significant. But they do not cease to be claims processors at five o'clock. Their participation is not something they simply turn off when they leave. Its effects on their experience are not restricted to the specific context of their engagement. It is a part of who they are that they always carry with them and that will surface if, for instance, they themselves happen to go to the doctor, fill out an insurance form, or call a customer service center. In this sense, participation goes beyond direct engagement in specific activities with specific people. It places the negotiation of meaning in the context of our forms of membership in various communities. It is a constituent of our identities. As such, participation is not something we turn on and off.

From this perspective, our engagement with the world is social, even when it does not clearly involve interactions with others. Being in a hotel room by yourself preparing a set of slides for a presentation the next morning may not seem like a particularly social event, yet its meaning is fundamentally social. Not only is the audience there with you as you attempt to make your points understandable to them, but your colleagues are there too, looking over your shoulder, as it were, representing for you your sense of accountability to the professional standards of your community. A child doing homework, a doctor making a decision, a traveler reading a book – all these activities implicitly involve other people who may not be present. The meanings of what we do are always social. By "social" I do not refer just to family dinners, company picnics, school dances, and church socials. Even drastic isolation – as in solitary confinement, monastic seclusion, or writing – is given meaning through social participation. The concept of participation is meant to capture this profoundly social character of our experience of life.

Reification

The term *reification* is less common than participation. But I hope to show that, in conjunction with participation, reification is a very useful concept to describe our engagement with the world as productive of meaning. Again, it will help to start with Webster's definition of reification: "To treat (an abstraction) as substantially existing, or as a concrete material object."[6]

Etymologically, the term reification means "making into a thing." Its usage in English has a significant twist, however: it is used to convey the idea that what is turned into a concrete, material object is not properly a concrete, material object. For instance, we make representations of "justice" as a blindfolded maid holding a scale, or use expressions such as "the hand of fate."

In everyday discourse, abstractions like "democracy" or "the economy" are often talked about as though they were active agents. When a newscast reports that "democracy took a blow during a military coup," or that "the economy reacted slowly to the government's action," the process of reification provides a shortcut to communication.

This succinctness derives from a slight illusion of excessive reality, but it is useful because it focuses the negotiation of meaning. This is the subtle idea I want to capture by using the term reification. We project our meanings into the world and then we perceive them as existing in the world, as having a reality of their own. For example, my own use of the term reification in the context of this book is itself a case in point. The term is a projection of what I mean. It is an abstraction. It does not do the work by itself. But after a while, as I use it to think with, it starts talking to me as though it were alive. Whereas in participation we recognize ourselves in each other, in reification we project ourselves onto the world, and not having to recognize ourselves in those projections, we attribute to our meanings an independent existence. This contrast between mutuality and projection is an important difference between participation and reification.

The concept of reification

I will use the concept of reification very generally to refer to the process of giving form to our experience by producing objects that congeal this experience into "thingness." In so doing we create points of focus around which the negotiation of meaning becomes organized. Again my use of the term reification is its own example. I am introducing it into the discourse because I want to create a new distinction to serve as a point of focus around which to organize my discussion. Writing down a law, creating a procedure, or producing a tool is a similar process. A certain understanding is given form. This form then becomes a focus for the negotiation of meaning, as people use the law to argue a point, use the procedure to know what to do, or use the tool to perform an action.

I would claim that the process of reification so construed is central to every practice. Any community of practice produces abstractions, tools, symbols, stories, terms, and concepts that reify something of that practice in a congealed form. Clearly, I want to use the concept of reification in a much broader sense than its dictionary definition. But I want to preserve the connotations of excessive concreteness and projected reality that are suggested by the dictionary definition. Indeed, no abstraction, tool, or symbol actually captures in its form the practices in the context of which it contributes to an experience of meaning. A medical claim, for instance, reifies in its form a complex web of conventions, agreements, expectations, commitments, and obligations, including (on the part of medical professionals) the right to bill for certain services and the obligation to do so in a standardized way and (on the part of the insurance company) the right to decide if the claim is legitimate and duly filled out, together with the obligation to honor the claim if it is.[7]

With the term reification I mean to cover a wide range of processes that include making, designing, representing, naming, encoding, and describing, as well as perceiving, interpreting, using, reusing, decoding, and recasting. Reification occupies much of our collective energy: from entries in a journal to historical records, from poems to encyclopedias, from names to classification systems, from dolmens to space probes, from the Constitution to a signature on a credit card slip, from gourmet recipes to medical procedures, from flashy advertisements to census data, from single concepts to entire theories, from the evening news to national archives, from lesson plans to the compilation of textbooks, from private address lists to sophisticated credit reporting databases, from tortuous political speeches to the yellow pages. In all these cases, aspects of human experience and practice are congealed into fixed forms and given the status of object.

Reification shapes our experience. It can do so in very concrete ways. Having a tool to perform an activity changes the nature of that activity. A word processor, for instance, reifies a view of the activity of writing, but also changes how one goes about writing. The effects of reification can also be less obvious. Reifying the concept of gravity may not change its effect on our bodies, but it does change our experience of the world by focusing our attention in a particular way and enabling new kinds of understanding. Similarly, reifying the concept of body weight as a measure of self-worth does not make us heavier but can weigh heavily on our sense of self. The reification of claims processing through the type of forms and procedures described in Vignette II can detach work activities from other personal experiences to the point where the generally reificative nature of the work gives the job of claims processing a particular character. Even the regularly scheduled breaks reify what is work and what is not.

Again, I should clarify a few points about my use of the concept of reification before proceeding.

- Reification can refer both to a process and its product, and I will use the term in both senses. This liberty is not just a lack of rigor, but part of the point. If meaning exists only in its negotiation then, at the level of meaning, the process and the product are not distinct. Reification is not just objectification; it does not end in an object. It does not simply translate meaning into an object. On the contrary, my use of the concept is meant to suggest that such translation is never possible, and that the process and the product always imply each other.
- Claims processors are not the designers of the rules and forms they use, yet they must absorb them into their practice. In an institutional environment such as a claims processing site, a very large portion of the reification involved in work practices comes from outside the communities of workers. Even so, however, reification must be re-appropriated into a local process in order to become meaningful.[8]
- The process of reification does not necessarily originate in design. A detective may spend much time studying fingerprints on a doorknob; an archaeologist is fascinated by traces of ancient life in a cave. Most human activities produce marks in the physical world. These marks are vestiges. They freeze fleeting moments of engagement in practice into monuments, which persist and disappear in their own time. Whether intentionally produced or not, they can then be reintegrated as reification into new moments of negotiation of meaning.
- Reification can take a great variety of forms: a fleeting smoke signal or an age-old pyramid, an abstract formula or a concrete truck, a small logo or a huge information-processing system, a simple word jotted on a page or a complex argument developed in a whole book, a telling glance or a long silence, a private knot on a handkerchief or a controversial statue on a public square, an impressionist painting of a butterfly or a scientific specimen in an entomological collection.

What is important about all these objects is that they are only the tip of an iceberg, which indicates larger contexts of significance realized in human practices. Their character as reification is not only in their form but also in the processes by which they are integrated into these practices. Properly speaking, the products of reification are not simply concrete, material objects. Rather, they are reflections of these practices, tokens of vast expanses of human meanings.

The double edge of reification

As an evocative shortcut, the process of reification can be very powerful. A politician can reify voters' inarticulate longings in one phrase that galvanizes support. A good tool can reify an activity so as to amplify its effects while making the activity effortless. A procedure can reify a concept so that its application is automatic. A formula can express in a few terms a regularity that pervades the universe.

But the power of reification – its succinctness, its portability, its potential physical persistence, its focusing effect – is also its danger. The politician's slogan can become a substitute for a deep understanding of and commitment to what it stands for. The tool can ossify activity around its inertness. Procedures can hide broader meanings in blind sequences of operations. And the knowledge of a formula can lead to the illusion that one fully understands the processes it describes.

The evocative power of reification is thus double-edged. Classifying people under broad categories can focus attention on a kind of diversity, but the reification can give differences and similarities a concreteness they do not actually possess. Similarly, if an organization displays a statement of values in its lobby, it has created a reification of something that does or should pervade the organization. Though this "something" is probably much more diffuse and intangible in practice, it gains a new concreteness once framed in the lobby. It becomes something people can point to, refer to, strive for, appeal to, and use or misuse in arguments. Yet, as a reification, it may seem disconnected, frozen into a text that does not capture the richness of lived experience and that can be appropriated in misleading ways. As a focus of attention that can be detached from practice, the reification may even be seen with cynicism, as an ironic substitute for what it was intended to reflect.

Indeed, my use of the term reification does not assume an inherent correspondence between a symbol and a referent, a tool and a function, or a phenomenon and an interpretation. On the contrary, the concept of reification suggests that forms can take a life of their own, beyond their context of origin. They gain a degree of autonomy from the occasion and purposes of their production. Their meaningfulness is always potentially expanded and potentially lost. Reification as a constituent of meaning is always incomplete, ongoing, potentially enriching, and potentially misleading. The notion of assigning the status of object to something that really is not an object conveys a sense of mistaken solidity, of projected concreteness. It conveys a sense of useful illusion. The use of the term reification stands both as a tribute to the generative power of the process and as a gentle reminder of its delusory perils.

The duality of meaning

In their interplay, participation and reification are both distinct and complementary, as suggested by the illustration in Figure 1.1.[9] The reification of a Constitution is just a form; it is not equivalent to a citizenry. Yet it is empty without the participation of the citizens involved. Conversely, the production of such a reification is crucial to the kind of negotiation that is necessary for them to act as citizens and to bring together the multiple perspectives, interests, and interpretations that participation entails.

As the figure suggests, participation and reification cannot be considered in isolation: they come as a pair. They form a unity in their duality. Given one, it is a useful heuristic to wonder where the other is. To understand one, it is necessary to understand the other. To enable one, it is necessary to enable the other. They come about through each other, but they cannot replace each other. It is through their various combinations that they give rise to a variety of experiences of meaning.

We don't usually think of the experience of meaning as a duality because the interplay of participation and reification remains largely unproblematic. Processes of reification and participation can be woven so tightly that the distinction between them seems almost blurred. The use of language in face-to-face interactions is a good example. Words as projections of human meaning are certainly a form of reification. In face-to-face interactions, however, speech is extremely evanescent; words affect the negotiation of meaning through a process that seems like pure participation. As a consequence, words can take advantage of shared participation among interlocutors to create shortcuts to communication. It is this tight interweaving of reification and participation that makes conversations such a powerful form of communication.

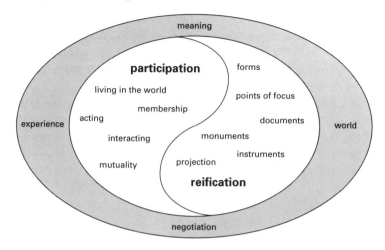

Figure 1.1. The duality of participation and reification.

More generally, the negotiation of meaning weaves participation and reification so seamlessly that meaning seems to have its own unitary, self-contained existence: a medical claim is a medical claim; a smile is a smile; a joke is a joke. Of course, it is often convenient to act as though meanings are in actions or artifacts themselves. So a medical claim is indeed a medical claim; it was produced to be a medical claim; it exists for us in a civilization where everything concurs to make it a medical claim. And yet what it is to be a medical claim is always defined with respect to specific forms of participation that contextualize meaning. It cannot be assumed to be intrinsic or universal.

The complementarity of participation and reification

Although seamlessly woven into our practices, the complementarity of participation and reification is something familiar. We use it as a matter of course in order to secure some continuity of meaning across time and space. Indeed, in their complementarity, participation and reification can make up for their respective limitations. They can compensate for each other's shortcomings, so to speak.

- On the one hand, participation makes up for the inherent limitations of reification. We send ambassadors with our treaties and hire judges to interpret our laws; we offer 800 numbers as customer service for our products in addition to our careful documentation; we convene a meeting to introduce a new policy in order to avoid misunderstandings; we discuss what we read in order to compare and enrich our interpretations. Participation is essential to repairing the potential misalignments inherent in reification. When the stiffness of its form renders reification obsolete, when its mute ambiguity is misleading, or when its purpose is lost in the distance, then it is participation that comes to the rescue.

• On the other hand, reification also makes up for the inherent limitations of participation. We create monuments to remember the dead; we take notes to remind ourselves of decisions made in the past; we share our notes with colleagues who could not attend a meeting; we are surprised by the way someone else describes a common event or object; we clarify our intentions with explanations and representational devices; we coordinate our coming and going with clocks. Mirroring the role of participation, reification is essential to repairing the potential misalignments inherent in participation: when the informality of participation is confusingly loose, when the fluidity of its implicitness impedes coordination, when its locality is too confining or its partiality too narrow, then it is reification that comes to the rescue.

One advantage of viewing the negotiation of meaning as constituted by a dual process is that we can consider the various trade-offs involved in the complementarity of participation and reification. Indeed, given an action or an artifact, it becomes a relevant question to ask how the production of meaning is distributed, that is, what is reified and what is left to participation.

• A computer program, for instance, could be described as an extreme kind of reification, which can be interpreted by a machine incapable of any participation in its meaning.

• A poem, by contrast, is designed to rely on participation, that is, to maximize the work that the ambiguity inherent in its form can do in the negotiation of meaning.

From such a perspective, communication is not just a quantitative issue. Indeed, what says more: the few lines of a tightly written poem or a volume of analytical comments on it? The communicative ability of artifacts depends on how the work of negotiating meaning is distributed between reification and participation. Different mixes become differentially productive of meaning.

The complementarity of participation and reification yields an obvious but profound principle for endeavors that rely on some degree of continuity of meaning – communication, design, instruction, or collaboration. Participation and reification must be in such proportion and relation as to compensate for their respective shortcomings. When too much reliance is placed on one at the expense of the other, the continuity of meaning is likely to become problematic in practice.

- If participation prevails – if most of what matters is left unreified – then there may not be enough material to anchor the specificities of coordination and to uncover diverging assumptions. This is why lawyers always want everything in writing.
- If reification prevails – if everything is reified, but with little opportunity for shared experience and interactive negotiation – then there may not be enough overlap in participation to recover a coordinated, relevant, or generative meaning. This helps explain why putting everything in writing does not seem to solve all our problems.

In cases of mismatches, it is necessary to analyze the situation in terms of the duality and to redress any imbalance. Merely adding more participation to participation or more reification to reification may not help much, because a form of participation or reification is by itself unlikely to correct its own shortcomings: not just another memo, not just another meeting . . . .

A fundamental duality

The duality of participation and reification will appear again and again as I develop my argument in this book. This duality is a fundamental aspect of the constitution of communities of practice, of their evolution over time, of the relations among practices, of the identities of participants, and of the broader organizations in which communities of practice exist.

In this context, as I tried to emphasize with the diagram of Figure 1.1, it is important *not* to interpret the duality of participation and reification in terms of a simple opposition. I will end this chapter by expanding this point. If you are in a hurry and feel that enough has been said already, you may want to skip the fine points I am making here and move on to the next chapter. But if you have the patience and the inclination, then reading on will help clarify both the nature of the relation between participation and reification and, more generally, what I mean by a duality as opposed to a dichotomy. The latter clarification will be useful since I will introduce a number of dualities in the coming chapters. Indeed, thinking in terms of complex dualities rather than mere dichotomies is fundamental to the conceptual framework of this book.

As suggested by Figure 1.1, a duality is a single conceptual unit that is formed by two inseparable and mutually constitutive elements whose inherent tension and complementarity give the concept richness and dynamism. In what follows, I will clarify this idea by contrasting the duality of participation and reification with related, more traditional dichotomies of opposites – for example, tacit versus explicit, formal versus informal, individual versus collective, private versus public, conscious versus unconscious, or people versus things. I will do so via a list of statements, in each case saying both what the duality of participation and reification is and what it is not.

◆ *Participation and reification are a duality, not opposites.*

Participation and reification are not defined merely by opposition to each other. The tacit is that which is not made explicit; the informal that which is not formalized; the unconscious that which is not conscious. But participation is not merely what is not reified. Both participation and reification are processes defined each in their own terms. As a result, they are not mutually exclusive. On the contrary, they take place together; they are two constituents intrinsic to the process of negotiation of meaning, and their complementarity reflects the inherent duality of this process.

Participation and reification both require and enable each other. On the one hand, it takes our participation to produce, interpret, and use reification; so there is no reification without participation. On the other hand, our participation requires interaction and thus generates shortcuts to coordinated meanings that reflect our enterprises and our takes on the world; so there is no participation without reification.

◆ *Participation and reification are two dimensions that interact; they do not define a spectrum.*

One way to avoid thinking starkly in terms of opposites is to consider a spectrum. Knowledge can be more or less explicit; learning can be more or less formal; an impression can be more or less conscious; a meaning can be more or less individual. While a continuum does allow more nuanced distinctions, it is still a relation between opposites.

Moving to one side implies leaving the other. More of one implies less of the other.

With an interacting duality, by contrast, both elements are always involved, and both can take different forms and degrees. In particular, there can be both intense participation and intense reification. In fact, the creative genius of great scientists and artists can be construed as stemming from their ability to bring the two together: on the one hand, an intense involvement with the reificative formalisms of their discipline; and on the other, a deep participative intuition of what those formalisms are about. This is true of a scientist like Albert Einstein, who insisted on the importance of exploring ideas intuitively as well as being able to give them mathematical expression. It is as true of a musician like Johann Sebastian Bach, who combined intricate forms of musical structure with melodic inspiration.

Such a perspective has pedagogical implications for teaching complex knowledge: an excessive emphasis on formalism without corresponding levels of participation, or conversely a neglect of explanations and formal structure, can easily result in an experience of meaninglessness.

♦ *Participation and reification imply each other; they do not substitute for each other.*

Increasing the level of participation or reification does not dispense with the other. On the contrary, it will tend to increase the requirements for the other.

Indeed, reification always rests on participation: what is said, represented, or otherwise brought into focus always assumes a history of participation as a context for its interpretation. In turn, participation always organizes itself around reification because it always involves artifacts, words, and concepts that allow it to proceed.

Explicit knowledge is thus not freed from the tacit. Formal processes are not freed from the informal. In fact, in terms of meaningfulness, the opposite is more likely. To be understood meaningfully as a representation of a piece of physics knowledge, an abstract reification like $E = mc^2$ does not obviate a close connection to the physics community but, on the contrary, requires it. In general, viewed as a reification, a more abstract formulation will require more intense and specific participation to remain meaningful, not less.

From such a perspective, it is not possible to make everything explicit and thus get rid of the tacit, or to make everything formal and thus get rid of the informal. It is possible only to change their relation.

♦ *Participation and reification transform their relation; they do not translate into each other.*

A dichotomy tends to suggest that there must be a process by which one can move from one to the other by translation into a different but equivalent state. We can transform tacit knowledge into explicit knowledge or vice versa; we can formalize a learning process; we can share our thoughts; we can make our emotions more conscious. By contrast, a change in the relations of participation and reification is never neutral; it always transforms the possibilities for negotiating meaning.

• Participation is never simply the realization of a description or a prescription. Participating in an activity that has been described is not just translating the description into embodied experience, but renegotiating its meaning in a new context.
• Reification is not a mere articulation of something that already exists. Writing down a statement of values, expressing an idea, painting a picture, recounting an event, articulating an emotion, or building a tool is not merely giving expression to existing meanings, but in fact creating the conditions for new meanings.

As a consequence, such processes as making something explicit, formalizing, or sharing are not merely translations; they are indeed transformations – the production of a new context of both participation and reification, in which the relations between the tacit and the explicit, the formal and the informal, the individual and the collective, are to be renegotiated.

♦ *Participation and reification describe an interplay; they are not classificatory categories.*

There is a fundamental difference between using a distinction to classify things (e.g., meanings, thoughts, knowledge, learning) as one pole or the other and using a distinction to describe an inherent interplay.

In a duality, what is of interest is understanding the interplay, not classifying. The duality of participation and reification is not a classificatory scheme. It does not classify meanings, thoughts, knowledge, or learning as tacit or explicit, formal or informal, conscious or unconscious, individual or collective. Rather, it provides a framework to analyze the various ways in which they are always both at once.

Traditional dichotomies are useful distinctions when they are used to highlight an aspect of a process that has not received enough attention. But when it comes to issues like meaning, knowing, or learning, dichotomies cannot provide clean classificatory categories because they focus on surface features rather than on fundamental processes. For instance, the contrast between explicit and tacit knowledge is quite useful because it is important to recognize the existence of aspects of knowledge that we cannot easily articulate; hence, being able to *tell* and being able to *do* are not equivalent.

Classifying knowledge as explicit or tacit runs into difficulties, however, because both aspects are always present to some degree. For example, people who know how to ride a bicycle often cannot articulate how they keep their balance. In particular, they cannot say which way they steer in order to avoid falling, even though they do it right.[10] To classify riding a bicycle as tacit knowledge is tricky because people are not exactly speechless about the process. They can tell you, for instance, that you must pedal and steer, hold the bar, and not wiggle too much or sit backward unless you're a pro. Classifying knowledge then becomes a matter of deciding what counts as explicit, and that depends on the enterprise we are involved in.

Walking is a very embodied knowledge, but if someone tells me to walk, I can do it. Requiring only this yields a good enough relation between the explicit and the tacit for certain purposes, though probably not good enough for an orthopedist who needs to know which muscles I use to keep my balance and move my legs – but that is a different enterprise altogether. Conversely, I'd bet that physicists, whose knowledge many of us would consider very explicit, would have as hard a time articulating exactly how they make sense of concepts such as force and space–time as we have explaining how we ride a bicycle. When it comes to meaningful knowing in the context of any enterprise, the explicit must always stop somewhere. It is always possible to find aspects that are not explicit, and this is exactly what a duality of participation and reification would predict: we produce precisely the reification we need in order to proceed with the practices in which we participate.

The duality of participation and reification is more fundamental than our ability to put things in words, create formalisms, articulate our feelings, or share our thoughts. It is therefore important not to reduce participation and reification to any of the dichotomies I have mentioned.

- For instance, participation is not just tacit, informal, or unconscious, because our participation includes actions like having a conversation, teaching a formalized curriculum, or reflecting on our motives.
- Reification is not just explicit, because there are many ways of reifying that are not simply putting things into words. A painting, for

instance, reifies a perception of the world, an understanding. It is an expression that makes a statement and focuses our attention in specific ways. But it is difficult to say whether this expression is explicit or tacit. Similarly, building a tool or systematically ignoring people to let them know they are outsiders are acts of reification that cannot easily be classified as tacit or explicit.

- Neither participation nor reification can be easily thought of in terms of contrasts of individual versus collective, or private versus public. Participation is clearly a social process, but it is also a personal experience. Reification allows us to coordinate our actions and is therefore of a collective character, but it shapes our own perceptions of the world and ourselves.
- Reification can be public to the extent that it produces tangible objects, but participation can also be public to the extent that our actions are observable. Moreover, the effects of both on our experience are not so visible or easily classified as public or private.

Finally, the duality of participation and reification is not just a distinction between people and things. It is true that participation is something we do as persons, and reification has to do with objects. But the duality of participation and reification suggests precisely that, in terms of meaning, people and things cannot be defined independently of each other.

- On the one hand, we experience the world as we make it amenable to our practices. I remember being awed by the complex system of distinctions and nuances that wine tasters have developed to describe what to most people is merely a better or worse glass of wine.
- On the other hand, our sense of ourselves includes the objects with which we identify because they furnish our practices. Mastering the wine-tasting vocabulary and being able to appreciate and discuss all the nuances of a good wine can become a source of distinction, pride, and identity.

What it means to be a person and what it means to be a thing both involve an interplay of participation and reification. From this perspective, people and things do not have to be posited as a point of departure. They need not be assumed as given to start with. It is engagement in social practice that provides the baseline. Through the negotiation of meaning, it is the interplay of participation and reification that makes people and things what they are.

In this interplay, our experience and our world shape each other through a reciprocal relation that goes to the very essence of who we are. The world as we shape it, and our experience as the world shapes it, are like the mountain and the river. They shape each other, but they have their own shape. They are reflections of each other, but they have their own existence, in their own realms. They fit around each other, but they remain distinct from each other. They cannot be transformed into each other, yet they transform each other. The river only carves and the mountain only guides, yet in their interaction, the carving becomes the guiding and the guiding becomes the carving.

Chapter 2
Community

The negotiation of meaning, I have argued, is the level of discourse at which the concept of practice should be understood. The second piece of necessary groundwork is to associate practice with the formation of communities. By associating practice with community, I am not arguing that everything anybody might call a community is defined by practice or has a practice that is specific to it; nor that everything anybody might call practice is the defining property of a clearly specifiable community. A residential neighborhood, for instance, is often called "the community" but it is usually not a community of practice. Playing scales on the piano is often called practice – as in "practice makes perfect" – but it does not define what I would call a community of practice. Rather, I am claiming that associating practice and community does two things.

1) It yields a more tractable characterization of the concept of practice – in particular, by distinguishing it from less tractable terms like culture, activity, or structure.
2) It defines a special type of community – a community of practice.

Because its constituent terms specify each other in this way, the term *community of practice* should be viewed as a unit. In Part I, when I use the term *community* or the term *practice* by itself, it is just an abbreviation to make the text less cumbersome. In Part II, however, things will become more complicated because I will start to talk about other types of communities.

To associate practice and community, I will describe three dimensions of the relation by which practice is the source of coherence of a community, as summarized in Figure 2.1:

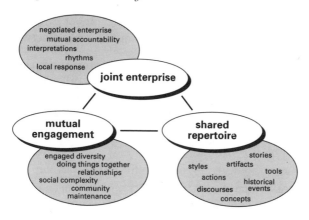

Figure 2.1. Dimensions of practice as the property of a community.

1) mutual engagement
2) a joint enterprise
3) a shared repertoire.

I will spend the bulk of this chapter talking about each of these three dimensions of communities of practice, saying what they are and what they are not, and specifying what characteristics of practice and community they entail and do not entail.

Mutual engagement

The first characteristic of practice as the source of coherence of a community is the mutual engagement of participants. Practice does not exist in the abstract. It exists because people are engaged in actions whose meanings they negotiate with one another. In this sense, practice does not reside in books or in tools, though it may involve all kinds of artifacts. It does not reside in a structure that precedes it, though it does not start in a historical vacuum. The history of claims processing started long before Ariel and her colleagues arrived on the scene, and yet what they do together is not just a cookie-cutter realization of a historical schema. Practice resides in a community of people and the relations of mutual engagement by which they can do whatever they do.

Membership in a community of practice is therefore a matter of mutual engagement. That is what defines the community. A community of practice is not just an aggregate of people defined by some characteristic. The term is not a synonym for group, team, or network.

- Membership is not just a matter of social category, declaring allegiance, belonging to an organization, having a title, or having personal relations with some people.
- A community of practice is not defined merely by who knows whom or who talks with whom in a network of interpersonal relations through which information flows.[1]
- Neither is geographical proximity sufficient to develop a practice. Of course, mutual engagement requires interactions, and geographical proximity can help. But it is not because claims processors work in the same office that they form a community of practice. It is because they sustain dense relations of mutual engagement organized around what they are there to do.

Enabling engagement

Whatever it takes to make mutual engagement possible is an essential component of any practice. For claims processors, for instance, coming to the office is a key element of their practice. So is being able (and allowed) to talk and interact while they work.[2] For a family, it can be having dinner together, taking trips on weekends, or cleaning the house on Saturdays. Given the right context, talking on the phone, exchanging electronic mail, or being connected by radio can all be part of what makes mutual engagement possible.

Being included in what matters is a requirement for being engaged in a community's practice, just as engagement is what defines belonging. What it takes for a community of practice to cohere enough to function can be very subtle and delicate. Certainly, for claims processors to work together, it is difficult to distinguish between the value of a specific piece of information and the value of the atmosphere of friendliness they create, or between bits of talk about work and the personal exchanges that are woven into their conversations. In order to be a full participant, it may just be as important to know and understand the latest gossip as it is to know and understand the latest memo.

The kind of coherence that transforms mutual engagement into a community of practice requires work. The work of "community maintenance" is thus an intrinsic part of any practice. It can, however, be much less visible than more instrumental aspects of that practice. As a result, it is easily undervalued or even totally unrecognized. I described in Vignette I how Roberta helped make daily work more bearable for everyone by providing an endless supply of snacks. Her generosity contributed to building the community and keeping it going. But she never got a bonus for her tireless dedication. Even when there is much in common in the respective backgrounds of participants, the specific coordination necessary to do things together requires constant attention.

Diversity and partiality

If what makes a community of practice a community is mutual engagement, then it is a kind of community that does not entail homogeneity. Indeed, what makes engagement in practice possible and productive is as much a matter of diversity as it is a matter of homogeneity. Claims processors, for instance, form an ill-defined group of people brought together by employment ads in the classified sections of newspapers. Many applied for the job simply because the ad stipulated that no previous experience was necessary and that training would be provided. Hardly anyone ever mentioned a specific interest in medical insurance as a reason for being there. Some are young, some old; some conservative, some liberal; some outgoing, some introverted. They are different from one another and have different personal aspirations and problems. Thus, claims processing takes on a unique significance in each of their individual lives. Even so, their responses to dilemmas and aspirations are connected by the relations they create through mutual engagement. They work together, they see each other every day, they talk with each other all the time, exchange information and opinions, and very directly influence each other's understanding as a matter of routine. What makes a community of practice out of this medley of people is their mutual engagement in claims processing as they make it happen at Alinsu.

Not only are claims processors different to start with, but working together creates differences as well as similarities. They specialize, gain a reputation, make trouble, and distinguish themselves, as much as they develop shared ways of doing things. As an obvious example, the unit supervisor and assistant supervisor are undoubtedly members of the community of practice (they rose from the ranks and are still very engaged in the details of processing), but they have acquired very different status with respect to daily work, authority, and relations to the corporation. More generally, each participant in a community of practice finds a unique place and gains a unique identity, which is both further integrated and further defined in the course of engagement in practice. These identities become interlocked and articulated with one another through mutual engagement, but they do not fuse.[3] Mutual relations of engagement are as likely to give rise to differentiation as to homogenization. Crucially, therefore, homogeneity is neither a requirement for, nor the result of, the development of a community of practice.

Mutual engagement involves not only our competence, but also the competence of others. It draws on what we do and what we know, as well as on our ability to connect meaningfully to what we don't do and what we don't know – that is, to the contributions and knowledge of others. In this sense, mutual engagement is inherently partial; yet, in the context of a shared practice, this partiality is as much a resource as it is a limitation. This is rather obvious when participants have different roles, as in a medical operating team, where mutual engagement involves *complementary* contributions. But it is also true among claims processors, who have largely *overlapping* forms of competence. Because they belong to a community of practice where people help each other, it is more important to know how to give and receive help than to try to know everything yourself.

In both types of communities, developing a shared practice depends on mutual engagement. Yet, the two types of communities have different effects because their practices are constituted by different relations of partiality among members. In fact, it is often useful to belong to both types at once in order to achieve the synergy of the two forms of engagement. For example, a specialist on a team made up of complementary competences will usually benefit from also belonging to a community of practice of peers who share their specialization.

Mutual relationships

Mutual engagement does not entail homogeneity, but it does create relationships among people. When it is sustained, it connects participants in ways that can become deeper than more abstract similarities in terms of personal features or social categories. In this sense, a community of practice can become a very tight node of interpersonal relationships.

Because the term "community" is usually a very positive one,[4] I cannot emphasize enough that these interrelations arise out of engagement in practice and not out of an idealized view of what a community should be like. In particular, connotations of peaceful coexistence, mutual support, or interpersonal allegiance are not assumed, though of course they may exist in specific cases. Peace, happiness, and harmony are therefore not necessary properties of a community of practice. Certainly there are plenty of disagreements, tensions, and conflicts among claims processors. In spite of Alinsu's rather successful "corporate culture" of personableness, there are jealousies, gossips, and cliques.

Most situations that involve sustained interpersonal engagement generate their fair share of tensions and conflicts. In some communities of practice, conflict and misery can even constitute the core characteristic of a shared practice, as they do in some dysfunctional families. A community of practice is neither a haven of togetherness nor an island of intimacy insulated from political and social relations. Disagreement, challenges, and competition can all be forms of participation. As a form of participation, rebellion often reveals a greater commitment than does passive conformity.

A shared practice thus connects participants to each other in ways that are diverse and complex. The resulting relations reflect the full complexity of doing things together. They are not easily reducible to a single principle such as power, pleasure, competition, collaboration, desire, economic relations, utilitarian arrangements, or information processing. In real life, mutual relations among participants are complex mixtures of power and dependence, pleasure and pain, expertise and helplessness, success and failure, amassment and deprivation, alliance and competition, ease and struggle, authority and collegiality, resistance and compliance, anger and tenderness, attraction and repugnance, fun and boredom, trust and suspicion, friendship and hatred. Communities of practice have it all.

Joint enterprise

The second characteristic of practice as a source of community coherence is the negotiation of a joint enterprise. I will make three points about the enterprise that keeps a community of practice together.

1) It is the result of a collective process of negotiation that reflects the full complexity of mutual engagement.

2) It is defined by the participants in the very process of pursuing it. It is their negotiated response to their situation and thus belongs to them in a profound sense, in spite of all the forces and influences that are beyond their control.

3) It is not just a stated goal, but creates among participants relations of mutual accountability that become an integral part of the practice.

A negotiated enterprise

The enterprises reflected in our practices are as complex as we are. They include the instrumental, the personal, and the interpersonal aspects of our lives. The practice of claims processors, for instance, reflects their attempt to create a context in which to proceed with their working lives. That involves, among other things, making money, being an adult, becoming proficient at claims processing, having fun, doing well, feeling good, not being naive, being personable, dealing with boredom, thinking about the future, keeping one's place. Although their job does not carry much status, claims processors struggle to maintain a sense of self they can live with. Toward this end, they carefully fold into their practice their sense of marginality with respect to the institution, cultivating a subdued cynicism and a tightly managed distance from the job and from the company.

Their enterprise, therefore, is not just to process claims, as defined by Alinsu or by the unit supervisor. Of course, claims processing so defined does enter into their practice as a very significant component. They endeavor to earn money by satisfying Alinsu's demand that claims processing take place. The supervisor is a symbol of that demand. But the enterprise as actually defined by claims processors through their mutual engagement in practice is much more complex because it includes all the energy they spend – within the stricture of their tight institutional context and also in spite of it – not only in making claims processing possible in practice, but also in making the place habitable for themselves. Their daily practice, with its mixture of submission and assertion, is a complex, collectively negotiated response to what they understand to be their situation.

Because mutual engagement does not require homogeneity, a joint enterprise does not mean agreement in any simple sense. In fact, in some communities, disagreement can be viewed as a productive part of the enterprise. The enterprise is joint not in that everybody believes the same thing or agrees with everything, but in that it is communally negotiated. To say that some claims processors share an enterprise is not merely to say that they share working conditions, that they have dilemmas in common, or that they create similar responses. Their individual situations and responses vary, from one person to the next and from one day to the next. But their responses to their conditions – similar or dissimilar – are interconnected because they are engaged together in the joint enterprise of making claims processing real and livable. They must find a way to do that together, and even living with their differences and coordinating their respective aspirations is part of the process. Their understanding of their enterprise and its effects in their lives need not be uniform for it to be a collective product.

An indigenous enterprise

Communities of practice are not self-contained entities. They develop in larger contexts – historical, social, cultural, institutional – with specific resources and constraints. Some of these conditions and requirements are explicitly articulated. Some are implicit but are no less binding. Yet even when the practice of a community is profoundly shaped by conditions outside the control of its members, as it always is in some respects, its day-to-day reality is nevertheless produced by participants within the resources and constraints of their situations. It is their response to their conditions, and therefore *their* enterprise.

Calling attention to the claims processors' own definition of their enterprise is not to deny the following.

1) *Their position within a broader system.* Their job is part of a large industry and the result of a long historical development. They did not invent claims processing, nor do they have much influence on its institutional constitution.

2) *The pervasive influence of the institution that employs them.* The company's efforts to maintain control over their practice is mostly successful. The formidable shadow of Alinsu is ever-present. It follows them even to their lunch break, as they keep talking about their production quotas and their quality ratings.

Even though their practice does not transcend or transform its institutional conditions in any dramatic fashion, it nonetheless responds to these conditions in ways that are not determined by the institution. To do what they are expected to do, the claims processors produce a practice with an inventiveness that is all theirs. Their inventive resourcefulness applies equally to what the company probably wants and to what it probably does not want.

- On the one hand, claims processors invent local ways of processing claims effectively – for instance, as Ariel learns from Nancy in Vignette I, by finding more or less appropriate categories under which they can classify cases in order to proceed rapidly. Their pragmatic resourcefulness sometimes surprised me in my newcomer's eagerness to be thorough, but I had to admit that the job could not reasonably get done without it.

- On the other hand, and with the same inventive resourcefulness, they devise ways to escape Alinsu's control (e.g., with the treatment of errors in "Q" claims as described in Vignette I). They also learn to create some space for themselves. Even while processing information, and even while looking at the clock, they do manage to have fun, to feel hopeless, to laugh at an accident report, to share their boredom, to be angry at a customer, to spread rumors, to discuss their views, to enjoy a snack, to be proud of a processing prowess, to exchange stories, to feel the pain of uncertainty, to be alive.

In sum, it is only as negotiated by the community that conditions, resources, and demands shape the practice. The enterprise is never fully determined by an outside mandate, by a prescription, or by any individual participant. Even when a community of practice arises in response to some outside mandate, the practice evolves into the community's own response to that mandate. Even when specific members have more power than others, the practice evolves into a communal response to that situation. Even when strict submission is the response, its form and its interpretation in practice must be viewed as a local collective creation of the community. Because members produce a practice to deal with what they understand to be their enterprise, their practice as it unfolds belongs to their community in a fundamental sense.

Again, saying that communities of practice produce their practice is not saying that they cannot be influenced, manipulated, duped, intimidated, exploited, debilitated, misled, or coerced into submission; nor is it saying that they cannot be inspired, helped, supported, enlightened, unshackled, or empowered. But it is saying that the power – benevolent or malevolent – that institutions, prescriptions, or individuals have over the practice of a community is always mediated by the community's production of its practice. External forces have no direct power over this production because, in the last analysis (i.e., in the doing through mutual engagement in practice), it is the community that negotiates its enterprise.

A regime of mutual accountability

The enterprise of a community of practice is not just a statement of purpose. In fact, it is not primarily by being reified that it animates the community. Negotiating a joint enterprise gives rise to relations of mutual accountability among those involved. These relations of accountability include what matters and what does not, what is important and why it is important, what to do and not to do, what to pay attention to and what to ignore, what to talk about and what to leave unsaid, what to justify and what to take for granted, what to display and what to withhold, when actions and artifacts are good enough and when they need improvement or refinement.

I have argued that, for claims processors, accountability to their enterprise includes not only processing claims but also being personable, treating information and resources as something to be shared, and being responsible to others by not making their lives more difficult. Responsibility with respect to what makes life harder for others, for instance, is something they enforce among themselves, sometimes quite vocally, because they all understand that making their work life bearable is part of their joint enterprise. That these relations of mutual accountability are sometimes taken to be violated only confirms their influence as a communal regime.[5]

This communal regime of mutual accountability plays a central role in defining the circumstances under which, as a community and as individuals, members feel concerned or unconcerned by what they are doing and what is happening to them and around them, and under which they attempt, neglect, or refuse to make sense of events and to seek new meanings.

While some aspects of accountability may be reified – rules, policies, standards, goals – those that are not are no less significant. Becoming good at something involves developing specialized sensitivities, an aesthetic sense, and refined perceptions that are brought to bear on making judgments about the qualities of a product or an action. That these become shared in a community of practice is what allows participants to negotiate the appropriateness of what they do.[6]

The regime of accountability becomes an integral part of the practice. As a result, it may not be something that anyone can articulate very readily, because it is not primarily by being reified that it pervades a community.[7] Even when the enterprise is reified into a statement, the practice evolves into a negotiated interpretation of that statement. In fact, the practice includes the ways that participants interpret reified aspects of accountability and integrate them into lived forms of participation. Being able to make distinctions between reified standards and competent engagement in practice is an important aspect of becoming an experienced member.[8]

Defining a joint enterprise is a process, not a static agreement. It produces relations of accountability that are not just fixed constraints or norms. These relations are manifested not as conformity but as the ability to negotiate actions as accountable to an enterprise. The whole process is as generative as it is constraining. It pushes the practice forward as much as it keeps it in check. An enterprise both engenders and directs social energy. It spurs action as much as it gives it focus. It involves our impulses and emotions as much as it controls them. It invites new ideas as much as it sorts them out. An enterprise is a resource of coordination, of sense-making, of mutual engagement; it is like rhythm to music.

Rhythm is not random, but it is not just a constraint either. Rather, it is part of the dynamism of music, coordinating the very process by which it comes into being. Extracted from the playing, it becomes fixed, sterile, and meaningless, but in the playing, it makes music interpretable, participative, and sharable. It is a constitutive resource intrinsic to the very possibility of music as a shared experience. An enterprise is part of practice in the same way that rhythm is part of music.

Shared repertoire

The third characteristic of practice as a source of community coherence is the development of a shared repertoire. Over time, the joint pursuit of an enterprise creates resources for negotiating meaning. In claims processing, medical terms take on a specific usage, the height of certain piles of paper on desks indicates the state of processing, the seating arrangement reflects relationships among people and reactions of management to these relationships. The enterprise of claims processing is what gives coherence to the medley of activities, relations, and objects involved. That is why claim forms on the computer and photos of dogs on the wall can be part of the same practice. That is why taking a spelling test and shooting spitballs can be part of the same practice. The elements of the repertoire can be very heterogeneous. They gain their coherence not in and of themselves as specific activities, symbols, or artifacts, but from the fact that they belong to the practice of a community pursuing an enterprise.

The repertoire of a community of practice includes routines, words, tools, ways of doing things, stories, gestures, symbols, genres,[9] actions, or concepts that the community has produced or adopted in the course of its existence, and which have become part of its practice. The repertoire combines both reificative and participative aspects. It includes the discourse by which members create meaningful statements about the world, as well as the styles by which they express their forms of membership and their identities as members.

Negotiation: history and ambiguity

I call a community's set of shared resources a *repertoire* to emphasize both its rehearsed character and its availability for further engagement in practice.[10] The repertoire of a practice combines two characteristics that allow it to become a resource for the negotiation of meaning:

1) it reflects a history of mutual engagement
2) it remains inherently ambiguous.

Histories of interpretation create shared points of reference, but they do not impose meaning. Things like words, artifacts, gestures, and routines are useful not only because they are recognizable in their relation to a history of mutual engagement, but also because they can be re-engaged in new situations. This is true of linguistic and nonlinguistic elements, of words as well as chairs, ways of walking, claim forms, or laughter.[11] All have well-established interpretations, which can be re-utilized to new effects, whether these new effects simply continue an established trajectory of interpretation or take it in unexpected directions.

The fact that actions and artifacts have recognizable histories of interpretation is not exclusively, or even primarily, a constraint on possible meanings, but also a resource to be used in the production of new meanings. The spontaneous creation of metaphors is a perfect example of the kind of resource provided by a renegotiable history of usage. When combined with history, ambiguity is not an absence or a lack of meaning. Rather, it is a condition of negotiability and thus a condition for the very possibility of meaning. It is how history remains both relevant and meaningful.

Resources of mutual engagement

This inherent ambiguity makes processes like coordination, communication, or design on the one hand difficult, in continual need of repair, and always unpredictable; and on the other hand, dynamic, always open-ended, and generative of new meanings. The need for coordinating perspectives is a source of new meanings as much as it is a source of obstacles. From this perspective, ambiguity is not simply an obstacle to overcome; it is an inherent condition to be put to work. Effective communication or good design, therefore, are not best understood as the literal transmission of meaning. It is useless to try to excise all ambiguity; it is more productive to look for social arrangements that put history and ambiguity to work. The real problem of communication and design then is to situate ambiguity in the context of a history of mutual engagement that is rich enough to yield an opportunity for negotiation.

Because the repertoire of a community is a resource for the negotiation of meaning, it is shared in a dynamic and interactive sense. In particular, shared beliefs – in the sense of same mental objects or models – are not what shared practice is about.[12] Agreement in the sense of literally shared meaning is not a precondition for mutual engagement in practice, nor is it its outcome. Indeed, mismatched interpretations or misunderstandings need to be addressed and resolved directly only when they interfere with mutual engagement. Even then, they are not merely problems to resolve, but occasions for the production of new meanings. Sustained engagement in shared practice is a dynamic form of coordination, one that generates "on the fly" the coordinated meanings that allow it to proceed.

Negotiating meaning in practice

A community of practice need not be reified as such to be a community: it enters into the experience of participants through their very engagement. The three dimensions discussed here need not be the focus of explicit attention to create a context for the negotiation of meaning.

1) Through mutual engagement, participation and reification can be seamlessly interwoven.
2) A joint enterprise can create relations of mutual accountability without ever being reified, discussed, or stated as an enterprise.
3) Shared histories of engagement can become resources for negotiating meaning without the constant need to "compare notes."

Still, most of us have experienced the kind of social energy that the combination of these three dimensions of shared practice can generate.

Conversely, we may also have experienced how this social energy can prevent us from responding to new situations or from moving on. The importance of our various communities of practice can thus be manifested in two ways: their ability to give rise to an experience of meaningfulness; and, conversely, to hold us hostages to that experience.

As a consequence, saying that communities of practice provide a privileged context for the negotiation of meaning should not be misconstrued as romanticizing them.

1) I have insisted that shared practice does not itself imply harmony or collaboration.
2) Moreover, asserting as I have that these kinds of communities produce their own practices is not asserting that communities of practice are in any essential way an emancipatory force.

The local coherence of a community of practice can be both a strength and a weakness. The indigenous production of practice makes communities of practice the locus of creative achievements and the locus of inbred failures; the locus of resistance to oppression and the locus of the reproduction of its conditions; the cradle of the self but also the potential cage of the soul.

Communities of practice are not intrinsically beneficial or harmful. They are not privileged in terms of positive or negative effects. Yet they are a force to be reckoned with, for better or for worse. As a locus of engagement in action, interpersonal relations, shared knowledge, and negotiation of enterprises, such communities hold the key to real transformation – the kind that has real effects on people's lives. From this perspective, the influence of other forces (e.g., the control of an institution or the authority of an individual) are no less important, but they must be understood as mediated by the communities in which their meanings are to be negotiated in practice.

Chapter 3

Learning

The negotiation of meaning is a fundamentally temporal process, and one must therefore understand practice in its temporal dimension. Some communities of practice exist over centuries – for example, communities of artisans who pass their craft from generation to generation. Some are shorter-lived but intense enough to give rise to an indigenous practice and to transform the identities of those involved. For instance, such communities may form as people come together to handle a disaster. The development of practice takes time, but what defines a community of practice in its temporal dimension is not just a matter of a specific minimum amount of time. Rather, it is a matter of sustaining enough mutual engagement in pursuing an enterprise together to share some significant learning. From this perspective, *communities of practice can be thought of as shared histories of learning.*

In this chapter I discuss the internal dynamics that constitute these shared histories of learning. Toward this end, I will take up the themes introduced in the last two chapters, but with a focus on time and learning.

1) I will first talk about participation and reification as forms of memory, as sources of continuity and discontinuity, and thus as channels by which one can influence the evolution of a practice.
2) I will then discuss the development of practice with reference to the three dimensions introduced in Chapter 2. I will argue that learning along these three dimensions is what produces practice as an emergent structure.
3) Finally, I will turn to the learning by which newcomers can join a practice, that is, by which generational discontinuities are also continuities.

In this chapter, I will mostly talk about learning as a characteristic of practice. The learning of individual participants is a topic that I will address more directly in Part II, when I discuss issues of identity in terms of trajectories of participation.

The dual constitution of histories

Practices evolve as shared histories of learning. History in this sense is neither merely a personal or collective experience nor just a set of enduring artifacts and institutions, but a combination of participation and reification intertwined over time.

Participation and reification are dual modes of existence through time. They interact, but they exist through time in different realms. If a claims processor like Ariel, for instance, has new aspirations and feels completely alienated by her work, perhaps even quits, then the computer system still contains the data she entered – even if, in specific instances, no one can make sense of some of the notes she appended to customer files. Likewise, if the computer system suddenly fails, Ariel will remain a participant in her community – even if, in her practice, computer downtime is a serious disruption.

What I am saying here is that the world and our experience are in motion, but they don't move in lockstep. They interact, but they do not fuse.

- Coming back after many years to the neighborhood we grew up in, we find that little has changed. Yet our transformed eyes are strangely surprised to see the same street, the same buildings, the same trees, the same bent signpost, the same dents in the sidewalk, as though their very constancy has rendered them unrecognizably foreign.
- Or conversely, the street has been paved, the house remodeled, the old oak felled; the store is a supermarket and the playground a parking structure. And yet we feel that the old neighborhood lives on, unpaved and unpavable – not only in our past, but in our present; not only in our memories, but in our actions – still unfolding, an indelible part of our enduring identity.

In other words, forms of participation and reification continually converge and diverge. In moments of negotiation of meaning, they come into contact and affect each other. But converging in such moments is the extent of their connection. They shape each other in such moments, but they are not bound to each other. They are not otherwise essentially coupled in time. They do not lock in. They unfold in different media until they meet again in new moments of negotiation.

Remembering and forgetting

The disjunction of participation and reification through time is almost too obvious to belabor, but it is quite fundamental to understanding the role of the negotiation of meaning in the constitution of practice. As distinct modes of existence in time, participation and reification act as distinct forms of memory and distinct forms of forgetting. They act as distinct sources of both continuity and discontinuity. We can shred documents, but it is not so easy to erase our memories. We can forget events, but the marks they leave in the world can bring them back to us.

- *Reification* is a source of remembering and forgetting by producing forms that persist and change according to their own laws. In particular, the combination of malleability and rigidity characteristic of physical objects yields a memory of forms that allows our engagement in practice to leave enduring imprints in the world. The persistence of these imprints focuses the future around them. The process of reification thus compels us to renegotiate the meaning of its past products, in the same way that a scar keeps bringing a past foolishness or heroic deed into conversations.

  This process is not closed, however. It is open-ended in the sense that the shapes of the world change and vanish, and because – not carrying their own meaning – such shapes are open to reinterpretation and to multiple interpretations. In fact, the moment they are produced, forms start taking a life of their own, as does a word that we regret, an old forgotten letter we find in the attic, or a quick sketch in which, once it is in front of us, we suddenly start seeing the germ of a great design. The persistence of forms inherent in reification is not just a reminder of the past; it can refocus our attention in new ways, surprise us, and force us into new relations with the world.

- *Participation* is a source of remembering and forgetting, not only through our memories, but also through the fashioning of identities and thus through our need to recognize ourselves in our past. Our brains convert our experiences of participation into replayable memories, and we subsume these memories and their interpretations under the fashioning of a trajectory that we (as well as others) can construe as being one person.[1] Our interpretation of memory in terms of an identity is as important as marks in the brain in creating continuity in our lives.

Of course, this process too is open-ended – not only because we forget or remember partially, but also because our forms of participation change, our perspectives change, and we experience life in new ways.

Remembering and forgetting in practice stem from the interaction of participation and reification, and we are connected to our histories by this dual process. The study of an ancient piece of pottery provides an example. On the one hand, it was produced as part of a practice long ago, and preserved under volcanic ashes for centuries; on the other hand, our identities have in time become such that today we are interested in archeology. We are connected to our histories through the forms of artifacts that are produced, preserved, weathered, reappropriated, and modified through the ages, and also through our experience of participation as our identities are formed, inherited, rejected, interlocked, and transformed through mutual engagement in practice from generation to generation. The constitution of histories of learning is the continual intertwining of these two processes.

Continuity and discontinuity

Over time, communities of practice become invested in both participation and reification.

- In the process of sustaining a practice, we become invested in what we do as well as in each other and our shared history. Our identities become anchored in each other and what we do together. As a result, it is not easy to become a radically new person in the same community of practice. Conversely, it is not easy to transform oneself without the support of a community, as reflected by the countless support groups proposed by the self-help industry.
- Communities of practice are also invested in reification. Tools, representational artifacts, concepts, and terms all reflect specific perspectives they tend to reproduce. Because of this investment of practice, artifacts tend to perpetuate the repertoires of practices beyond the circumstances that shaped them in the first place. Unwieldy spellings can survive through generations of dismayed students, because it is still easier to learn any kind of spelling than to change the whole language and all the practices invested in it. Similarly, American inches and gallons can withstand the logical onslaught of meters and liters. And the "QWERTY" keyboard, whose layout was determined

by the locking of adjacent hammers in early typewriters, lives on in the computer age.

The simultaneous investment of practice in participation and reification can be a source of both continuity and discontinuity. In fact, since both participation and reification are inherently limited in scope, they inevitably create discontinuities in the evolution of practices. Participants move on to new positions, change direction, find new opportunities, become uninterested, start new lives. Among claims processors there is a substantial turnover, but even in communities where participants remain for life, they eventually retire and die, making room for new generations of members. Similarly, new artifacts, ideas, terms, concepts, images, and tools are produced and adopted as old ones are used up, made obsolete, or discarded.

In a community of practice, what can be considered a "generation" depends on its reproduction cycles. Among claims processors at Alinsu, high turnover means that new generations of members come in rather frequently (there are usually several training classes every year), even though a complete reproduction cycle is much longer. It takes two to four years from the time one is a trainee to the time one becomes a level 8 and so can serve as an instructor, quality reviewer, or back-up trainer. But the generational spread is actually slightly broader, because it can take six to ten years before one can move up from processing to a technical or managerial position.

Because a community of practice is a system of interrelated forms of participation, discontinuities propagate through it. When newcomers join a community of practice, generational discontinuities spread through multiple levels; relations shift in a cascading process. Relative newcomers become relative old-timers. Last year's trainee now helps the new trainee. These promotions are mostly unmarked and often hardly talked about, yet they can have significant effects. Participants forge new identities from their new perspectives. These changes can be encouraging or unsettling. They can reveal progress that had remained unnoticed: you suddenly see all that you have learned because you are in a position to help someone. But they can also create new demands: all of a sudden, you are looked up to and expected to know more than you are sure you do. As these successive generations interact, some of the history of the practice remains embodied in the generational relations that structure the community. The past, the present, and the future live together.

Reification too can have generations that cause discontinuities. The installation of a computer system in the claims processing center was a discontinuity of major proportions. The few old-timers who were there at the time still talk about the radical transformation it caused in their practice. They reminisce with archeological amusement (but no nostalgia) about the huge file cabinets full of customer files, which they had to locate in order to start processing a claim. They laugh about the amounts of paper they had to handle and all the running around. They think of those days as a different era altogether, associated with simpler procedures and less medical jargon. A decade later, there is talk of a new generation of systems that can gather data directly from the doctor's office and process some of the simpler claims automatically. The introduction of such a system will have broad ramifications and will again transform claims processing almost beyond recognition. A whole array of tools, concepts, and artifacts will become obsolete in a ripple of replacements. Because practice is invested in reification, these discontinuities too create cascades of transformations through the practice.

The politics of participation and reification

I have argued that participation and reification are dual modes of existence in time, dual modes of remembering and forgetting, and dual sources of continuity and discontinuity. In consequence, as communities of practice become invested in them, participation and reification provide dual avenues for exercising influence on what becomes of a practice. They offer two kinds of lever available for attempts to shape the future – to maintain the status quo or conversely to redirect the practice.

1) You can seek, cultivate, or avoid specific relationships with specific people.
2) You can produce or promote specific artifacts to focus future negotiation of meaning in specific ways.

In this sense, participation and reification are two distinct channels of power available to participants (and to outside constituencies). They constitute two distinct forms of politics.

1) The politics of *participation* include influence, personal authority, nepotism, rampant discrimination, charisma, trust, friendship, ambition.

2) Of a different nature are the politics of *reification*, which include legislation, policies, institutionally defined authority, expositions, argumentative demonstrations, statistics, contracts, plans, designs.

Ensuring the cohesion of a team through friendship is different from outlining a set of goals, a schedule, and a work plan; calling upon the moral commitment of participants is different from presenting a statistical demonstration of consistent injustice. Though recourse to each can create a very different atmosphere, both avenues can be effective in influencing the development of a practice.

Because of the complementarity of participation and reification, the two forms of politics can be played off each other. Each can be employed to circumvent, or to compensate for abuses in, the other.

1) Convincing powerful people of a special case can provide a way to bend the bureaucratic rigidities of policies when their reificative stiffness becomes counterproductive.
2) However, the reification of explicit policies may be necessary in order to combat the various forms of partiality that can bias the politics of participation.

Claims processors, for instance, do count on their personal relations with their supervisors in order to adapt company policies to their specific situations. On the other hand, they enjoy the idea that their performances are calculated automatically on the basis of their production in purely quantitative terms. This reificative form of assessment was a feature of their employment contract that many claimed attracted them to the job initially. Within this rigid structure – over which they have no say, but according to which they can make claims to promotions – they feel more in control of their destiny, protected to some extent from arbitrary decisions by those directly in charge of their employment.

As a result of this complementarity, control over practice usually requires a grip on both forms of politics; one is rarely effective without the other. It takes both the participation of a supervisor and the reification of a set of policies to ensure control over claims processing. On a different scale, writing legislation to protect the environment does not replace instilling in our children a love and respect for nature.

• To be effective, the politics of reification requires participation because reification does not itself ensure any effect. Reification has to be adopted by a community before it can shape practice in significant ways.

- Conversely, the politics of participation must include the power to wield reification, since reification creates the points of focus around which people negotiate what matters.

Because the negotiation of meaning is the convergence of participation and reification, controlling both participation and reification affords control over the kinds of meaning that can be created in a certain context and the kinds of person that participants can become. It is no surprise, then, that totalitarian regimes endeavor both to burn books and restrict the right of association.

The combination of the two forms of politics is powerful indeed when it affords a hold on the development of a practice. It can be a source of stability when power differentials favor specific perspectives. It can be a destabilizing factor when power shifts. Yet, because meaning is always negotiated anew and because participation and reification are not locked in, there is always an uncertainty, an opening for a "slippage" of practice. No form of control over the future can be complete and secured. In order to sustain the social coherence of participation and reification within which it can be exercised, control must constantly be reproduced, reasserted, renegotiated in practice.

Histories of learning

Now that I have talked about the forms of memory available to constitute a practice, I can describe practice as a shared history of learning. I will make three points.

1) Practice is not stable, but combines continuity and discontinuity.
2) Learning in practice involves the three dimensions introduced in Chapter 2.
3) Practice is not an object but rather an emergent structure that persists by being both perturbable and resilient.

Continuities and discontinuities

The practice of claims processing is located in a long history of increasingly detailed institutional control, including more recently computerization. One might expect this long institutional evolution to have created a very stable practice. Yet I was amazed to find a brew of adaptation and invention that belied the label of routine work that management – and often even the claims processors themselves – put on their job. Even in a setting so historically and institutionally determined, communities must tune their practice constantly in their attempt to get the job done.

Because the world is in flux and conditions always change, any practice must constantly be reinvented, even as it remains "the same practice." When asked about the challenges of their job, claims processors almost inevitably speak about change: changes in policies, insurance plans, and medical practice, as well as changes in internal organization and procedures. In the office, memos come in continually that change this or that rule, this or that procedure, this or that feature of the computer system – or even to change a recent change. In conjunction with this constant evolution of the practice, there is also a substantial turnover of personnel that constantly brings in new faces.

Claims processors have to respond to the demands of a world in constant flux, but it would be an oversimplification to understand their learning strictly in terms of responses to new circumstances. The process of change reflects not only adaptation to external forces, but an investment of energy in what people do and in their mutual relations. Even though claims processors may have good reasons not to invest themselves very deeply in their job, there is an uncheckable inventiveness as they struggle to do their work and maintain an atmosphere they can live in. A question gives rise to discussion; a conversation sparks a proposal; new ways are tried out; the office is rearranged; a unit meeting is called to discuss a problem; people are moved around; someone has an idea, which is taken up; things improve; things worsen. In the community, people renegotiate their mutual relationships and forms of participation. They reach their goals, they fall short. Friendships start, friendships are broken. Conflicts erupt, conflicts are resolved. Rumors spread, rumors are denied. Given the routine reputation of the job, the inherent, self-generated restlessness and inventiveness of the community is striking.

Constant change is so much a part of day-to-day engagement in practice that it largely goes unnoticed. Even when it causes a discontinuity or a crisis, it rarely leads to a breakdown. The community does not fall apart. Similarly, departures and arrivals are not just discontinuities. People are replaced; new recruits are progressively absorbed into the community as they start contributing to its practice. There is a stake in continuity – at the level of the institution, and at the level of the community of practice as well. Everyone and everything concur to sustain this sense of continuity in the midst of discontinuities. This combination of discontinuity and continuity creates a dynamic equilibrium that can be construed, by participants and by the encompassing institution, as stable and as the same practice.

Learning in practice

Claims processors and managers rarely talk about the job as learning. They talk about change, about new ideas, about performance levels, about the old days. The concept of learning is not absent from the claims processing office, but it is used mainly for trainees. And yet, when I posed the question directly to them, claims processors all agreed that they were learning continually. One reason they do not think of their job as learning is that what they learn *is* their practice. Learning is not reified as an extraneous goal or as a special category of activity or membership. Their practice is not merely a context for learning something else. Engagement in practice – in its unfolding, multidimensional complexity – is both the stage and the object, the road and the destination. What they learn is not a static subject matter but the very process of being engaged in, and participating in developing, an ongoing practice.

If, from the characterization of the last chapter, practices are histories of mutual engagement, negotiation of an enterprise, and development of a shared repertoire, then learning in practice includes the following processes for the communities involved.

* *Evolving forms of mutual engagement:* discovering how to engage, what helps and what hinders; developing mutual relationships; defining identities, establishing who is who, who is good at what, who knows what, who is easy or hard to get along with.
* *Understanding and tuning their enterprise:* aligning their engagement with it, and learning to become and hold each other accountable to it; struggling to define the enterprise and reconciling conflicting interpretations of what the enterprise is about.
* *Developing their repertoire, styles, and discourses:* renegotiating the meaning of various elements; producing or adopting tools, artifacts, representations; recording and recalling events; inventing new terms and redefining or abandoning old ones; telling and retelling stories; creating and breaking routines.

Although this perspective takes learning to be ongoing, it does not trivialize the concept by saying that everything we do is learning. Significant learning affects these dimensions of practice. It is what changes our ability to engage in practice, the understanding of why we engage in it, and the resources we have at our disposal to do so. This kind of learning is not just a mental process – such as neurological memory, information processing in the brain, or mechanical habituation[2] – though mental processes are surely involved. Such learning has to do with the development of our practices and our ability to negotiate meaning. It is not just the acquisition of memories, habits, and skills, but the formation of an identity. Our experience and our membership inform each other, pull each other, transform each other. We create ways of participating in a practice in the very process of contributing to making that practice what it is.

Emergent structure

Learning is the engine of practice, and practice is the history of that learning. As a consequence, communities of practice have life cycles that reflect such a process. They come together, they develop, they evolve, they disperse, according to the timing, the logic, the rhythms, and the social energy of their learning. Thus, unlike more formal types of organizational structures, it is not so clear where they begin and end. They do not have launching and dismissal dates. In this sense, a community of practice is a different kind of entity than, say, a task force or a team. Whereas a task force or a team starts with an assignment and ends with it, a community of practice may not congeal for a while after an assignment has started, and it may continue in unofficial ways far beyond the original assignment. Based on joint learning rather than reified tasks that begin and end, a community of practice takes a while to come into being, and it can linger long after an official group is disbanded.

To assert that learning is what gives rise to communities of practice is to say that learning is a source of social structure. But the kind of structure that this refers to is not an object, which exists in and of itself and can be separated from the process giving rise to it. Rather, it is an emergent structure.[3]

Indeed, practice is ultimately produced by its members through the negotiation of meaning. The negotiation of meaning is an open process, with the constant potential for including new elements. It is also a recovery process, with the constant potential for continuing, rediscovering, or reproducing the old in the new. The result is that, as an emergent structure, practice is at once highly perturbable and highly resilient.

- The three dimensions of learning just described are interdependent and interlocked into a tight system. Each dimension can disrupt the others. For instance, the inclusion of new members can, as I described earlier, create a ripple of new opportunities for mutual engagement; these new relationships can awaken new interests that translate into a renegotiation of the enterprise; and the process can produce a whole generation of new elements in the repertoire. Because of this combination of an open process (the negotiation of meaning) and a tight system of interrelations, a small perturbation somewhere can rapidly have repercussions throughout the system.[4] Among claims processors, for instance, an interesting rumor will spread very fast and get everyone talking. So will a good idea from a respected source.

• In a community of practice, mutual relationships, a carefully understood enterprise, and a well-honed repertoire are all investments that make sense with respect to each other. Participants have a stake in that investment because it becomes part of who they are. From that standpoint, practice is an investment in learning. The community then will tend to reorganize itself around novelty so that its investment can be brought to bear. As the proverb goes, if you have a hammer, the world looks like a nail. But for a community of practice, this is not just a matter of habits mechanically reproducing themselves, though habits too must be taken into account because they have their place in the practice. More fundamentally, it is a matter of investment of one's identity and thus of negotiating enough continuity to sustain an identity. From this perspective, practice is different from a physical system, because people do not merely act individually or mechanically, but by negotiating their engagement with one another with respect to their shared practice and their interlocked identities.[5]

The combination of perturbability and resilience is a characteristic of adaptability. Learning involves a close interaction of order and chaos.[6] The continuity of an emergent structure derives not from stability but from adaptability. Indeed, as an emergent structure, practice is neither inherently stable nor inherently unstable. It is not a structure that remains the same unless something is done to cause a change. But neither is it merely "messy" or disorderly, changing wildly and randomly unless some external structuring is imposed on its unfolding.[7]

Stability and destabilization can occur, but they cannot be assumed. They must be explained.

• Obviously, there can be factors of stability that affect the evolution of practice. Alinsu has built a whole apparatus of stability to ensure that claims are processed according to its policies with a strict consistency. Claims processors themselves have produced local policies to coordinate the treatment of specific clients. I have also argued that one participant with a disproportionate amount of power and influence can create a kind of stability by discouraging negotiation. But stability requires work; it is not a default case that sustains itself unless disturbed. It requires as much work as transformation.

- Conversely, there can be destabilizing events. When Alinsu decided to move some of its operations to a small town with a more favorable labor market, or when it installed its computer system, it caused serious disruptions in the practice of claims processors. A hiring raid by a competitor that would cause the old-timers to quit would likewise be a serious disruption. A whim of a person in power can throw things off. Destabilizing events do take place, but communities of practice reorganize their histories around them, developing specific responses to them that honor the continuity of their learning.

Change and learning, by contrast, are in the very nature of practice; they can be assumed to occur, but they always involve continuity as well as discontinuity. In dealing with communities of practice – whether living within one or being in charge of one – it is thus essential always to assume learning. Otherwise, practice may seem stubbornly stable or randomly transformable.

- Someone who assumes stability but understands the need for change would regard communities of practice as a source of resistance.
- Someone who assumes instability would be concerned that things left to themselves will slip into disorder, and may be tempted to devise overly detailed measures to maintain order. From this perspective, practice is unreliable; it lacks structure and is therefore unproblematically malleable.

Under both assumptions, seeking specific discontinuities or striving to maintain specific forms of stability may thus work against, rather than with, the change that is already taking place and the continuity that is already assured. The negotiation of meaning is never mere continuity or mere discontinuity. Close scrutiny will usually reveal good reasons – functional or dysfunctional – for a practice to be the way it is, without having to resort to blanket assumptions of inherent stability or instability. In other words: it is a mistake to assume that practice is inherently a conservative force, and it is also a mistake to assume that practice is erratic or can be modified by decree.

Generational discontinuities

The existence of a community of practice does not depend on a fixed membership. People move in and out. An essential aspect of any long-lived practice is the arrival of new generations of members. As long as membership changes progressively enough to allow for sustained generational encounters, newcomers can be integrated into the community, engage in its practice, and then – in their own way – perpetuate it. These encounters between generations are the aspect of practice that is most often understood as learning. Here I will argue that practice can be shared across generational discontinuities precisely because it already is fundamentally a social process of shared learning.

Generational encounters

In the claims processing center, the learning of newcomers is a recognized necessity. Being a trainee is a marked category, both during the training class and later, during an initial period in the community. Because the company has an interest in maintaining the practice, it has put in place an official process of selection and training to ensure that new recruits are going to work as old-timers do. The official training, however, is not the main locus of the generational encounter. Although the trainees have their class in a separate room, they are in the same office as their more established colleagues, take breaks in the same lounge, ride the same elevators, and use the same bathrooms. They quickly become part of the scene. And after they complete their classes and start working "on the floor," their integration into the community of practice really begins.

ETIENNE How do you think you gained [your own] understanding [of claims processing]? Was it from the training class?
SHEILA Actually from doing the claims, I think. Actually the processing itself.
MARY Yeah, more repetition, more times you do it.
MAUREEN In training they give you the, whatever, just a feel for it. And then you go down there, and the more you do it, kind of, the more you understand. They don't actually tell us the contracts.
ETIENNE Is it from doing it or from conversations with people?
SHEILA Doing it, and then if you don't understand, you talk to somebody about it and they can explain it to you. And then you do it and you say "Oh yeah, that worked, you know, I get it now," or something.

For claims processors, the passage from classroom to actual processing is a difficult transition. These difficulties have prompted comments that the training is too short. I would argue that the real problem lies in their difficulty in entering their new community of practice. Separated from their classmates, they have to get enough attention and create enough relationships with busy old-timers to gain access to the community and its practice. Only then can they start to become full participants. Old-timers do spend energy introducing these newcomers into the actual practice of their community, but there is little official recognition for their efforts and they are under their own production pressures. So it may very well be that recognizing these efforts, encouraging them, and otherwise facilitating the process would be more effective than extending the training.

In our book on this topic, Jean Lave and I used the term "legitimate peripheral participation" to characterize the process by which newcomers become included in a community of practice. The term is a bit unwieldy, but it does capture important conditions under which people can become members of communities of practice. We wanted to point out that the required learning takes place not so much through the reification of a curriculum as through modified forms of participation that are structured to open the practice to nonmembers. Peripherality and legitimacy, we argued, were two types of modification required to make actual participation possible.[8]

- Peripherality provides an approximation of full participation that gives exposure to actual practice. It can be achieved in various ways, including lessened intensity, lessened risk, special assistance, lessened cost of error, close supervision, or lessened production pressures. It can involve explanations and stories, but there is a big difference between a lesson that is *about* the practice but takes place outside of it, and explanations and stories that are *part of* the practice and take place within it. Observation can be useful, but only as a prelude to actual engagement. To open up a practice, peripheral participation must provide access to all three dimensions of practice: to mutual engagement with other members, to their actions and their negotiation of the enterprise, and to the repertoire in use. No matter how the peripherality of initial participation is achieved, it must engage newcomers and provide a sense of how the community operates. Note that the curriculum is then the community of practice itself. Teachers, masters, and specific role models can be important, but it is by virtue of their membership in the community as a whole that they can play their roles.

- In order to be on an inbound trajectory, newcomers must be granted enough legitimacy to be treated as potential members. If a community like that of claims processors rejected a newcomer for some reason, that person would have a hard time learning. Again, legitimacy can take many forms: being useful, being sponsored, being feared, being the right kind of person, having the right birth. A new squire may have only cleaned armors and fed horses. But the legitimacy granted by his birth was enough for the peripherality of his menial activities to warrant the prospect of becoming a knight. In traditional apprenticeship, the sponsorship of a master is usually required for apprentices to be able to have access to the practice. The standing of the master in the community is therefore crucial. Today, doctoral students have professors who give them entry into academic communities. Granting the newcomers legitimacy is important because they are likely to come short of what the community regards as competent engagement. Only with enough legitimacy can all their inevitable stumblings and violations become opportunities for learning rather than cause for dismissal, neglect, or exclusion.

Note that peripherality and legitimacy are achievements that involve both a community and its newcomers and that do not presuppose a generational encounter free of conflicts; on the contrary, this perspective integrates the generational encounter into the processes of negotiation by which a practice evolves. I have argued that communities of practice are not havens of peace and that their evolution involves politics of both participation and reification. Generational differences add an edge to these politics by including the distinct perspectives that successive generations bring to bear on the history of a practice. The working out of these perspectives involves a dynamics of continuity and discontinuity that propels the practice forward. In Chapter 6 I will expand on this issue and discuss the generational encounter in terms of trajectories and identities.

Practice as learning

There is a subtle point underlying the foregoing discussion. From this perspective, educational processes based (like apprenticeship) on actual participation are effective in fostering learning not just because they are better pedagogical ideas, but more fundamentally because they are "epistemologically correct," so to speak. There is a match between knowing and learning, between the nature of competence and the process by which it is acquired, shared, and extended.

Practice is a shared history of learning that requires some catching up for joining. It is not an object to be handed down from one generation to the next. Practice is an ongoing, social, interactional process, and the introduction of newcomers is merely a version of what practice already is. That members interact, do things together, negotiate new meanings, and learn from each other is already inherent in practice – that is how practices evolve. In other words, communities of practice reproduce their membership in the same way that they come about in the first place. They share their competence with new generations through a version of the same process by which they develop. Special measures may be taken to open up the practice to newcomers, but the process of learning is not essentially different.[9]

Chapter 4
Boundary

In the previous chapter, I characterized communities of practice as shared histories of learning. Over time, such histories create discontinuities between those who have been participating and those who have not. These discontinuities are revealed by the learning involved in crossing them: moving from one community of practice to another can demand quite a transformation. But practice does not create only boundaries. At the same time as boundaries form, communities of practice develop ways of maintaining connections with the rest of the world.

So far, I have focused almost exclusively on communities of practice as if they were isolated. But that focus was artificial. Communities of practice cannot be considered in isolation from the rest of the world, or understood independently of other practices. Their various enterprises are closely interconnected. Their members and their artifacts are not theirs alone. Their histories are not just internal; they are histories of articulation with the rest of the world.

As a result, engagement in practice entails engagement in these external relations. For a job like claims processing, which is considered by many to be relatively narrow, the range of related communities of practice as well as constituencies without a shared practice is actually rather complex. It involves, among others, claims technicians, underwriters, system designers, and various levels of management at Alinsu; beyond the company, there are other claims processors, patients, benefit representatives, accounting clerks, and a variety of medical and legal professionals. Newcomers to claims processing quickly become initiated to this set of relations. Joining a community of practice involves entering not only its internal configuration but also its relations with the rest of the world.

Whereas the continuities and discontinuities of the previous chapter concerned the historical development of a practice, here I will talk about continuities and discontinuities in the social landscape defined by the boundaries of various practices.[1] I will use a structure similar to that of the previous chapter, rehearsing the themes of Chapters 1 and 2 as they relate to issues of boundary.

1) I will discuss how participation and reification act as sources of social discontinuity and as connections that can create continuities across boundaries.

2) I will then consider communities of practice themselves, both as sources of boundary and contexts for creating connections.

3) I will end by looking at the social landscape created by the weaving of boundaries and peripheries.

Here I will focus on continuities and discontinuities defined through practice. In other words, I will focus on the local constitution and crossing of boundaries. But the relations of communities of practice to the rest of the world are not only local. In Part II, I will introduce mechanisms by which communities of practice can define themselves in broader contexts, such as contributing to a broader enterprise or belonging to an organization.

The duality of boundary relations

Participation and reification can both contribute to the discontinuity of a boundary. In some cases, the boundary of a community of practice is reified with explicit markers of membership, such as titles, dress, tattoos, degrees, or initiation rites. Of course, the degree to which these markers actually act as boundary depends on their effect on participation. Moreover, the absence of obvious markers does not imply the absence or the looseness of boundaries. The status of outsider can be reified in subtle and not so subtle ways – through barriers to participation – without a reification of the boundary itself. On the school playground, the unmarked but sharp boundary of a clique can be a cruel reality, one for which well-meaning parents and teachers are of little help. The nuances and the jargon of a professional group distinguish the inside from the outside as much as do certificates. Not having the style and the connections can be as detrimental to an ambitious employee as the lack of a degree from a major business school. A "glass ceiling" is sometimes more impenetrable in practice than any official policy or entrance requirement.

At the same time, however, participation and reification can also create continuities across boundaries, as illustrated in Figure 4.1.

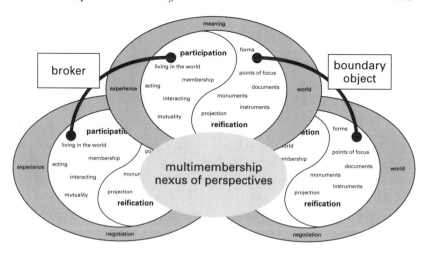

Figure 4.1. Participation and reification as connections.

- The products of reification can cross boundaries and enter different practices. Alinsu's office building, for instance, is part of the practice of claims processors, but it is also part of the practices of architects, city planners, postal employees, maintenance personnel, real estate and financial professionals. It is appropriated and reified in different ways in each of these practices. As an artifact, the building is a nexus of perspectives, and on various occasions can provide a form of coordination among these perspectives.
- We can participate in multiple communities of practice at once. Among claims processors, the unit supervisor belongs both to local management and to her own unit. Spanning that boundary is one of her main functions. Whether or not we are actively trying to sustain connections among the practices involved, our experience of multimembership always has the potential of creating various forms of continuity among them.

I will start my discussion of these issues by presenting two types of connections:

1) *boundary objects* – artifacts, documents, terms, concepts, and other forms of reification around which communities of practice can organize their interconnections
2) *brokering* – connections provided by people who can introduce elements of one practice into another.

Through these two forms of connections, practices influence each other, and the politics of participation and reification extend beyond their boundaries.

Boundary objects

Sociologist of science Leigh Star coined the term *boundary object* to describe objects that serve to coordinate the perspectives of various constituencies for some purpose.[2] In this sense, the claim forms that arrive in the office translate medical consultations and services into reports that can be processed. This standardized reification serves as a coordinating mechanism between claims processors and different – and largely disjoint – constituencies, some of which are communities of practice, some of which are not. In this sense, these claim forms are used as boundary objects that connect the practice of claims processing with the rest of the world.

More generally, reification lies at the heart of claims processing and its relations with the world. In a narrow but – at some level – real sense, claims processing is an information-processing function. The job of claims processors is to take some standardized information about medical services and then transform this information – using other available information about contracts, regulations, and procedures – into information about payments due. Even the checks eventually issued are physically printed and dispatched somewhere else. The thrust of much of what is happening in the office is to make tractable the information necessary to perform this transformation: forms and manuals of all kinds, streams of memos, thick ringbinders, lists, reference books, medical dictionaries, the computer system with its enormous data bases, and, beyond Alinsu, administrative and medical records that are only a phone call away. As a result of dealing with standardized information, claims processors – like many of their peers in parallel service industries – have only an indirect relation to the meanings of their work in the broader world. They process claims submitted by people they do not know and whose medical conditions they have never witnessed; they receive reports about medical procedures in which they have not been involved; they enforce contracts in order to sustain relations to which they are not parties; and they compute amounts of money earned and spent in circumstances about which they have no idea.

Even though claims processors are not connected in very direct ways to the content of the claims they process, they are still able to do their work. In order to make this possible, the office is replete with boundary objects that connect its function with a wide range of communities of practice and constituencies without a specific shared practice. One could picture the claims processing office as a walled computation center, with parades of carefully crafted boundary objects being shipped in and out, in and out.[3]

These connections are reificative, not in the sense that they do not involve participation, but that they use forms of reification to bridge disjoint forms of participation. As a result, these boundary objects both connect and disconnect. They enable coordination, but they can do so without actually creating a bridge between the perspectives and the meanings of various constituencies.

In everyday life we constantly deal with artifacts that connect us in various ways to communities of practice to which we do not belong. The kind of standardization of information typical of a claim form is only one of a number of characteristics that Leigh Star discusses as enabling artifacts to act as boundary objects.

1) *Modularity:* each perspective can attend to one specific portion of the boundary object (e.g., a newspaper is a heterogeneous collection of articles that has something for each reader).

2) *Abstraction:* all perspectives are served at once by deletion of features that are specific to each perspective (e.g., a map abstracts from the terrain only certain features such as distance and elevation).

3) *Accommodation:* the boundary object lends itself to various activities (e.g., the office building can accommodate the various practices of its tenants, its caretakers, its owners, and so forth).

4) *Standardization:* the information contained in a boundary object is in a prespecified form so that each constituency knows how to deal with it locally (for example, a questionnaire that specifies how to provide some information by answering certain questions).

A boundary object is not necessarily an artifact or encoded information. A forest can be a boundary object around which hikers, logging interests, conservationists, biologists, and owners organize their perspectives and seek ways of coordinating them. Not all objects are boundary objects, whether by design or in their use. Nevertheless, to the degree that they belong to multiple practices, they are nexus of perspectives and thus carry the potential of becoming boundary objects if those perspectives need to be coordinated. When a boundary object serves multiple constituencies, each has only partial control over the interpretation of the object. For instance, an author has jurisdiction over what is written, but readers have jurisdiction over what it comes to mean to them. Jurisdiction over various aspects of a boundary object is thus distributed among the constituencies involved, and using an artifact as a boundary object requires processes of coordination and translation between each form of partial jurisdiction.

Because artifacts can appear as self-contained objects, it is easy to overlook that they are in fact nexus of perspectives, and that it is often in the meeting of these perspectives that artifacts obtain their meanings. If one writes a memo for wide distribution, for instance, it is easy to assume that the memo tells its story and to overlook that the meanings to which it gives rise are in fact a function of the relations between the practices involved. When a person reads the memo, what is really going on involves not merely a relation between the person and the memo, but also a relation between communities of practice: those where the memo originated and those to which the person belongs. The problem of communication is then one of both participation and reification, to be dealt with in terms of opportunities for the negotiation of meaning within and among communities of practice.

In this context, the design of artifacts – documents, systems, tools – is often the design of boundary objects. When designers of computer systems, for instance, are concerned about issues of use, they often talk about "the user," a generic term of mythical proportions in their jargon. From this perspective, "use" is a relation between a user and an artifact. But that user engages in certain practices and is thus a member of certain communities of practice. Artifacts, then, are boundary objects, and designing them is designing for participation rather than just use. The crucial issue is the relationship between the practices of design and the practices of use. Connecting the communities involved, understanding practices, and managing boundaries become fundamental design tasks.[4] It is then imperative to consider a broader range of connections beyond the artifact itself, both to reconcile various perspectives in the nexus and to take advantage of their diversity.

Brokering

Not all the connections of claims processing to other practices are through reification. For instance, the supervisor of the local technical unit, who had transferred to the claims processing center from another office, noticed that a procedure had been interpreted differently. He was able to understand the difference and to convince everyone to adopt the interpretation of his old unit. I will call this use of multimembership to transfer some element of one practice into another *brokering*. This is a term that my colleague Penelope Eckert introduced to describe how school kids constantly introduce new ideas, new interests, new styles, and new revelations into their clique.[5] Note that multimembership does not entail brokering. There are forms of participation that we keep separate.

Brokering is a common feature of the relation of a community of practice with the outside. Employees at companies that have strict safety programs often bring their learning home and make their understanding about safety part of family practice – for instance, noting exit signs or wearing protective glasses.[6] Inside organizations, people in charge of special projects across functional units often find themselves brokering.[7] The role of managers is often construed in terms of directing people, but it is worth noting that a good part of their activities have more to do with brokering across boundaries between practices.

Brokers are able to make new connections across communities of practice, enable coordination, and – if they are good brokers – open new possibilities for meaning. Although we all do some brokering, my experience is that certain individuals seem to thrive on being brokers: they love to create connections and engage in "import–export," and so would rather stay at the boundaries of many practices than move to the core of any one practice.

The job of brokering is complex. It involves processes of translation, coordination, and alignment between perspectives. It requires enough legitimacy to influence the development of a practice, mobilize attention, and address conflicting interests.[8] It also requires the ability to link practices by facilitating transactions between them, and to cause learning by introducing into a practice elements of another. Toward this end, brokering provides a participative connection – not because reification is not involved, but because what brokers press into service to connect practices is their experience of multimembership and the possibilities for negotiation inherent in participation.

Brokering often entails ambivalent relations of multimembership. For the supervisor of the claims processing unit, spanning the boundary between workers and management is not always comfortable. She belongs at the same time to both practices and to neither. She is not quite a manager, either in management's eyes or in the eyes of claims processors, who think of her as "just a glorified processor." Nevertheless, her position of authority isolates her to a substantial extent from the rest of the unit.

Uprootedness is an occupational hazard of brokering. Because communities of practice focus on their own enterprise, boundaries can lack the kind of negotiated understanding found at the core of practices about what constitutes competence. That makes it difficult to recognize or assess the value of brokering. As a consequence, brokers sometimes interpret the uprootedness associated with brokering in personal terms of individual adequacy. Reinterpreting their experience in terms of the occupational hazards of brokering is useful both for them and for the communities involved. It can also allow brokers to recognize one another, seek companionship, and perhaps develop shared practices around the enterprise of brokering. That is one way people can deal with uprootedness.

Brokers must often avoid two opposite tendencies: being pulled in to become full members and being rejected as intruders. Indeed, their contributions lie precisely in being neither in nor out. Brokering therefore requires an ability to manage carefully the coexistence of membership and nonmembership, yielding enough distance to bring a different perspective, but also enough legitimacy to be listened to.

Complementary connections

Participation and reification can each create connections across boundaries, but they provide distinct channels of connection. The sharing of objects does not imply overlaps in participation, and participants in multiple communities do not necessarily carry their paraphernalia from one to the other. Participation and reification provide very different sorts of connections and present different characteristics, advantages, and problems, reflecting their complementarity.

Reificative connections can transcend the spatiotemporal limitations inherent in participation. We cannot be all over the world, but we can read the newspaper. We cannot live in the past, but we can wonder at monuments left behind by long-gone practices. In this respect, reificative connections afford seemingly limitless possibilities. But the ambiguity inherent in reification presents new challenges when this ambiguity is uprooted from the practices in which it functions as an interactional resource. With no (or limited) mutual engagement, one must carefully consider the potentials and limits of reification:

1) the ability of reification to travel, that is, to break free from the physical limitations of mutual engagement and spread widely (e.g., a piece of information on the Internet) – but also the limited distance that reification, if unaccompanied by people, can in fact travel through time and space without the risk of divergent interpretations

2) the ambiguity that allows reification to accommodate different viewpoints – but also the possible misunderstandings and incompatible assumptions that can remain undetected

3) the ability of reification to make people take a stand by requiring interpretation and coordination (e.g., a new policy) – but also the risk of its embodying and thus reinforcing the very boundaries it is meant to cross (e.g., the language of the policy is typical of its authors' reputation and serves only to confirm the cynicism of the intended audience).

Participative connections offer possibilities for negotiation that can give them the vivid character of a vicarious experience. We know all about rock climbing because our best friend is a fanatic; we have a personal sense of Sudanese culture because our neighbors are from there; we are privy to the questions, the mysteries, and the politics of microbiology because we usually have lunch with a group of microbiologists in the lab's cafeteria; we go to school with our children during supper time; we are half a mason, half a lawyer, half a nurse, or half an engineer, because our better half is the real thing. But our knowledge of these practices inherits the partiality of those who give us peripheral access to them:

1) no single member is fully representative of the practice as a whole

2) what people remember depends on their experience of the moment

3) in the absence of the practice and the rest of the community, isolated representatives cannot fully act and function as they do when engaged in actual practice.

In order to take advantage of the complementarity of participation and reification, it is often a good idea to have artifacts and people travel together. Accompanied artifacts stand a better chance of bridging practices. A document can give a less partial view of a topic, and a person can help interpret the document and negotiate its relevance. When combined, the ambiguity of reification and the partiality of participation can compensate for each other by becoming productive interactional resources. Given enough legitimacy, visitors with a carefully composed paraphernalia of artifacts can provide a substantial connection indeed.

Boundary encounters and the negotiation of meaning

Boundary encounters – such as meetings, conversations, and visits – can take various forms, which are illustrated in Figure 4.2. Each form can serve a different purpose. In terms of negotiation of meaning, the connecting effects of boundary encounters depends on the distribution of internal and boundary relations among those involved.

- A one-on-one conversation between two members of two communities involves only the boundary relation between them. The advantage of such private conversations is that interlocutors are by themselves and can therefore be candid about their own practices in an effort to advance the boundary relation. As I have remarked, though, the connection created is hostage to the partiality of each interlocutor.
- One way to enrich the boundary encounter is to visit a practice. This kind of immersion provides a broader exposure to the community of practice being visited and to how its members engage with one another. By themselves, visitors must "background" their home membership in order to advance the boundary relation and maximize exposure to or influence on the practice of the visited community. This process, however, provides mostly a one-way connection. The host practice is unlikely to witness in any significant way how visitors function in their home practice.
- When delegations of a number of participants from each community are involved in an encounter, the negotiation of meaning takes place at the same time among members within each practice and across the boundary. Keeping the negotiation of meaning alive along these multiple dimensions at the same time has two advantages.

    1) Negotiating the meaning of elements from the other side can be accomplished by a process of negotiation within a practice – that is, with outsiders and among insiders at the same time.

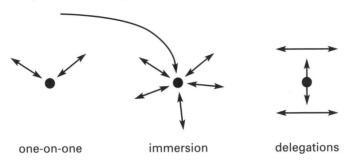

one-on-one   immersion   delegations

Figure 4.2. Types of boundary encounter.

2)   This process allows each side to get a sense of how the negotia-
     tion of meaning takes place in the other community.

Delegations do provide two-way connections, but the problem with
this arrangement is that participants may cling to their own internal
relations, perspectives, and ways of thinking.

Here, I described boundary encounters as single or discrete events that
provide connections. But connections can also be longer-lived and thus
become part of a practice, a possibility to which I now turn.

Practice as connection

Practice is the source of its own boundary through all three
dimensions introduced in Chapter 2.

1)   Participants form close relationships and develop idiosyncratic
     ways of engaging with one another, which outsiders cannot
     easily enter.
2)   They have a detailed and complex understanding of their en-
     terprise as they define it, which outsiders may not share.
3)   They have developed a repertoire for which outsiders miss
     shared references.

Note that the boundary is not only for outsiders; it also keeps insiders
in. When pursuing an enterprise, it makes sense to spend time in mutual
engagement with others who also pursue it, and to ignore what is not
directly relevant to it in terms of interests and resources. Even when
interacting with an outsider, it may make sense to gloss over difficult
points and not waste energy engaging them with internal issues.

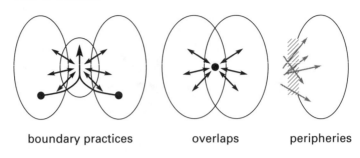

boundary practices   overlaps   peripheries

Figure 4.3. Types of connection provided by practice.

In addition to being a source of boundary for outsiders and insiders, practice can also become a form of connection. Practice has the advantage of offering something to do together, some productive enterprise around which to negotiate diverging meanings and perspectives. People can engage in practice rather than simply talk about it. Over time, the connection itself gains a history:

1) sustained mutual engagement builds relationships
2) maintaining connections becomes part of the enterprise
3) the repertoire begins to include boundary elements that articulate the forms of membership involved.

In all these ways, practice can offer connections that go beyond boundary encounters. I will describe three ways that practice itself can become a connection: boundary practices, overlaps, and peripheries (see Figure 4.3).

Boundary practices

The first type of practice-based connection I will describe is an identifiable boundary practice. If a boundary encounter – especially of the delegation variety – becomes established and provides an ongoing forum for mutual engagement, then a practice is likely to start emerging. Its enterprise is to deal with boundaries and sustain a connection between a number of other practices by addressing conflicts, reconciling perspectives, and finding resolutions. The resulting boundary practice becomes a form of collective brokering.

Boundary practices are common in organizations; examples include task forces, executive committees, and cross-functional teams. In the claims processing center, the office managers and the representatives from the regional headquarters coordinated local activities with the rest of the corporation through a boundary practice, though not much of what they did was shared with claims processors. Boundary practices can be less official. Engineers of a supplier company working with engineers of a customer company may over time create a community of practice that reflects deep working relations and creates an indispensable bridge between their respective practices – and between the organizations to the point of blurring allegiances.

The idea of a boundary practice works only if the process does not become completely self-involved. Boundary practices combine participation and reification, and thus solve some of the problems of boundary objects and isolated brokers. Yet, they present the danger of gaining so much momentum of their own that they become insulated from the practices they are supposed to connect. One way to look at training classes, for instance, is as boundary practices between some communities and the rest of the world. But if their practices cease to be boundary practices then they fail to create connections to anything beyond themselves. One teacher, isolated from other practitioners and immersed in classroom issues, ceases to be representative of anything else; and artifacts gain local meanings that do not point anywhere.

Becoming a community of practice in its own right is a risk of boundary practices that may thwart their roles in creating connections – but this risk is also their potential. Many long-lived communities of practice have their origin in an attempt to bring two practices together. New scientific disciplines, for instance, are often born of the interaction of established ones, a fact sometimes reflected in their unwieldy names: sociolinguistics, biochemistry, neuropsychoimmunology. It is difficult to establish criteria for what is valuable at the fringes of established practices, and the burgeoning of promising new practices is not always easy to recognize because they do not fit well within existing regimes of accountability.

Overlaps

The second type of practice-based connection does not require a specific boundary enterprise, but is provided by a direct and sustained overlap between two practices. I will illustrate this idea with a story from the claims processing center. Two types of employees process claims at Alinsu. Claims processors do the bulk of the claims; and claims technicians take care of special claims, which processors cannot or are not allowed to deal with because of the extensive research, legal issues, or very large amounts of money involved. A processor who finds such a claim refers it to the technical unit.

It used to be that every claims processing unit had its resident claims technicians. Even though the technician's primary allegiance was to a different community of practice – that of their technical colleagues – they were physically working among the claims processors who referred cases to them. The situation worked well, but management became concerned that technicians were too spread out to handle claims uniformly and so decided to group them together in their own office. The intent was that they could then communicate better and probably handle cases more uniformly.

In this new situation, claims to be referred to the technical unit were just dumped in a basket, collected once a day, processed by a technician, and later returned with instructions about what actions to take. A new problem developed, however. In their own office, technicians were becoming increasingly isolated. They were losing their awareness of the problems faced by claims processors, and they were unable to share their wisdom with claims processors in order to enable them to handle more claims themselves. Without the reassurance of direct contacts with the technical unit and because of the threat of "voids" by quality review, claims processors started to refer any claim that presented even the slightest problem. The technical unit was becoming inundated with claims that, under the old arrangement, would not have been referred at all.

After a few years, the technical unit became so overwhelmed with claim referrals that management was compelled to send the technicians back on the floor. The technicians agreed because – even though they enjoyed their isolation – they had to acknowledge that the problem was real. But they decided to remain a unit of their own, with their own relations, their own practice, their own meetings, and their own administrative structure. They joined claims processing units in small groups, so they had each other at hand, and they all kept in touch regularly as a technical unit. In addition, they also participated in the life of their "unit of residence," engaging in conversations, answering questions, and attending unit meetings. Claims processors who had a problem that called for technical help could now walk the claim up to the desk of one of their technicians, discuss the problem, and try to resolve it together. They would leave the claim with the technician only if some research had to be carried out or if some other technical task was necessary. Once that task was accomplished – by the technician usually or perhaps by a colleague with special expertise – the technician was again able to discuss the results with the claims processor rather than just write down an instruction. Because the presence of technicians among claims processors again provided an overlap between these two communities of practice, claims processors were able to handle a broader spectrum of claims themselves.

The participation of the claims technicians in specific units did not merge the two communities. They remained distinct, with distinct enterprises and distinct practices. But their engagement in both communities at once created not so much an identifiable boundary practice as an overlap between their practices. In assembling the technicians in one place, management had overlooked the amount of learning, for both communities, enabled by this overlap.

Peripheries

The third type of practice-based connection is the opening of a periphery. Communities of practice can connect with the rest of the world by providing peripheral experiences – of the kind I argued newcomers need – to people who are not on a trajectory to become full members. The idea is to offer them various forms of casual but legitimate access to a practice without subjecting them to the demands of full membership. This kind of peripherality can include observation, but it can also go beyond mere observation and involve actual forms of engagement.

The periphery of a practice is thus a region that is neither fully inside nor fully outside, and surrounds the practice with a degree of permeability. Professional communities of practice, for instance, often organize themselves to let outsiders in to some extent, usually in the course of providing or receiving a service, but also in efforts of public relations or under requirements of public scrutiny. Good architects, for instance, will discuss the reasons for their designs with their clients. Trials will be public or even broadcast on television.

The ability to have multiple levels of involvement is an important characteristic of communities of practice, one that presents opportunities for learning both for outsiders and for communities. Indeed, because it is defined by engagement rather than a reification of membership, a community of practice can offer multiple, more or less peripheral forms of participation.

From this perspective, a community of practice is a node of mutual engagement that becomes progressively looser at the periphery, with layers going from core membership to extreme peripherality. The interaction of all these levels affords multiple and diverse opportunities for learning. Different participants contribute and benefit differently, depending on their relations to the enterprise and the community.

In fact, combining these layers is a source of dynamism. I have argued in the previous chapter that practice is both perturbable and resilient. As a consequence, the periphery is a very fertile area for change:

1) it is partly outside and thus in contact with other views
2) it is partly inside and so perturbations are likely to propagate.

The practice then develops as the community constantly renegotiates the relations between its core and its periphery.

The landscape of practice

As communities of practice differentiate themselves and also interlock with each other, they constitute a complex social landscape of shared practices, boundaries, peripheries, overlaps, connections, and encounters. I want to conclude with two points that are by now rather obvious but cannot be overstated. First, the texture of continuities and discontinuities of this landscape is defined by practice, not by institutional affiliation; second, the landscape so defined is a weaving of both boundaries and peripheries.

Practice as boundary

Because communities of practice define themselves through engagement in practice, they are essentially informal. By "informal" I do not mean that the practice is disorganized or that communities of practice never have any formal status. What I mean is that, since the life of a community of practice as it unfolds is, in essence, produced by its members through their mutual engagement, it evolves in organic ways that tend to escape formal descriptions and control. The landscape of practice is therefore not congruent with the reified structures of institutional affiliations, divisions, and boundaries. It is not independent of these institutional structures, but neither is it reducible to them.

- On the one hand, the boundaries of communities of practice do not necessarily follow institutional boundaries, because membership is not defined by institutional categories. Who belongs and who does not, how the boundaries are defined, and what kinds of periphery are open are all matters of engagement in practice over time, of the need to get things done, and of the formation of viable identities.
- On the other hand, an institutional boundary does not necessarily outline a community of practice. Careful scrutiny of its day-to-day existence may reveal that a work group, classroom, committee, or neighborhood does not actually constitute a community of practice. It may consist of multiple communities of practice, or it may not have developed enough of a practice of its own.

An institutional boundary may therefore correspond to one community of practice, to a number of them, or to none at all. In addition, communities of practice can also be found spread throughout organizations (e.g., a community of practice of specialists in one area of expertise who work in different units but manage to stay in close contact) or straddling the boundaries of organizations (e.g., communities of practice formed around an emerging technology by professionals from competing companies). Communities of practice that bridge institutional boundaries are often critical to getting things done in the context of – and sometimes in spite of – bureaucratic rigidities.

Thus, even when communities of practice live and define themselves within an institutional context, their boundaries may or may not coincide with institutional boundaries. And even when communities of practice are formed more or less along institutional boundaries, they entertain all sorts of relations of peripherality that blur those boundaries. Institutional boundaries draw clear distinctions between inside and outside. By contrast, boundaries of practice are constantly renegotiated, defining much more fluid and textured forms of participation.

Boundaries and peripheries

The terms *boundaries* and *peripheries* both refer to the "edges" of communities of practice, to their points of contact with the rest of the world, but they emphasize different aspects. Boundaries – no matter how negotiable or unspoken – refer to discontinuities, to lines of distinction between inside and outside, membership and nonmembership, inclusion and exclusion. Peripheries – no matter how narrow – refer to continuities, to areas of overlap and connections, to windows and meeting places, and to organized and casual possibilities for participation offered to outsiders or newcomers.

Boundaries and peripheries are woven together. I was allowed to enter the community of practice of claims processors with an openness that at times felt like full participation, but every so often elements of boundary would creep in to remind me that I was an outsider: an expression I could not understand, a mistrusting look from the supervisor, a reference to a past event, someone's panicking concern about production quotas (to which I was not subjected), or even a claims processor's sigh of relief at five o'clock when I knew that I still had to go to my office and type up my notes.

Peripherality is thus an ambiguous position. Practice can be guarded just as it can be made available; membership can seem a daunting prospect just as it can constitute a welcoming invitation; a community of practice can be a fortress just as it can be an open door. Peripherality can be a position where access to a practice is possible, but it can also be a position where outsiders are kept from moving further inward.

The access that claims processors have to medical professionals, medical records, and medical jargon as a matter of routine is a form of periphery that does affect their own doctor–patient relations. But their own experience of their peripheral access to medical practices reflects all the ambivalence of peripherality, as illustrated by the following dialogue.

ETIENNE   Does that make a difference for you now, when you go see a doctor. Do you feel different?
MAUREEN   No.
SHEILA   Well, you know more about what they are talking about. I think it's ... when I went to the dentist yesterday, he told me that this joint and everything is kind of weak. And I knew exactly it was TMJ. I knew exactly. The way he was wording it.
MAUREEN   You're sort of, self-diagnosing yourself.
SHEILA   Yeah, exactly. I think I pay more attention going to the doctor. Look at all these people who get sick, you know, maybe I should go. Maybe, I don't know if ... I haven't gone to the doctor in a long time, so.
MAUREEN   You read an operative report. "Oh, I think I got this," you know.
SHEILA   Or I think I get to be a hypochondriac. Oh, that sounds like me, better go to the doctor.

Claims processors do not become doctors. In fact, they usually keep a low profile about the knowledge they gain through their peripheral access to medical information. An old-timer, who was the mother of a young child, told me that knowing all the terms and having read many reports gave her critical insights into the work of the medical professionals she dealt with. Yet, with a tacit awareness of her need to cooperate in maintaining a traditional doctor–patient relation, she also confided that she usually tried not to show her own knowledge and not to ask too many technical questions. Along with the periphery, the boundary clearly remained. By weaving boundaries and peripheries, a landscape of practice forms a complex texture of distinction and association, possibilities and impossibilities, opening and closing, limits and latitude, gates and entries, participation and non-participation.

Chapter 5
Locality

Is claims processing in general a community of practice? Should any work group be considered a community of practice? What about a whole company? What about an academic department or a classroom? What about a single individual or a family? What about a couple of lovers who see each other once a week or an older couple who have lived their entire lives together? What about a hitchhiker and a motorist who share a ride? What about a nation, Asians, or the English-speaking world? What about the commuters on a transit system or the theater-going crowd in New York? What about a tribe of mountain gorillas? Some of these configurations fit the concept of community of practice squarely, some are more or less marginal cases, and some really stretch the idea.

Calling every imaginable social configuration a community of practice would render the concept meaningless. On the other hand, encumbering the concept with too restrictive a definition would only make it less useful. It is not necessary, for instance, to develop a simple metric that would yield a clear-cut answer for each of the social configurations just listed by specifying exact ranges of size, duration, proximity, amount of interaction, or types of activities.

I find it more important to explore, as I have done so far, the perspective that underlies the concept of practice, and thus develop a framework by which to articulate to what degree, in which ways, and to what purpose it is (or is not) useful to view a social configuration as a community of practice. In this chapter, I will build on what I have done so far to clarify a bit more explicitly how the concept of community of practice constitutes a level of analysis.

1) I will first discuss the locality of practice and the scope of relevance of the concept of community of practice.
2) I will then introduce the concept of a constellation of practices as a simple way to start considering other levels of analysis.

122

3) Finally, I will discuss the interactions between the local and the global as suggested by different levels of analysis.

Though I will start to speak about different levels of analysis in this chapter, I will still do so strictly in terms of engagement in practice, again leaving for Part II the discussion of other processes. Talking about other levels of social structure has two advantages.

1) Equipped with related alternatives, one is less tempted to try to account for everything by stretching the relevance of one single concept (such as community of practice) beyond recognition or usefulness.
2) At the same time, such related alternatives give the concept more distinctiveness by contrast and more systematicity by locating it within a broader framework.

The locality of practice

Different ways of looking at the world reveal different sources of continuity and discontinuity. Focusing on one level of structure or another brings out distinctions that are relevant for a given purpose. I have considered claims processors who work together a community of practice because I was interested in understanding how they made sense of their daily activities at work. They have a sustained history of mutual engagement. They negotiate with one another what they are doing there, how they should behave, their relation with the company, and the meanings of the artifacts they use. They have developed local routines and artifacts to support their work together. They know who to ask when they need help. And they introduce into their community new trainees who want to become proficient at their practice.

There were other configurations that I could have considered: friendship groups of two or three claims processors who sometimes go to lunch together, the entire office, or the profession of claims processing as a whole. All are reasonable candidates as the home base of a practice.

1) Going to lunch can become a routine, with conversations that refer to past ones or even extend over a number of days.
2) The office has established procedures, rules, and regulations that everyone must adhere to; people are transferred among units, and friendships are established.
3) As a profession, claims processing is probably not all that different at Alinsu's competitors.

In all three cases, there is an experience of participation: the animated discussions at lunch, the rather intimate atmosphere of the office Christmas party, and the development of professional identities all reflect a sense of belonging. Yet there are factors that weaken the case of all three candidates.

- The lunch groups are not very steady and do not build up into conversations, relationships, enterprises, and shared histories that are distinct from broader participation in the unit.
- Although the entire office follows similar patterns, each unit is self-contained enough to develop its own practices. On a day-to-day basis, the office as a whole is more a physical and organizational context for the job than a focus of engagement by claims processors.
- Similarly, the profession of claims processing is mostly an abstraction, and its regularities have little to do with the mutual engagement of claims processors. Except for brief phone conversations with colleagues at other companies and the prospect of other employment, the profession does not enter as a significant component in their daily work. Processors do not seek to know very much about the history of their trade in general; this history is delivered to them mostly in the form of company policies.

Although there are arguments in favor of the three candidates just discussed, I would not consider the whole company a good candidate for a community of practice. Not only is Alinsu as a company a rather distant abstraction for claims processors, but it is also composed of very different (and largely disconnected) practices. The same can be said about the less gigantic business division, and even the smaller regional organization to which their office reports. It would be stretching the definition quite thin to consider any of these levels of organization a community of practice, even though all are social configurations in which claims processors are implicated at some level, and even though claims processors have a clear sense that their work is part of these configurations. In fact, viewing these levels of aggregation as communities of practice would likely be misleading because it would overlook the multiplicity and the substantial disconnectedness of the perspectives involved.

A level of analysis

As an analytical tool, the concept of community of practice is a midlevel category. It is neither a specific, narrowly defined activity or interaction nor a broadly defined aggregate that is abstractly historical and social.

- Viewing a specific interaction (e.g., a conversation or an activity) as a transient community of practice might seem like a way to capture the ephemeral history of learning that can become a local resource in negotiating meaning. But this view would attribute too much importance to the moment. Interactions and activities take place in the service of enterprises and identities whose definition is not confined to single events. This view would overlook broader continuities in time and among people. It would overlook the communities where enterprises are defined and where learning events are consolidated and integrated into the formation of practices and identities.

- Conversely, viewing a nation, a culture, a city, or a corporation as one community of practice might seem like a way to capture the processes of learning that constitute these social configurations. Yet it would miss crucial discontinuities among the various localities where relevant learning takes place. It would place too much emphasis on the overarching continuity of a configuration reified by its name. Learning and the negotiation of meaning are ongoing within the various localities of engagement, and this process continually creates locally shared histories. This is true even when there are no serious conflicts or ruptures between localities, and a fortiori when there are.

Because a community of practice need not be reified as such in the discourse of its participants, indicators that a community of practice has formed would include:

1) sustained mutual relationships – harmonious or conflictual
2) shared ways of engaging in doing things together
3) the rapid flow of information and propagation of innovation
4) absence of introductory preambles, as if conversations and interactions were merely the continuation of an ongoing process
5) very quick setup of a problem to be discussed
6) substantial overlap in participants' descriptions of who belongs
7) knowing what others know, what they can do, and how they can contribute to an enterprise
8) mutually defining identities
9) the ability to assess the appropriateness of actions and products
10) specific tools, representations, and other artifacts
11) local lore, shared stories, inside jokes, knowing laughter
12) jargon and shortcuts to communication as well as the ease of producing new ones

13)   certain styles recognized as displaying membership
14)   a shared discourse reflecting a certain perspective on the world.

These characteristics indicate that the three dimensions of a community of practice introduced in Chapter 2 – a community of mutual engagement, a negotiated enterprise, and a repertoire of negotiable resources accumulated over time – are present to a substantial degree.

- It is not necessary that all participants interact intensely with everyone else or know each other very well – but the less they do, the more their configuration looks like a personal network or a set of interrelated practices rather than a single community of practice.
- It is not necessary that everything participants do be accountable to a joint enterprise, or that everyone be able to assess the appropriateness of everyone's actions or behavior. But the less that is the case, the more questionable it is that there is a substantial enterprise that brings them together and that they have spent some effort negotiating what it is they are trying to accomplish.[1]
- It is not necessary that a repertoire be completely locally produced. In fact, the bulk of the repertoire of most communities of practice is imported, adopted, and adapted for their own purpose – if only the language(s) they speak. But if there is hardly any local production of negotiable resources, and if hardly any specific points of reference or artifacts are being created in that context, then one would start to wonder whether there is really something that the people involved are doing together and around which they engage with one another in a sustained way.

So characterized, the notion of practice refers to a level of social structure that reflects shared learning. Note that this is a level both of analysis and of experience. Since communities of practice can form without being named or otherwise reified, most people do not think about their lives and their identities in these terms. In this sense, communities of practice are an analytical category, but not merely an esoteric analytical category that refers to abstract kinds of social aggregates. By referring to structures that are within the scope of our engagement, this category captures a familiar aspect of our experience of the world and so is not merely analytical.

Constellations of practices

Some configurations are too far removed from the scope of engagement of participants, too broad, too diverse, or too diffuse to be usefully treated as single communities of practice. This is true not only of very large configurations (the global economy, speakers of a language, a city, a social movement) but also of some smaller ones (a factory, an office, or a school). Whereas treating such configurations as single communities of practice would gloss over the discontinuities that are integral to their very structure, they can profitably be viewed as *constellations* of interconnected practices.

A large company like Alinsu is a good example of such a constellation. Belonging to the same organization is a form of continuity reinforced by an institutional apparatus, but – at the level of practice – claims processing centers, underwriting offices, upper management, sales teams, and various cross-functional teams all have their own communities, with their own enterprises and their own interpretations of the overall organization.

A broader and more diffuse establishment like health insurance similarly arises out of the practices of many local communities – in business, in the medical and legal professions, in government agencies, and many others. Each of these communities is in many ways similar to the communities of claims processors, with its own practice and its own specific focus. And each contributes in its own way to the constitution of the overall constellation. The same is true of a profession, a religion, a sport, a language, or a nation.

The term *constellation* refers to a grouping of stellar objects that are seen as a configuration even though they may not be particularly close to one another, of the same kind, or of the same size. A constellation is a particular way of seeing them as related, one that depends on the perspective one adopts. In the same way, there are many different reasons that some communities of practice may be seen as forming a constellation, by the people involved or by an observer. These include:

1) sharing historical roots
2) having related enterprises
3) serving a cause or belonging to an institution
4) facing similar conditions
5) having members in common
6) sharing artifacts
7) having geographical relations of proximity or interaction
8) having overlapping styles or discourses
9) competing for the same resources.

All these relations can create continuities that define broader configurations than a single community of practice. A given community of practice can be part of any number of constellations. The practice of claims processors is part of the corporation, the local office, the occupants of their building, the profession of claims processing, the claims processors in their county, the "pink collar" workforce, and a host of others I could come up with. Communities of practice define themselves in part by the way they negotiate their place within the various constellations they are involved in, a theme to which I will return later in the book.

As a simple way to account for a level of continuity that cuts across communities of practice, the concept of constellation can remain fairly broad in its application.

- Belonging to a constellation need not be reified within the discourse of any of the practices involved. A given constellation may or may not be recognized by participants; it may or may not be named.
- There may or may not be people who endeavor to keep the constellation together. There may be an overarching enterprise around which the practices of the communities involved are primarily organized, as in the case of a social movement or a corporation, or their connections may be merely incidental to their own practices, as in the case of the tenants of an office building.
- The connections that tie communities of practice may take intentional forms, such as the deliberate straddling of boundaries by a supervisor, or they may be due to emerging circumstances, as in the case of sharing a cafeteria.

Interactions among local communities can affect their practices without an explicit sense of participation in a constellation. All the people who use a rare word, whose close colleagues are all near retirement age, or who belong to a family in which everyone has read a certain novel may not have the sense of belonging to a constellation of practices, though it may be useful to view them this way for some purposes. The combined effects of many local interconnections is not always easy or useful to perceive.

Practices, discourses, and styles

A constellation of practices consists of communities and boundaries that define two kinds of diversity.

1) *Diversity internal to practice and defined through mutual engagement.* I have argued that shared practice does not entail uni-

formity, conformity, cooperation, or agreement, but it does entail a kind of diversity in which perspectives and identities are engaged with one another.

2) *Diversity caused by boundaries and stemming from lack of mutual engagement.* I have argued that boundaries are not sharp lines of demarcation, but they do reflect the specificity of various enterprises and the ongoing production of local meanings.

When a social configuration is viewed as a constellation rather than a community of practice, the continuity of the constellation must be understood in terms of interactions among practices:

1) boundary objects and brokering, including individual trajectories, patterns of migrations, and diaspora of communities of practice
2) boundary practices, overlaps, and peripheries
3) elements of styles that spread as people copy, borrow, imitate, import, adapt, and reinterpret ways of behaving in the process of constructing an identity
4) elements of discourses that travel across boundaries and combine to form broader discourses as people coordinate their enterprises, convince each other, reconcile their perspectives, and form alliances.

Styles and discourses are aspects of the repertoire of a practice that are exportable. Elements of style and discourse can be detached from specific enterprises. They can be imported and exported across boundaries, and reinterpreted and adapted in the process of being adopted within various practices.

• If a group of children imitate the style of a movie star or of some other adult, those same ways of behaving are integrated into a different enterprise and given different meanings.
• When claims processors adopt elements of medical discourse into their own practice, these terms and concepts take on very specific meanings that are related to their meanings in a medical context but are specialized to claims processing.

Because styles and discourses can spread across an entire constellation, they can create forms of continuity that take on a global character. However, styles and discourses are not practices in themselves. They are available material – resources that can be used in the context of various practices. As material for the negotiation of meaning and the formation of identities, styles and discourses can be shared by multiple practices. But that does not mean that they are integrated in these various practices in the same ways once they are put in the service of different local enterprises. In the course of producing their own histories, therefore, communities of practice also produce and reproduce the interconnections, styles, and discourses through which they form broader constellations.

The geography of practice

Constellations define relations of locality, proximity, and distance, which are not necessarily congruent with physical proximity, institutional affiliations, or even interactions. Claims processors are in important ways "closer" to claims processors in other companies than they are to the customers who call them on the phone or to the janitors in their own building. And their regular contacts with the medical profession can bring them closer to the medical establishment than they are to upper-level management in their own company.[2]

Engagement in practice not only reflects these relations, it also modifies them. Engineers on different projects may be closer to each other than they are to the marketing people on their own teams. Yet with enough shared engagement, even engineers can become good at marketing. In other words, the geography of practice reflects histories of learning, but learning continues to reconfigure relations of proximity and distance.

- Relations of proximity and distance may facilitate or hinder learning. For instance, people who have related backgrounds will probably be able to form a community of practice with less mutual engagement than people whose prior practices are more distant to start with.
- The members of an incipient community of practice may belong to very different localities of practice to start with, but – after sustaining enough mutual engagement – they will end up creating a locality of their own, even if their backgrounds have little in common.

Introducing the concept of constellations of practices into the framework adds notions of locality, proximity, and distance to those of boundaries and peripheries. My argument is not that physical proximity, institutional affiliation, or frequency of interaction are irrelevant, but rather that the geography of practice cannot be reduced to them. Practice is always located in time and space because it always exists in specific communities and arises out of mutual engagement, which is largely

dependent on specific places and times. Yet the relations that constitute practice are primarily defined by learning. As a result, the landscape of practice is an emergent structure in which learning constantly
creates localities that reconfigure the geography.

The local and the global

There is a widespread assumption – in social theory as well as
in more popular writing – that the history of modern times involves a
transition from local communities to global societies.[3] From that perspective, the concept of community of practice and the local character
of mutual engagement may seem obsolete. By contrast, in the context
of constellations of practices, the local and the global are not different
historical moments in an expanding world. Instead, they are related
levels of participation that always coexist and shape each other. The
relevance of communities of practice is therefore not diminished by
the formation of broader and broader configurations.

In this context, it is important to reiterate here the distinction made
in Chapter 1 between participation and engagement. We can develop
new ways of participating in the global, but we do not engage with it.
Claims processors participate in Alinsu, but they do not engage with
the company as a whole; they engage with their own community of
practice and a few other people. The cosmopolitan character of a practice, for instance, does not free it from the locality of engagement. Day-
to-day work in an office at UN headquarters is still local in its own
way, even though it deals with international affairs that have broad
ramifications.

Our scope of engagement is not fixed, for sure, but it is not indiscriminately expandable either. Technological developments have provided
means for pushing its limits, with transforming innovations in areas
such as transportation, telecommunication and networking, automation and organizational techniques, systematic record keeping, and access to information. These technological developments, however, are
not simply straightforward expansions of our scope of engagement;
rather, they involve trade-offs. For instance, reificative tools such as
statistical or financial analysis afford a dramatic increase in the scope of
complexity of perceivable patterns, but at the cost of giving up participation in the complexity of situations and their local meanings. You can
tell how many marriages end in divorce, but that tells you little about
the story of any given marriage.

Similarly, the production reports that claims processors fill out every day reify their activities for consumption outside their practice. Limiting the report to numbers of claims processed is a way to enforce a specific, exportable interpretation on a day of work, but the number of claims processed that day leaves out much of what happened. A whole day of work, negotiation of meaning, boredom, inventiveness, rebellion, conversation, and community building has been reified into a number, which – even in terms of what has been done specifically for the company – is a very restricted representation of that day. These numbers are abstracted from the processors' practice for the calculations of other practices, such as operations management and finance. They can be combined to build encompassing models and reveal broad patterns. Yet, because the reification that makes them exportable from one practice to another entails a loss of content and context, the practices that make use of these numbers to create a global picture of the organization are in their own way as local as claims processing. The broad view they attempt to achieve involves trade-offs in complexity. They can see more only by seeing less. What they end up knowing is something different, which has its own relevance in its own context, but which does not subsume the perspectives it attempts to incorporate.

In these trade-offs, one kind of complexity replaces another, one kind of limitation is overcome at the cost of introducing another. We travel to the four corners of the world but we hardly know our neighbors; we coordinate our work in huge organizations but we find it difficult to know whom to trust; we have instant access to a worldwide web of connected computers, but we long for ways to sort out what to pay attention to and what to ignore in order to maintain a sense of coherence and personal trajectory. My point here is not nostalgia. Your neighbor may not be worth knowing; trusting your fellow worker can mean being cheated; and surfing the web can be a way to discover new horizons and form new communities. My point is rather that changing the scope of our engagement is not so much expanding its range as it is a series of trade-offs between forms of complexity.

Recognizing the scope of mutual engagement and its importance in the negotiation of meaning does not imply a glorification of localism. Claiming that communities of practice are a crucial locus of learning is not to imply that the process is intrinsically benevolent. In this regard, it is worth repeating that communities of practice should not be romanticized: they can reproduce counterproductive patterns, injustices, prejudices, racism, sexism, and abuses of all kinds. In fact, I would argue that they are the very locus of such reproduction.

On the other hand, the discourses that tie our communities of practice into broader constellations do not replace practice. For example, institutions like religion, science, and law have created discourses that reify certain enterprises on a large scale. The discourses of these institutions connect the practices of different communities where they find realizations that may or may not be congruent. Talking about styles and discourses on the one hand and practices on the other – without assuming congruence between them – is neither a positivist despising of the local nor a relativist glorifying of it.[4]

On this view, communities of practice can neither be dismissed as a relic of the past nor be unquestionably trusted as an idyllic promise. Rather than idealizing or vilifying them in general terms, we must recognize them as a fact of social life. They are important places of negotiation, learning, meaning, and identity. Focusing on the level of communities of practice is not to glorify the local, but to see these processes – negotiation of meaning, learning, the development of practices, and the formation of identities and social configurations – as involving complex interactions between the local and the global.

Coda I

Knowing in practice

I will end this first part of the book with a brief essay on the nature of knowing in practice. This essay, which is philosophical but in a light-hearted kind of way, will allow me to provide a summary of the themes introduced in Part I in the context of discussing a specific topic. Focusing on knowing for this purpose is a useful topic, but this choice should not be interpreted as assuming that knowing is all that communities of practice are about, especially if by "knowing" one refers to some instrumental kind of expertise. Communities of practice should not be reduced to purely instrumental purposes. They are about knowing, but also about being together, living meaningfully, developing a satisfying identity, and altogether being human.

Flowers and bits

I will start with two odd questions. The first one was concocted long ago by Zen teachers to help their students think more sharply: What does a flower know about being a flower? The second question is the information-age version of the first: What does a computer know about being a flower?[1]

The question of what a flower knows about being a flower is somewhat troubling because there seem to be two contradictory answers. Being a flower is to no one as transparent, immediately obvious, fully internalized, and natural as it is to a flower: spreading those leaves, absorbing that specific spectrum of light from the sun, taking the energy in, building protein, sucking nutrients from its roots, growing, budding, blooming, being visited by a bee. One might then be tempted to say that the flower knows more than anyone could ever know about being a flower. But ask the flower to teach a botany class, and it will just stand there, knowing nothing about being a flower, not the first thing – not that its leaves are green, not that it is absorbing energy to perform photosynthesis, not even that it has a sweet smell.

134

At the other extreme, type the word "flower" into the encyclopedia program of your computer. Up comes all the information you could ever need. Type "photosynthesis," "petal," "stem," and so on: perfect answers. The knowledge is all there. Or better yet, buy an interactive, multimedia educational program on botany and give it to the class the poor flower could not teach, and let the students explore. They will become experts. But if – as a reward for teaching the class – you buy your computer a half-dozen roses, then the computer will sit there, awaiting some input. It knows nothing.

Of course, these are two extreme examples, and using them just for rhetorical purposes may seem unfair. The flower, because it is a flower, is very good at being a flower; its experience of being a flower, whatever it is, is sufficient unto itself. The computer is simply responding properly to a given input according to its program, which is what we expect. But that is exactly the point. When we ask what the flower or the computer knows about being a flower, we find ourselves in a conundrum, not because it is a profound, intriguing, or difficult question but because knowing is not definable in the abstract. It cannot be taken as the point of departure.

Rather than starting with knowing, then, let me start with practice. Reviewing the characterizations of practice I have given in each chapter will allow me to make better sense of why knowing is undefined for flowers and computers and, by contrast, how it becomes defined for us.

Experience of meaning

Taking practice as the point of departure, the first observation to make is that neither the flower nor the computer is in a position to have an experience of meaning, which I argued in Chapter 1 is what practice is about. I also argued that meaning arises out of a process of negotiation that combines both participation and reification.

The flower may have an experience as a living entity, and it may even have some kind of relationship with us, but it cannot deal with our reifications. It remains impermeable to the concepts, images, classification schemes, and words – even the word *flower* – that we use to negotiate meaning and thus to make sense of our experience. But such reifications are an intrinsic part of our practices. They are indispensable to the process of negotiation that sustains those practices, and thus to the experiences of meaning we can achieve.

By contrast, computers can deal very well with certain types of reification, such as elements of discourse. Because they can handle enormous amounts of information at very high speeds, they can adapt their outputs to their inputs in a wide variety of ways, provided they have been programmed in a sophisticated enough fashion. But this prodigious dexterity does not translate into an ability to negotiate the meanings of their basic terms. They remain dependent on programmers and users to deal with the meanings of their electronic activities. What these machines lack in order to take some responsibility for meaning is not additional information or processing power but an experience of participation. They can do the right thing according to a reified definition of what the right thing is. They can interpret commands and data correctly. They can play their part in activities competently. But they do not have an identity of participation with which to take responsibility for the meanings of what they process.

By lacking – in opposite ways – the ability to combine participation and reification in a process of negotiation, both the flower and the computer lack the capability to have an experience of meaning.

Regimes of competence

One way to give the flower and the computer an experience of meaning would be to give them membership in a community of practice. They could then combine participation and reification, and so develop the kind of identity that allows us to have an experience of meaning. But that attempt would run into difficulties because membership in a community of practice is not something that can be granted arbitrarily, even if (say, out of curiosity) a community were to agree to the experiment. The competence required is neither merely individual nor abstractly communal. It is not something that we can claim as individuals because it implies a negotiated definition of what the community is about. But neither is it something that is just a property of a community in the abstract, that can be awarded through some decision, because this competence is experienced and manifested by members through their own engagement in practice.

This competence is not merely the ability to perform certain actions, the possession of certain pieces of information, or the mastery of certain skills in the abstract. Going back to the three dimensions of a community of practice discussed in Chapter 2, competent membership would include:

1) *mutuality of engagement* – the ability to engage with other members and respond in kind to their actions, and thus the ability to establish relationships in which this mutuality is the basis for an identity of participation

2) *accountability to the enterprise* – the ability to understand the enterprise of a community of practice deeply enough to take some responsibility for it and contribute to its pursuit and to its ongoing negotiation by the community

3) *negotiability of the repertoire* – the ability to make use of the repertoire of the practice to engage in it. This requires enough participation (personal or vicarious) in the history of a practice to recognize it in the elements of its repertoire. Then it requires the ability – both the capability and the legitimacy – to make this history newly meaningful.

Again, it is by its very practice – not by other criteria – that a community establishes what it is to be a competent participant, an outsider, or somewhere in between. In this regard, *a community of practice acts as a locally negotiated regime of competence.* Within such a regime, knowing is no longer undefined. It can be defined as what would be recognized as competent participation in the practice. That does not mean that one can know only what is already known. A community's regime of competence is not static. Even knowing something entirely new, and therefore even discovering, can be acts of competent participation in a practice.

Learning: experience and competence

If displaying a definition on a screen at the right time were competence enough, then the computer would know what it is to be a flower. If being a good-smelling flower were competence enough, then the flower would know what it is to be a flower. Why not leave it at that? Indeed, I said in Chapter 3 that, for learning purposes, a community can offer peripheral forms of participation that are considered legitimate without fulfilling all the conditions of full membership.

This is where, again, both our flower and our computer fall short. To become even a peripheral member of a community of practice, one must do some learning along the three dimensions of competence in practice just listed. This remains true whether a community of practice is forming, whether someone is joining one, or whether someone remains at the periphery. Such learning is not just a matter of competence, but a matter of experience of meaning as well.

Because the flower and the computer cannot combine reification and participation and thus cannot have an experience of meaning, they are barred from learning along all three dimensions.

1) They cannot engage with members of a community of practice in a way that would allow true mutuality because there is no experience of meaning to recognize and address in them.

2) They cannot understand a community's enterprise because, in the final analysis, an experience of meaning is what any enterprise is about.

3) They cannot negotiate the repertoire because, ultimately, experiences of meaning are what elements of the repertoire refer to.

For learning in practice to be possible, an experience of meaning must be in interaction with a regime of competence. Although experience and competence are both constituents of learning – and thus of knowing – they do not determine each other. They may be out of alignment in either direction.

• *Competence may drive experience.* Sometimes, our experience must align itself with a regime of competence. This is what happens to newcomers to a practice. In order to achieve the competence defined by a community, they transform their experience until it fits within the regime. But old-timers, too, need to catch up as the practice evolves.

• *Experience may drive competence.* Imagine that one or more members have had some experience that currently falls outside the regime of competence of a community to which they belong – for instance, because there are no words for it or because it puts the enterprise in question. As a way of asserting their membership, they may very well attempt to change the community's regime so that it includes their experience.[2] Toward this end, they have to negotiate its meaning with their community of practice. They invite others to participate in their experience; they attempt to reify it for them. They may need to engage with people in new ways and transform relations among people in order to be taken seriously; they may need to redefine the enterprise in order to make the effort worthwhile; they may need to add new elements to the repertoire of their practice. If they have enough legitimacy as members to be successful, they will have changed the regime of competence – and created new knowledge in the process.

This two-way interaction of experience and competence is crucial to the evolution of practice. In it lies the potential for a transformation of both experience and competence, and thus for learning, individually and collectively. In fact, learning – taken to be a transformation of knowing – can be characterized as a change in the alignment between experience and competence, whichever of the two takes the lead in causing a realignment at any given moment.

Boundaries

I can now prove, before I leave them alone, that I have nothing against flowers and computers – they each make my life more interesting in their uncanny ways. And for all my arguments, I certainly cannot claim to know much about their experience, or even if they have any. This is exactly the point. The embodied experience of the flower and the disembodied competence of the computer are too foreign for me to fathom. Precisely because they are extreme examples, the conundrum that they are either very knowledgeable or completely ignorant is in fact a point not about them but about boundaries.

If you allow yourself to cross boundaries of practice recklessly enough, then any experience or any competence can be defined as knowledge or ignorance, understanding or shallowness, consciousness or unconsciousness, or awareness or oblivion; all you have to do is change the regime of competence. This is what I meant in Coda 0 when I argued that the relation of claims processors to the COB worksheet of Vignette II can be viewed as one of transparency and one of opacity, depending on how you look at it – it can be made into knowledge or ignorance simply by varying the regime of competence:

1) by taking advantage of the partiality enabled by mutual engagement and not requiring everyone to share in the understanding of everything; if the worksheet was transparent to only one person to whom others could have access, that was good enough for all

2) by changing the enterprise and making the processors accountable here to their calculations, here to the customers, here to

the insurance industry, here to my analysis of their community, here to each other

3) by introducing new terms or concepts (e.g., "reification") and then stating that claims processors do not understand the worksheet as a reification.

Similarly, asking someone which way they turn to keep their balance on a bicycle (as discussed in Chapter 1) is changing the regime of competence. In a practice where the regime of competence included being able to tell which way to turn the steering bar, I bet everyone would be able to articulate this well enough. Contrasts like explicit versus tacit are often brought to the fore by boundary encounters. Any practice – even the most verbal – will have tacit aspects that are revealed by demands outside its regime of competence. By overlooking issues of boundary, schemes for classifying knowledge into types often place too much emphasis on individual cognition and thus on solutions to problems that do not take advantage of the landscape of practices. (The business literature supplies two more examples worthy of discussion.[3])

To say that the concept of knowing is not defined outside a regime of competence is not to say that boundaries cannot be crossed. I spent the bulk of Chapter 4 discussing all sorts of ways in which boundaries could be crossed. But that can take place only when participants are able to recognize an experience of meaning in each other and to develop enough of a shared sense of competence to do some mutual learning. Learning thus depends on the kinds of relations – locality, proximity, distance – introduced in Chapter 5. The point is that learning is impaired when experience and competence are too close *and* when they are too distant. In either case, they do not pull each other.

Crossing boundaries between practices exposes our experience to different forms of engagement, different enterprises with different definitions of what matters, and different repertoires – where even elements that have the same form (e.g., the same words or artifacts) belong to different histories. By creating a tension between experience and competence, crossing boundaries is a process by which learning is potentially enhanced, and potentially impaired.

The local and the global

I have so far abstained from talking about knowledge, restricting myself to terms like experience, competence, and knowing in practice. This is because "knowledge" is a tricky word. As a regime of competence, every practice is in some sense a form of knowledge, and knowing is participating in that practice.[4] But that is not a very satisfying way to talk, for two reasons.

- First, the practice of many communities includes ignorance, not only out of a lack of time and energy to explore everything, but also as an active principle of their enterprise. Claims processors, for instance, will not make what they would consider overly diligent efforts to know everything that an outside observer might think is relevant to their job. And in schools, some communities of practice organize their competence against the knowledge proposed by institutional curriculums.[5]
- Second, making knowledge practice-specific ignores the broader discourses by which we come to negotiate across practices what we consider to be knowledge. What we dare consider knowledge is not just a matter of our own experiences of meaning or even our own regimes of competence. It is also a matter of the positions of our practices with respect to the broader historical, social, and institutional discourses and styles (e.g., scientific, religious, political, artistic) to which we orient our practices in various ways and to which we can thus be more or less accountable.

What can be called knowledge, therefore, is not just a matter of local regimes of competence; it depends also on the orientation of these practices within broader constellations. Yet, whatever discourses we use to define what knowledge is, our communities of practice are a context of mutual engagement where these discourses can touch our experience and thus be given new life. In this regard, knowing in practice involves an interaction between the local and the global.

Well, this is what you get when you start wondering what flowers and computers know. Interestingly, but perhaps not surprisingly, it seems that you end up understanding more about your own knowing than about theirs. What transpires is that knowing is defined only in the context of specific practices, where it arises out of the combination of a regime of competence and an experience of meaning. Our knowing – even of the most unexceptional kind – is always too big, too rich, too ancient, and too connected for us to be the source of it individually. At the same time, our knowing – even of the most elevated kind – is too engaged, too precise, too tailored, too active, and too experiential for it to be just of a generic size. The experience of knowing is no less unique, no less creative, and no less extraordinary for being one of participation. As a matter of fact, on the face of it, it would probably not amount to much otherwise.

Part II
Identity

Intro II
A focus on identity

Issues of identity came up on a number of occasions in Part I, but I did not address the topic directly. It is now time to turn to it. Focusing on identity, however, is not a change of topic but rather a shift in focus within the same general topic. Issues of identity are an integral aspect of a social theory of learning and are thus inseparable from issues of practice, community, and meaning. Focusing on identity within this context extends the framework in two directions:

1) it narrows the focus onto the person, but from a social perspective
2) it expands the focus beyond communities of practice, calling attention to broader processes of identification and social structures.

In addition, focusing on identity brings to the fore the issues of nonparticipation as well as participation, and of exclusion as well as inclusion. Our identity includes our ability and our inability to shape the meanings that define our communities and our forms of belonging.

The individual and the collective

I will use the concept of identity to focus on the person without assuming the individual self as a point of departure. Building an identity consists of negotiating the meanings of our experience of membership in social communities. The concept of identity serves as a pivot between the social and the individual, so that each can be talked about in terms of the other. It avoids a simplistic individual–social dichotomy without doing away with the distinction. The resulting perspective is neither individualistic nor abstractly institutional or societal. It does justice to the lived experience of identity while recognizing its social character − it is the social, the cultural, the historical with a human face.

145

Talking about identity in social terms is not denying individuality but viewing the very definition of individuality as something that is part of the practices of specific communities. It is therefore a mistaken dichotomy to wonder whether the unit of analysis of identity should be the community or the person. The focus must be on the process of their mutual constitution. As I argued in Chapter 1, in a duality it is the interplay that matters most, not the ability to classify.

Indeed, in everyday life it is difficult – and, I would argue, largely unnecessary – to tell exactly where the sphere of the individual ends and the sphere of the collective begins. Each act of participation or reification, from the most public to the most private, reflects the mutual constitution between individuals and collectivities. Our practices, our languages, our artifacts, and our world views all reflect our social relations. Even our most private thoughts make use of concepts, images, and perspectives that we understand through our participation in social communities.

Taken separately, the notions of individual and community are reifications whose self-contained appearance hides their mutual constitution. We cannot become human by ourselves; hence a reified, physiologically based notion of individuality misses the interconnectedness of identity. Conversely, membership does not determine who we are in any simple way; hence generalizations and stereotypes miss the lived complexity of identity.

How Ariel experiences her job, how she interprets her position, what she understands about what she does, what she knows, doesn't know, and doesn't try to know – all of these are neither simply individual choices nor simply the result of belonging to the social category "claims processor." Instead, they are negotiated in the course of doing the job and interacting with others. It is shaped by belonging to a community, but with a unique identity. It depends on engaging in practice, but with a unique experience. In other words, it is as misleading to view identities as abstractly collective as it is to view them as narrowly individual.

Some assumptions to avoid

Before proceeding, I would like to discard at the outset two common assumptions about the relation between the individual and the social.

- The first assumption is that there is an inherent conflict between the individual and the collective:

1) that the two are fundamentally at odds, representing inherently diverging interests and incompatible tendencies, and consequently

2) that human life is a compromise by which each makes concessions to the other.

- The second, related assumption is that one is good and the other bad, one a source of problems and the other a source of solutions:

   1) that the individual is the source of freedom and creativity while the social is the source of constraints and limitations, or (conversely)

   2) that the social is the source of harmony and order while the individual is the source of discord and fragmentation.[1]

My discussion of the social formation of identities is not based on an assumption of either agreement or conflict. By refusing to assume an inherent divergence between the individual and the social, I am not saying that there is never any tension or conflict between the resources and demands of groups and the aspirations of individuals. In each specific case, there may be tensions, conflicts, or concessions; but, for every case where there is a conflict, you can find a case where individual and social developments enhance each other. Thus acknowledging that there can be specific tensions between individuals and collectivities is very different from positing a dichotomy with a fundamental divergence between them.

Similarly, by refusing to romanticize or revile either community or individuality in general terms, I am not saying that they are not sources of problems and solutions. But for each case in which an individual's creativity is squelched by a conformist community, there is another case in which a social activity is a source of insight. For each case in which individual conflicts create discord, you could find another case in which social peace depends on some individuals' willingness to take a stand against the pettiness of their own communities.

It is relatively easy to find counterexamples to these assumptions. But my purpose in disowning them up front is not so much to refute them as it is to state emphatically that they do not underlie my approach to the topic. Consequently, reading them into my text would only create confusion.

Structure of Part II

I will start by tying the topic of identity back to Part I, establishing a parallel between practice and identity. Then, in each chapter

I will introduce issues of identity that progressively complexify the picture, including but also extending beyond communities of practice. Our identities, even in the context of a specific practice, are not just a matter internal to that practice but also a matter of our position and the position of our communities within broader social structures.

- *Identity in practice.* Chapter 6 shows the relation between identity and practice by rehearsing the argument of Part I. By revisiting the various characteristics of practice introduced in each chapter, I will show how they can be construed as characteristics of identity. The result will be a characterization of identity that inherits the richness and complexity of practice.
- *Identities of participation and non-participation.* Chapter 7 introduces non-participation as a central aspect of the formation of identity. I will argue that non-participation can take many forms – being an outsider, being a peripheral participant, or being marginalized – each with different implications for the resulting identities.
- *Modes of belonging.* Chapter 8 extends the notion of belonging beyond local communities of practice. I will distinguish between three modes of belonging: engagement (which is already familiar from Part I), imagination, and alignment. I will describe the basic features of each of these modes of belonging, the kind of work they require, and finally the various kinds of communities to which they give rise.
- *Identification and negotiability.* Chapter 9 discusses issues of belonging in terms of identification with certain communities and also in terms of negotiability – that is, in terms of our ability to shape the meanings produced in the context of these communities. I will argue that the formation of communities inherently gives rise to "economies of meaning" in which various participants have various degrees of "ownership" of the meanings that define their communities. The dual processes of identification and negotiability make the notion of belonging a basis for talking about both identity and power in social terms.
- *Learning communities.* Coda II summarizes Part II by describing some basic features of what I will call a learning community, whose practice it is to keep alive the tension between competence and experience.

Chapter 6
Identity in practice

There is a profound connection between identity and practice. Developing a practice requires the formation of a community whose members can engage with one another and thus acknowledge each other as participants. As a consequence, practice entails the negotiation of ways of being a person in that context. This negotiation may be silent; participants may not necessarily talk directly about that issue. But whether or not they address the question directly, they deal with it through the way they engage in action with one another and relate to one another. Inevitably, our practices deal with the profound issue of how to be a human being. In this sense, the formation of a community of practice is also the negotiation of identities.

The parallels between practice and identity are summarized in Figure 6.1. To highlight them in this chapter, I will (as I did in Coda I) go through the themes of Part I, chapter by chapter, but recast them in terms of identity. This exercise will yield the following characterizations.

- Identity as *negotiated experience*. We define who we are by the ways we experience our selves through participation as well as by the ways we and others reify our selves.
- Identity as *community membership*. We define who we are by the familiar and the unfamiliar.
- Identity as *learning trajectory*. We define who we are by where we have been and where we are going.
- Identity as *nexus of multimembership*. We define who we are by the ways we reconcile our various forms of membership into one identity.
- Identity as *a relation between the local and the global*. We define who we are by negotiating local ways of belonging to broader constellations and of manifesting broader styles and discourses.

These parallels constitute a level of analysis that presents identity and practice as mirror images of each other. This strategy is, however, a

149

practice as ...	identity as ...
• negotiation of meaning (in terms of participation and reification)	• negotiated experience of self (in terms of participation and reification)
• community	• membership
• shared history of learning	• learning trajectory
• boundary and landscape	• nexus of multimembership
• constellations	• belonging defined globally but experienced locally

Figure 6.1. Parallels between practice and identity.

first approximation, which I will refine and expand in the following chapters.

Negotiated experience: participation and reification

In Vignette I, Ariel refers to herself as a "level 6." Alinsu has reified levels of claims processing – 4 through 8 – defined in terms of certain performance milestones. Correspondingly, there are official markers of transition. "Getting your level," as the transition from one level to another is called, is celebrated with a small ritual of both official decorum – delivery of a letter with encouraging remarks by an assistant director in front of the employee's unit – and sincere rejoicing – clapping and shouting. For claims processors, their level is a substantial aspect of their local identity. It represents the institution's view of their expertise and comes with certain responsibilities and privileges. But this institutional reification of competence hardly reflects the richness of the actual process of belonging to the community and contributing to its practice. The daily engagement of claims processors in their community of practice creates relations among them that constitute "who one is" in the office, who knows what, who is good at what, who is cool, who is funny, who is friendly, who is central, who is peripheral.

Engagement in practice gives us certain experiences of participation, and what our communities pay attention to reifies us as participants. Becoming a claims processor, for instance, is both taking on the label "claims processor" and giving this label specific meanings through engagement in practice. It is doing what claims processors do, being treated the way they are treated, forming the community they form, entertaining certain relations with other practices, and – in the details of this process – giving a personal meaning to the category of claims processor. If, as mentioned in Vignette I, Ariel is treated rudely by a customer, her engagement in practice suddenly brings into focus the humble status of her position in a striking way. She is working the front line and can be yelled at without compunction. Events like these can jolt our experience of participation and bring our identity into focus. Our very participation becomes reified, so to speak, and the labels we use take on deeper meanings.

The experience of identity in practice is a way of being in the world. It is not equivalent to a self-image; it is not, in its essence, discursive or reflective. We often think about our identities as self-images because we talk about ourselves and each other – and even think about ourselves and each other – in words. These words are important, no doubt, but they are not the full, lived experience of engagement in practice. I am not trying to belittle the importance of categories, self-images, and narratives of the self as constitutive of identity, but neither do I want to equate identity with those reifications. Who we are lies in the way we live day to day, not just in what we think or say about ourselves, though that is of course part (but only part) of the way we live. Nor does identity consist solely of what others think or say about us, though that too is part of the way we live. Identity in practice is defined socially not merely because it is reified in a social discourse of the self and of social categories, but also because it is produced as a lived experience of participation in specific communities. What narratives, categories, roles, and positions come to mean as an experience of participation is something that must be worked out in practice.

An identity, then, is a layering of events of participation and reification by which our experience and its social interpretation inform each other. As we encounter our effects on the world and develop our relations with others, these layers build upon each other to produce our identity as a very complex interweaving of participative experience and reificative projections. Bringing the two together through the negotiation of meaning, we construct who we are. In the same way that meaning exists in its negotiation, identity exists – not as an object in and of itself – but in the constant work of negotiating the self. It is in this cascading interplay of participation and reification that our experience of life becomes one of identity, and indeed of human existence and consciousness.

Community membership

I have argued that practice defines a community through three dimensions: mutual engagement, a joint enterprise, and a shared repertoire. Because a community of practice is not necessarily reified as such, our membership may not carry a label or other reified marker. But I have argued that our identity is formed through participation as well as reification. In this context, our membership constitutes our identity, not just through reified markers of membership but more fundamentally through the forms of competence that it entails. Identity in this sense is an experience and a display of competence that requires neither an explicit self-image nor self-identification with an ostensible community.

When we are with a community of practice of which we are a full member, we are in familiar territory. We can handle ourselves competently. We experience competence and we are recognized as competent. We know how to engage with others. We understand why they do what they do because we understand the enterprise to which participants are accountable. Moreover, we share the resources they use to communicate and go about their activities. These dimensions of competence, introduced in Chapter 2, become dimensions of identity.

* *Mutuality of engagement.* In a community of practice, we learn certain ways of engaging in action with other people. We develop certain expectations about how to interact, how people treat each other, and how to work together. We become who we are by being able to play a part in the relations of engagement that constitute our community. Our competence gains its value through its very partiality. As an identity, this translates into a form of individuality defined with respect to a community. It is a certain way of being part of a whole through mutual engagement. For instance, I have reported that among claims processors it is more important to give and receive help than to know everything oneself.[1] This results in a definition of individuality that differs from, say, forms of individuality in certain academic circles, where knowledge is a form of personal power and not knowing is largely construed as a personal deficit.[2]

* *Accountability to an enterprise.* As we invest ourselves in an enterprise, the forms of accountability through which we are able to contribute to that enterprise make us look at the world in certain ways. Being a claims processor, doctor, parent, social worker, salesperson, beggar, folk dancer, or photographer gives us a certain focus. It

moves us to understand certain conditions and to consider certain possibilities. As an identity, this translates into a perspective. It does not mean that all members of a community look at the world in the same way. Nonetheless, an identity in this sense manifests as a tendency to come up with certain interpretations, to engage in certain actions, to make certain choices, to value certain experiences – all by virtue of participating in certain enterprises.

• *Negotiability of a repertoire.* Sustained engagement in practice yields an ability to interpret and make use of the repertoire of that practice. We recognize the history of a practice in the artifacts, actions, and language of the community. We can make use of that history because we have been part of it and it is now part of us; we do this through a personal history of participation. As an identity, this translates into a personal set of events, references, memories, and experiences that create individual relations of negotiability with respect to the repertoire of a practice.

This translation of dimensions of competence into dimensions of identity has its inverse. When we come in contact with new practices, we venture into unfamiliar territory. The boundaries of our communities manifest as a lack of competence along the three dimensions I just described. We do not quite know how to engage with others. We do not understand the subtleties of the enterprise as the community has defined it. We lack the shared references that participants use. Our non-membership shapes our identities through our confrontation with the unfamiliar.

In sum, membership in a community of practice translates into an identity as a form of competence. An identity in this sense is relating to the world as a particular mix of the familiar and the foreign, the obvious and the mysterious, the transparent and the opaque. We experience and manifest our selves by what we recognize and what we don't, what we grasp immediately and what we can't interpret, what we can appropriate and what alienates us, what we can press into service and what we can't use, what we can negotiate and what remains out of reach. In practice, we know who we are by what is familiar, understandable, usable, negotiable; we know who we are not by what is foreign, opaque, unwieldy, unproductive.

Trajectories

I have argued that identity in practice arises out of an interplay of participation and reification. As such, it is not an object, but a constant becoming. The work of identity is always going on. Identity is not some primordial core of personality that already exists. Nor is it something we acquire at some point in the same way that, at a certain age, we grow a set of permanent teeth. Even though issues of identity as a focus of overt concern may become more salient at certain times than at others, our identity is something we constantly renegotiate during the course of our lives.

As we go through a succession of forms of participation, our identities form trajectories, both within and across communities of practice. In this section, I will use the concept of trajectory to argue that:

1) identity is fundamentally temporal
2) the work of identity is ongoing
3) because it is constructed in social contexts, the temporality of identity is more complex than a linear notion of time
4) identities are defined with respect to the interaction of multiple convergent and divergent trajectories.

In using the term "trajectory" I do not want to imply a fixed course or a fixed destination. To me, the term trajectory suggests not a path that can be foreseen or charted but a continuous motion – one that has a momentum of its own in addition to a field of influences. It has a coherence through time that connects the past, the present, and the future.[3]

In the context of communities of practice, there can be various types of trajectories.

- *Peripheral trajectories.* By choice or by necessity, some trajectories never lead to full participation. Yet they may well provide a kind of access to a community and its practice that becomes significant enough to contribute to one's identity.
- *Inbound trajectories.* Newcomers are joining the community with the prospect of becoming full participants in its practice. Their identities are invested in their future participation, even though their present participation may be peripheral.
- *Insider trajectories.* The formation of an identity does not end with full membership. The evolution of the practice continues – new events, new demands, new inventions, and new generations all create occasions for renegotiating one's identity.
- *Boundary trajectories.* Some trajectories find their value in spanning boundaries and linking communities of practice. Sustaining an identity across boundaries is one of the most delicate challenges of this kind of brokering work (see Chapter 4 and the next section in this chapter).

- *Outbound trajectories.* Some trajectories lead out of a community, as when children grow up. What matters then is how a form of participation enables what comes next. It seems perhaps more natural to think of identity formation in terms of all the learning involved in entering a community of practice. Yet being on the way out of such a community also involves developing new relationships, finding a different position with respect to a community, and seeing the world and oneself in new ways.

Learning as identity

The temporal dimension of identity is critical. Not only do we keep negotiating our identities, but they place our engagement in practice in this temporal context. We are always simultaneously dealing with specific situations, participating in the histories of certain practices, and involved in becoming certain persons. As trajectories, our identities incorporate the past and the future in the very process of negotiating the present.[4] They give significance to events in relation to time construed as an extension of the self. They provide a context in which to determine what, among all the things that are potentially significant, actually becomes significant learning. A sense of trajectory gives us ways of sorting out what matters and what does not, what contributes to our identity and what remains marginal.

For claims processors, being on a trajectory is an important aspect of their job. They know that improvement in their performance will mean advancement, and they value the fact that advancement is automatic because it gives them some degree of control over their trajectory. Moreover, their sense of trajectory extends beyond claims processing. Some of them view the job as their profession, hoping to move on to technical or managerial positions in due time; some are just paying their way through college and have no interest in a professional career in claims processing. These different trajectories give them very different perspectives on their participation and identities at work. So for them, processing a claim is not just a self-contained activity. Understanding something new is not just a local act of learning. Rather, each is an event on a trajectory through which they give meaning to their engagement in practice in terms of the identity they are developing.

Learning events and forms of participation are thus defined by the current engagement they afford, as well as by their location on a trajectory. A very peripheral form of participation, for instance, may turn out to be central to one's identity because it leads to something significant.

Paradigmatic trajectories

The progression of a career offered by the company is not the only way claims processors define their identity as a trajectory, even within the confines of their job. Their community, its history, and its evolution shape the trajectories they construct. More experienced peers are not merely a source of information about processing claims; they also represent the history of the practice as a way of life. They are living testimonies to what is possible, expected, desirable.

More generally, any community of practice provides a set of models for negotiating trajectories. These "paradigmatic" trajectories are not simply reified milestones, such as those provided by a career ladder or even by communal rituals. Rather, they embody the history of the community through the very participation and identities of practitioners. They include actual people as well as composite stories. Exposure to this field of paradigmatic trajectories is likely to be the most influential factor shaping the learning of newcomers. In the end, it is members – by their very participation – who create the set of possibilities to which newcomers are exposed as they negotiate their own trajectories. No matter what is said, taught, prescribed, recommended, or tested, newcomers are no fools: once they have actual access to the practice, they soon find out what counts.[5]

From this perspective, a community of practice is a field of possible trajectories and thus the proposal of an identity. It is a history and the promise of that history. It is a field of possible pasts and of possible futures, which are all there for participants, not only to witness, hear about, and contemplate, but to engage with. They can interact with old-timers, who offer living examples of possible trajectories. A community of practice is a history collapsed into a present that invites engagement. Newcomers can engage with their own future, as embodied by old-timers. As a community of practice, these old-timers deliver the past and offer the future, in the form of narratives and participation both. Each has a story to tell. In addition, the practice itself gives life to these stories, and the possibility of mutual engagement offers a way to enter these stories through one's own experience.

Of course, new trajectories do not necessarily align themselves with paradigmatic ones. Newcomers must find their own unique identities. And the relation goes both ways; newcomers also provide new models for different ways of participating. Whether adopted, modified, or rejected in specific instances, paradigmatic trajectories provide live material for negotiating and renegotiating identities.

Generational encounters

As a process of negotiating trajectories, the encounter between generations is much more complex than the mere transmission of a heritage. It is an interlocking of identities, with all the conflicts and mutual dependencies this entails; by this interlocking, individual trajectories incorporate in different ways the history of a practice. Different generations bring different perspectives to their encounter because their identities are invested in different moments of that history. With less past, there is less history to take into consideration. With less future, there is less urgency to reconsider history. Yet, the perspectives of old-timers and newcomers are not so simply delineated.

If learning in practice is negotiating an identity, and if that identity incorporates the past and the future, then it is in each other that old-timers and newcomers find their experience of history. Their perspectives on the generational encounter is not simply one of past versus future, of continuity versus discontinuity, or of old versus new.

- While newcomers are forging their own identities, they do not necessarily want to emphasize discontinuity more than continuity. They must find a place in relation to the past. In order to participate, they must gain some access – vicarious as it may be – to the history they want to contribute to; they must make it part of their own identities. As a result, newcomers are not necessarily more progressive than old-timers; they do not necessarily seek to change the practice more than established members do. They have an investment in continuity because it connects them to a history of which they are not a part. Their very fragility and their efforts to include some of that history in their own identity may push them toward seeking continuity.
- Conversely, old-timers have an investment in their practice, yet they do not necessarily seek continuity. Embroiled in the politics of their community and with the confidence derived from participation in a history they know too well, they may want to invest themselves in the future not so much to continue it as to give it new wings. They might thus welcome the new potentials afforded by new generations who are less hostage to the past.

Depending on how a community negotiates individuality, the generational encounter can have different effects – with different degrees of emphasis on continuity and discontinuity as old-timers and newcomers fashion their identities in their encounter. This encounter is always a complex meeting of the past and the future, one in which generations attempt to define their identities by investing them in different moments of the history of a practice. The new will both continue and displace the old.[6] In each other, generations find the partiality as well as the connectedness of their personal trajectories, that is, new dimensions of finitude and extension of their identities.

The temporality of identity in practice is thus a subtle form of temporality. It is neither merely individual nor simply linear. The past, the present, and the future are not in a simple straight line, but embodied in interlocked trajectories. It is a social form of temporality, where the past and the future interact as the history of a community unfolds across generations.

In summary, the temporal notion of trajectory characterizes identity as:

1) a work in progress
2) shaped by efforts – both individual and collective – to create a coherence through time that threads together successive forms of participation in the definition of a person
3) incorporating the past and the future in the experience of the present
4) negotiated with respect to paradigmatic trajectories
5) invested in histories of practice and in generational politics.

Nexus of multimembership

As I mentioned, we all belong to many communities of practice: some past, some current; some as full members, some in more peripheral ways. Some may be central to our identities while others are more incidental. Whatever their nature, all these various forms of participation contribute in some way to the production of our identities. As a consequence, the very notion of identity entails

1) an experience of multimembership
2) the work of reconciliation necessary to maintain one identity across boundaries.

Identity as multimembership

Our membership in any community of practice is only a part of our identity. Claims processors do not form their identities entirely at work. They came to their jobs as adults or youths, having belonged to many communities of practice. Some have other jobs concurrently;

some are students in community colleges; some are parents; some are church-goers; some are bar-goers; some have engrossing hobbies. In fact, for many of them, their work is a part of their identity that they tend to disparage.

Because our identities are not something we turn on and off, our various forms of participation are not merely sequences in time. Claims processors who are parents come to the office without their children, and they will return home at the end of the afternoon to be with them. Though there are sequential phases in their engagement in different locations, they certainly do not cease to be parents because they are at work. They talk about their kids; and, more generally, the tidbits of conversation they interweave with their exchanges of work-related information continually reflect their participation in other practices.

Our various forms of participation delineate pieces of a puzzle we put together rather than sharp boundaries between disconnected parts of ourselves.[7] An identity is thus more than just a single trajectory; instead, it should be viewed as a nexus of multimembership. As such a nexus, identity is not a unity but neither is it simply fragmented.

- On the one hand, we engage in different practices in each of the communities of practice to which we belong. We often behave rather differently in each of them, construct different aspects of ourselves, and gain different perspectives.
- On the other hand, considering a person as having multiple identities would miss all the subtle ways in which our various forms of participation, no matter how distinct, can interact, influence each other, and require coordination.

This notion of nexus adds multiplicity to the notion of trajectory. A nexus does not merge the specific trajectories we form in our various communities of practice into one; but neither does it decompose our identity into distinct trajectories in each community. In a nexus, multiple trajectories become part of each other, whether they clash or reinforce each other. They are, at the same time, one and multiple.

Identity as reconciliation

If a nexus of multimembership is more than just a fragmented identity, being one person requires some work to reconcile our different forms of membership. Different practices can make competing demands that are difficult to combine into an experience that corresponds to a single identity. In particular:

1) different ways of engaging in practice may reflect different forms of individuality
2) different forms of accountability may call for different responses to the same circumstances
3) elements of one repertoire may be quite inappropriate, incomprehensible, or even offensive in another community.

Reconciling these aspects of competence demands more than just learning the rules of what to do when. It requires the construction of an identity that can include these different meanings and forms of participation into one nexus. Understood as the negotiation of an identity, the process of reconciling different forms of membership is deeper than just discrete choices or beliefs. For a doctor working in a hospital, making decisions that do justice to both her professional standards and institutional bottom-line demands is not simply a matter of making discrete decisions; she must find an identity that can reconcile the demands of these forms of accountability into a way of being in the world.

The work of reconciliation may be the most significant challenge faced by learners who move from one community of practice to another. For instance, when a child moves from a family to a classroom, when an immigrant moves from one culture to another, or when an employee moves from the ranks to a management position, learning involves more than appropriating new pieces of information. Learners must often deal with conflicting forms of individuality and competence as defined in different communities.

The nexus resulting from reconciliation work is not necessarily harmonious, and the process is not done once and for all. Multimembership may involve ongoing tensions that are never resolved. But the very presence of tension implies that there is an effort at maintaining some kind of coexistence. By using the term "reconciliation" to describe this process of identity formation, I want to suggest that proceeding with life – with actions and interactions – entails finding ways to make our various forms of membership coexist, whether the process of reconciliation leads to successful resolutions or is a constant struggle. In other words, by including processes of reconciliation in the very definition of identity, I am suggesting that the maintenance of an identity across boundaries requires work and, moreover, that the work of integrating our various forms of participation is not just a secondary process. This work is not simply an additional concern for an independently defined identity viewed as a unitary object; rather, it is at the core of what it means to be a person. Multimembership and the work of reconciliation are intrinsic to the very concept of identity.

Social bridges and private selves

Multimembership is the living experience of boundaries. This creates a dual relation between identities and the landscape of practice: they reflect each other and they shape each other. In weaving multiple trajectories together, our experience of multimembership replays in our identities the texture of the landscape of practice. But this replay is not a passive reflection. On the contrary, as the boundaries of practice become part of our personal experience of identity, the work of reconciliation is an active, creative process. As we engage our whole person in practice, our identities dynamically encompass multiple perspectives in the negotiation of new meanings. In these new meanings we negotiate our own activities and identities, and at the same time the histories of relations among our communities of practice. The creative negotiation of an identity always has the potential to rearrange these relations. In this regard, multimembership is not just a matter of personal identity. The work of reconciliation is a profoundly social kind of work. Through the creation of the person, it is constantly creating bridges – or at least potential bridges – across the landscape of practice.

And yet, the work of reconciliation can easily remain invisible because it may not be perceived as part of the enterprise of any community of practice. Across boundaries, the parallelism between histories of practice and personal trajectories no longer holds. The experience of multimembership can require the reconciliation of a nexus that is unique and thus very personal. Indeed, this nexus may not, in its entirety, be relevant to any practice or even to any relationship we have with anyone. Even though each element of the nexus may belong to a community, the nexus itself may not. The careful weaving of this nexus of multimembership into an identity can therefore be a very private achievement. By incorporating into the definition of the person the diversity of the social world, the social notion of a nexus of multimembership thus introduces into the concept of identity a deeply personal dimension of individuality.

Local–global interplay

An important aspect of the work of any community of practice is to create a picture of the broader context in which its practice is located. In this process, much local energy is directed at global issues and relationships. For Ariel, belonging to the profession of claims processing or to an organization like Alinsu constitute relations whose meanings she negotiates through her participation in her community of practice. For instance, when one of her colleagues was fired for speaking against the company at a radio show, claims processors used each other as resources for making sense of this event. Their local community of practice became a productive context in which to discuss whether it was right for the claims processor to criticize her employer publicly or for the company to respond by firing her. Similarly, sports events and TV shows are the topics of frequent and animated conversations in the office. Although these conversations reflect outside interests and allegiances, they become part of the processors' participation in their local community. If the baseball fans or the television watchers worked among people for whom allegiance to a baseball team was a trivial concern and watching television a waste of time, their interests may well take on very different meanings for them.

More generally, what it means to be left-handed or right-handed, a woman or a man, good-looking or plain, a younger person or an older person, a high-school dropout or the holder of a doctorate, the owner of a BMW or of a beat-up subcompact, literate or illiterate, outcast or successful – these meanings are shaped by the practices where such categories are lived as engaged identities. Broader categories and institutions attract our attention because they are often more publicly reified than the communities of practice in which we experience them as part of a lived identity. Affiliation with a political party is more public than membership in a group that discusses politics over lunch, but the lunch discussions may have more impact on our thinking than the party's platform.

In the same way that a practice is not just local but connected to broader constellations, an identity – even in its aspects that are formed in a specific community of practice – is not just local to that community. In our communities of practice we come together not only to engage in pursuing some enterprise but also to figure out how our engagement fits in the broader scheme of things. Identity in practice is therefore always an interplay between the local and the global.

In summary, drawing a parallel between practice and identity has yielded a perspective on identity that inherits the texture of practice. Indeed, our identities are rich and complex because they are produced within the rich and complex set of relations of practice. The parallel has characterized identity in practice as follows.

1) *Lived.* Identity is not merely a category, a personality trait, a role, or a label; it is more fundamentally an experience that involves both participation and reification. Hence it is more diverse and more complex than categories, traits, roles, or labels would suggest.

2) *Negotiated.* Identity is a becoming; the work of identity is ongoing and pervasive. It is not confined to specific periods of life, like adolescence, or to specific settings, like the family.

3) *Social.* Community membership gives the formation of identity a fundamentally social character. Our membership manifests itself in the familiarity we experience with certain social contexts.

4) *A learning process.* An identity is a trajectory in time that incorporates both past and future into the meaning of the present.

5) *A nexus.* An identity combines multiple forms of membership through a process of reconciliation across boundaries of practice.

6) *A local–global interplay.* An identity is neither narrowly local to activities nor abstractly global. Like practice, it is an interplay of both.

Now that the link between individual engagement and the formation of communities of practice has produced a basic perspective on the concept of identity, I can start to explore further aspects of the concept that will shed further light on the link between practice and identity, as well as move beyond the confines of practice.

Chapter 7

Participation and non-participation

I have argued that we know who we *are* by what is familiar and by what we can negotiate and make use of, and that we know who we are *not* by what is unfamiliar, unwieldy, and out of our purview. This is an important point. We not only produce our identities through the practices we engage in, but we also define ourselves through practices we do not engage in. Our identities are constituted not only by what we are but also by what we are not. To the extent that we can come in contact with other ways of being, what we are not can even become a large part of how we define ourselves. For instance, we define ourselves in a small but not insignificant way by our regular contacts with various professionals from whom we receive services. Though we remain mostly non-participants, our service encounters often let us know just enough about their practices to gain some sense of what it is we are not, what we wish we were, what we would not dream of being, or what we are glad not to be. In other words, non-participation is, in a reverse kind of fashion, as much a source of identity as participation.

Our relations to communities of practice thus involve both participation and non-participation, and our identities are shaped by combinations of the two. In this chapter, I will explore the notion of identity of non-participation by:

1) defining a range of interactions between participation and non-participation, and in particular distinguishing between peripherality and marginality
2) distinguishing between various sources of participation and non-participation
3) using the example of claims processing to describe some institutional forms of non-participation and their effects on practice.

164

Identities of non-participation

Experiences of non-participation do not necessarily build up to an identity of non-participation. Because our own practices usually include elements from other practices, and because we inevitably come in contact with communities of practice to which we do not belong, non-participation is an inevitable part of living in a landscape of practices. In a world complexly structured by interlocked communities of practice, we are constantly passing boundaries – catching, as we peek into foreign chambers, glimpses of other realities and meanings; touching, as we pass by outlandish arrangements, objects of distant values; learning, as we coordinate our actions across boundaries, to live with decisions we have not made. Not all that we encounter becomes significant and not all that we meet carries our touch; yet these events can all contribute in their own ways to our experience of identity.

It would be absurd to think that we can or should identify with everyone and everything we meet. In a landscape defined by boundaries and peripheries, a coherent identity is of necessity a mixture of being in and being out. When participation and non-participation refer only to relations of insider and outsider, they simply reflect our membership in specific communities of practice and not in others. Realizing that you are not a claims processor may contribute in a small way to your sense of self but, unless you are trying to become one, that realization remains inconsequential. In such cases, participation and non-participation do not define each other and merely have distinct effects on our identities.

Experiences of non-participation are an inevitable part of life, but they take on a different kind of importance when participation and non-participation interact to define each other. For instance, for a novice not to understand a conversation between old-timers becomes significant because this experience of non-participation is aligned with a trajectory of participation. It is the interaction of participation and non-participation that renders the experience consequential.

More generally, it is useful to distinguish two cases of the interaction of participation and non-participation.

- In the case of *peripherality*, some degree of non-participation is necessary to enable a kind of participation that is less than full. Here, it is the participation aspect that dominates and defines non-participation as an enabling factor of participation.

- In the case of *marginality,* a form of non-participation prevents full participation. Here, it is the non-participation aspect that dominates and comes to define a restricted form of participation.

Peripherality and marginality both involve a mix of participation and non-participation, and the line between them can be subtle. Yet, they produce qualitatively different experiences and identities, so it would be wrong to associate them too closely. Consider, for example, the case of the COB worksheet of Vignette II.

- When the worksheet was initially introduced in the training class, it was not perceived as problematic. At this stage, the trainees were happy just to be told what to do and to adopt the activities, forms, and worksheets as presented. Non-participation was an initial relation that allowed them to become involved in their new job quickly, to do something relevant without waiting to know why. What was crucial was to find an entry point into the job.
- Only when they later became engaged in real work did the procedural character of their understanding of the worksheet become problematic. Though they could do the calculation, they did not feel that they had enough grasp of the procedure to do their job with confidence. As claims processors, they had gained enough participation to feel accountable for the results of their calculation and for their conversations with customers. With respect to their new form of participation, not having access to the technical meanings of the procedure became a relation of marginality.

The difference between peripherality and marginality must be understood in the context of trajectories that determine the significance of forms of participation.

- Newcomers, for instance, may be on an inbound trajectory that is construed by everyone to include full participation in its future. Non-participation is then an opportunity for learning. Even for people whose trajectory remains peripheral, non-participation is an enabling aspect of their participation because full participation is not a goal to start with.
- Conversely, long-standing members can be kept in a marginal position, and the very maintenance of that position may have become so integrated in the practice that it closes the future. We often find it hard to be grown-up participants within our own families of birth. Women who seek equal opportunity often find that the practices of

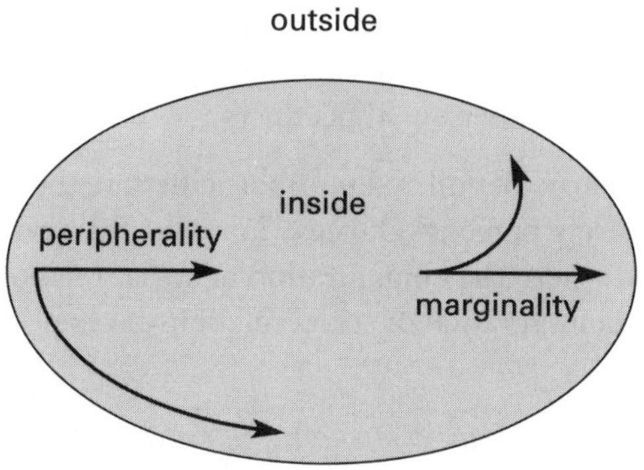

outside

Figure 7.1. Relations of participation and non-participation.

certain communities never cease to push them back into identities of non-participation. In such cases, forms of non-participation may be so ingrained in the practice that it may seem impossible to conceive of a different trajectory within the same community.

Hence, whether non-participation becomes peripherality or marginality depends on relations of participation that render non-participation either enabling or problematic. Of course, there are degrees of each. From this discussion emerges the notion of a range of forms of participation with four main categories, as illustrated in Figure 7.1: full participation (insider); full non-participation (outsider); peripherality (participation enabled by non-participation, whether it leads to full participation or remains on a peripheral trajectory); and marginality (participation restricted by non-participation, whether it leads to non-membership or to a marginal position).

Sources of participation and non-participation

The mix of participation and non-participation through which we define our identities reflects our power as individuals and communities to define and affect our relations to the rest of the world. It shapes such fundamental aspects of our lives as:

1) how we locate ourselves in a social landscape
2) what we care about and what we neglect
3) what we attempt to know and understand and what we choose to ignore

4)   with whom we seek connections and whom we avoid
5)   how we engage and direct our energies
6)   how we attempt to steer our trajectories.

As combinations of participation and non-participation, these aspects of our lives are not merely personal choices. They involve processes of community formation where the configuration of social relations is the work of the self. This configuration of social relations takes place at different levels.

- *Trajectories with respect to specific communities of practice.* These are the relations of participation and non-participation I have talked about so far. For instance, the two older women who were members of the claims processing unit kept an amused distance from many of the social interactions of the younger majority, although they were full participants in the community of practice by all other accounts. For different reasons, the two "guys" were also in a marginal position in the unit.
- *Boundary relations and the demands of multimembership.* Across boundaries between communities of practice, multimembership can also give rise to coexisting identities of participation and non-participation. For instance, when communities define themselves by contrast to others – workers versus managers; collaborating versus rebellious students; or, more broadly, one ethnic, religious, or political group versus another – being inside implies, and is largely defined in terms of, being outside. Non-participation then is a defining constituent of participation. This situation makes boundary crossing difficult, because each side is defined by opposition to the other and membership in one community implies marginalization in another. I argued that this kind of tension between mutually defining forms of participation and non-participation characterizes the position of the claims processing unit supervisor, caught between her former peers in the unit and her new peers among management. She ends up being marginal in both groups. For another example, children of immigrants can experience this coexistence of participation and non-participation intensely when they are torn between the conflicting values of their family practices and their new communities at school and on the street.
- *Our position and the position of our communities within broader constellations of practices and broader institutions.* Whereas certain members can be in marginal or peripheral positions with respect to a community

of practice, the community of practice itself can be in a peripheral or marginal position with respect to broader constellations and institutional arrangements. For instance, the marginality of claims processors is mostly a function of the position that their community occupies in the corporation and the insurance industry, a position that determines their ability to affect this context.

Institutional non-participation

It is often the case that, rather than being direct boundary relations between communities and people or among communities, relations of non-participation are mediated by institutional arrangements. This is true for claims processors. The low status of the job in the company, the meager salary, the lack of encouragement of initiative, the perception of repetitiousness, the pervasive use of standardized reifications to connect to the world, and the organization of the work in terms of narrow procedures all contribute to an experience of non-participation. But these relations of non-participation are not direct relations with the communities of practice implicated. Rather, they are mediated by institutional arrangements.

I will end this chapter by using the example of claims processors to illustrate how non-participation in an institutional context can become a defining characteristic of practice. Although this example represents a fairly common situation, not all institutional arrangements lead to marginalization.

Non-participation as institutional relation

Non-participation pervades the design of the institutional context in which processors work. It is anchored in the things they do every day, in why and how they do them. In the case of claims processors, institutional relations of non-participation can be interpreted from a number of perspectives.

- *Non-participation as compromise.* The atmosphere of non-participation is sustained by a reciprocal understanding on the part of management and claims processors. Overall, there is a striking complementarity between the attitudes of employees and management with regard to their respective involvement in each other's purpose. For instance, the office manager asked me to make sure I did not intrude in the employees' breaks: "It's *their* time," she declared. And indeed,

whereas my occasional tape recordings had encountered no opposition in the office, the group I usually went to breaks with refused to
have the recorder on during breaks because these recordings were
something they associated with work. "No way! We don't talk about
work during break." My own observation is that they do talk about
work quite a bit during their breaks – they just do not want to think
of their breaks in those terms. Admitting that they talk about work
on their own time would be admitting that they have identified themselves with work, that the separation they strive to maintain is threat-
ened. A balance seems to have been achieved: you give me your time
and I'll give you money; you don't invest yourself in me and I don't
invest myself in you. It is in the context of this mutual compromise
of non-participation that claims processors form their own community of practice and negotiate their identities as workers.

- *Non-participation as strategy.* As a pervasive subtext of the claims
  processors' relationship with the institution, non-participation is perceived with a fair amount of ambivalence; it is something they both
  resent and embrace. From their perspective, non-participation is construed as a source of disengagement and boredom, on the one hand,
  and on the other as a source of freedom and privacy – a cherished
  sphere of selfhood. They can feel profoundly bored and depressed,
  but the fact that they can leave their job behind as soon as they walk
  out of the office is an aspect of their relation to their work that they
  value. "I'm off. That's it!" They see their identity mainly outside
  their job. "I don't want it to be, like, my life is my job." What they describe as the worst possible situation is when the stress of work becomes such – as it sometimes does – that it spills over into their private time and they start thinking about claims processing while away
  from the office.

- *Non-participation as cover.* In a service industry dealing with pain-
  ful situations such as diseases, financial difficulties, and death, non-
  participation can also be a shield from broader conflicts. "It's kind of
  screwy, but you should not think of the person. You have to think of
  the company." When claims processors have to answer the phone
  and talk with displeased customers, they cannot take it too personally. As I mentioned in Vignette I, callers who have not received
  money they counted on can be rather unpleasant and, not infre-
  quently, even abusive, venting on claims processors their frustration
  with a bureaucratic system they do not trust. Non-participation pro-

vides protection for one's sensitivity from the broader moral issues and societal conflicts of interest one feels powerless to address – the "I just work here" syndrome.

These relations of non-participation underlie the artifacts that claims processors use: the forms, the rules, the production reports. Non-participation likewise pervades the relations they develop with customers and representatives of the corporation. When relations of non-participation are mediated by systematic institutional arrangements, they can reach deep into the definition of a practice.

Non-participation as practice

A significant amount of the processors' communal energy goes into making their time at work a livable realization of their marginality within the corporation and the insurance industry. Non-participation becomes an active aspect of their practice. The subtle cultivation of non-participation is not something claims processors talk much about, but it's in the air – a tacitly shared understanding. It manifests in the instantaneous legitimacy obtained by remarks about looking forward to the weekend or wishing it were four o'clock; in the mutually supportive way they inject into their working interactions spontaneous conversations about their private lives, hobbies, favorite TV shows, or personal relationships; and in the way they walk out and say good-bye at the end of the day, hurry toward the parking lot, and scatter toward their cars – becoming at once silent and animated as they go their separate ways. While they cultivate a rather friendly atmosphere at work, few of them sustain tight bonds of friendship with colleagues outside the office. In absorbing their experience of non-participation, their practice even creates a momentum that reproduces this relation.

Participation and non-participation are both constituents of their identities in interrelated ways. Whereas claims processors for the most part maintain a distance – and are maintained at a distance – from the institutional aspects of their job, they mostly identify with their shared practice and membership in their community. They identify with the enterprise of making their work possible and, if not always personally satisfying, at the very least habitable for the kinds of identities they construct. Their engagement in this shared practice engenders a commitment to each other and to their common conditions that amounts to a substantial expeperience of participation. In other words, the identities of non-participation that they develop with respect to the institution and to the content of their work are an integral part of their identities of participation in their own communities of practice. In dealing with their marginality, they place this complex mixture of participation and non-participation at the core of their practice and their identities as workers.

Chapter 8

Modes of belonging

In Chapter 6, I talked about identity in terms of belonging to communities of practice. But to make sense of the formation of identity in a context such as the institutional non-participation described in Chapter 7, it is necessary to consider modes of belonging other than engagement in practice. The claims processors' experience of both participation and non-participation is deeply part of their daily practice, but it also reaches beyond the walls of their office. In order to do their job, they must align their activities and their interpretations of events with structures, forces, and purposes beyond their community of practice and so find their place in broader business processes. Their identities as workers are affected by the picture they build of their position. They see themselves as participants in social processes and configurations that extend beyond their direct engagement in their own practice. They have to make some sense of many artifacts they encounter coming from practices they do not have access to. They may have to use their imagination to get a picture of these broader connections. They have an image of Alinsu, for instance, even though they have not had direct involvement with most of the practices that constitute the corporation. Yet this image is no less significant and, in a sense, no less real than their daily involvement at work.

To make sense of these processes of identity formation and learning, it is useful to consider three distinct modes of belonging (see Figure 8.1):

1) *engagement* – active involvement in mutual processes of negotiation of meaning
2) *imagination* – creating images of the world and seeing connections through time and space by extrapolating from our own experience

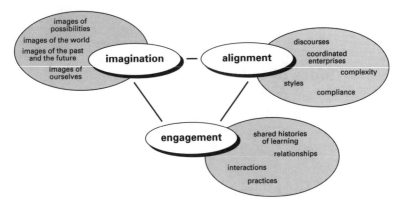

Figure 8.1. Modes of belonging.

3) *alignment* – coordinating our energy and activities in order to fit within broader structures and contribute to broader enterprises.

In this chapter, I will discuss the distinct mechanisms of belonging covered by these terms and lay out the kinds of trade-offs they involve. I will then speak of the different kinds of communities that are defined through these different modes of belonging. In conclusion, I will articulate the kind of community-building work associated with each mode of belonging.

Engagement

I have described engagement as a threefold process, which includes the conjunction of:

1) the ongoing negotiation of meaning
2) the formation of trajectories
3) the unfolding of histories of practice.

It is in the conjunction of all three processes – as they take place through each other – that engagement becomes a mode of belonging and a source of identity. Although the concept of engagement need not be defined in terms of specifiable communities of practice, the two concepts are closely linked since mutual engagement will give rise to communities of practice over time.

I have already talked at length about engagement as a source of identity, and I need not add much here. However, in order to create a contrast with the other two modes of belonging, I should emphasize again the bounded character of engagement. First, there are obvious physical limits in time and space: we can be only in one place at a time and dispose of only a finite number of hours per day. In addition, there are physiological limits to the complexity that each of us can handle, to the scope of activities we can be directly involved in, and to the number of people and artifacts with which we can sustain substantial relationships of engagement. This bounded character is both the strength and the weakness of engagement as a mode of belonging.

Trade-offs of engagement

The boundedness of engagement may seem like a limitation, but it is a crucial resource enabling the delicate process of negotiating viable identities. Within the mutuality it affords, we contribute to defining the enterprises through which we define ourselves. In other words, we both adopt and contribute to shaping the relations of accountability by which we define our actions as competent. Indeed, engagement transforms communities, practices, persons, and artifacts through each other. In this regard, engagement is an interesting dimension of power: it affords the power to negotiate our enterprises and thus to shape the context in which we can construct and experience an identity of competence.

Engagement, however, can also be narrow. The understanding inherent in shared practice is not necessarily one that gives members broad access to the histories or relations with other practices that shape their own practice. Through engagement, competence can become so transparent, locally ingrained, and socially efficacious that it becomes insular: nothing else, no other viewpoint, can even register, let alone create a disturbance or a discontinuity that would spur the history of practice onward. In this way, a community of practice can become an obstacle to learning by entrapping us in its very power to sustain our identity.

Imagination

Claims processing is a common profession. At Alinsu's office, everyone knows very well that many others do similar work at other locations and in other companies – all over the country and indeed all over the world. They have some direct and indirect contacts with other claims processors. They regularly talk to their colleagues at other companies when they must coordinate the benefits paid by different insurers for the same services. A few local claims processors have worked for other companies or in other Alinsu offices, and they have stories to tell. By extrapolating from their own experience, claims processors can imagine what the working lives of these other people are probably like. They can assume that they are colleagues and that their jobs are similar, with similar problems and similar solutions. Because of Alinsu's recruiting strategy, however, most claims processors are on their first job and this is all the processing experience they have with which to imagine the working lives of their peers elsewhere or to see themselves as one of a very large number of people who process claims day after day.

Imagination is an important component of our experience of the world and our sense of place in it. It can make a big difference for our experience of identity and the potential for learning inherent in our activities. This brings to mind the story about the two stonecutters who are asked what they are doing. One responds: "I am cutting this stone in a perfectly square shape." The other responds: "I am building a cathedral." Both answers are correct and meaningful, but they reflect different relations to the world. The difference between these answers does not imply that one is a better stonecutter than the other, as far as holding the chisel is concerned. At the level of engagement, they may well be doing exactly the same thing. But it does suggest that their experiences of what they are doing and their sense of self in doing it are rather different. This difference is a function of imagination. As a result, they may be learning very different things from the same activity.

My use of the concept of imagination refers to a process of expanding our self by transcending our time and space and creating new images of the world and ourselves. Imagination in this sense is looking at an apple seed and seeing a tree. It is playing scales on a piano, and envisioning a concert hall. It is entering a temple and knowing that the ritual you are performing is performed and has been performed by millions throughout the world. It is seeing your grandfather take out his dentures and knowing that you had better brush you teeth. It is visiting your mother's home farm and watching her as a little girl learning to love nature, the way she taught you to. It is reading a biography and recognizing yourself in the struggles of a character.

The term imagination is sometimes used to connote personal fantasies, withdrawal from reality, or mistaken as opposed to factual conclusions. My use of the term, however, emphasizes the creative process of producing new "images" and of generating new relations through time and space that become constitutive of the self. Calling this process imagination is, therefore, not to suggest that it produces aspects of our identity that are less "real" or "significant" than those based on mutual engagement. It is rather to suggest that imagination involves a different kind of work of the self – one that concerns the production of images of the self and images of the world that transcend engagement.

Imagination does include fantasies. But this is precisely because it is a creative process that reaches beyond direct engagement, not because it is inherently misleading. I remember once standing with my children around a globe and pointing proudly: "This is where we live." They were duly impressed – not for a moment doubtful, yet a little puzzled – and I started to reflect on the kind of process by which it made sense to indicate a point on a globe and claim it is where we live. It involved a kind of fantasy. It was the work of imagination, not in the pejorative sense of a fantasy but in the sense of creating a picture that was not obviously there. It was very different from entering a *house* and saying "we live here." It was not imagination as opposed to fact, because the issue was not whether what I was saying was factual. At issue was constructing a picture of the world such that it did make sense to point to a globe and say that we live "there." We talked about the earth, the solar system, and gravity, and from that perspective I think that it did seem rather exciting to them to think that, indeed, we live "there" – little stick figures glued to a huge revolving planet.

Of course, imagination can involve stereotypes that overlook the finer texture of practice – for example, assuming that every Scot is a miser, that every Swiss is squeaky clean, or that every American is a materialist. Again, such overgeneralizations are possible not because imagination is inherently misleading but because it can project our experience beyond the sounding board of mutual engagement. Of course, imagination can be mistaken, but then so can engagement. Being mistaken or nonfactual is not a defining characteristic of imagination. Through engagement, participants do not necessarily understand the world, each other's experiences, or their shared enterprise more accurately. Mutual engagement merely creates a shared reality in which to act and construct an identity. Imagination is another process for creating such a reality.

Finally, imagination as I use the term is not just an individual process. The stories that claims processors exchange about work in other offices and the discussions they have about their career prospects all nurture their collective imagination. The way nations use history to define a sense of common roots is a social process through and through, one that calls upon imagination to see the present as the continuation of a shared heritage. The creative character of imagination is anchored in social interactions and communal experiences. Imagination in this sense is not just the production of personal fantasies. Far from an individual withdrawal from reality, it is a mode of belonging that always involves the social world to expand the scope of reality and identity.

Trade-offs of imagination

Through imagination, we can locate ourselves in the world and in history, and include in our identities other meanings, other possibilities, other perspectives. It is through imagination that we recognize our own experience as reflecting broader patterns, connections, and configurations. It is through imagination that we see our own practices as continuing histories that reach far into the past, and it is through imagination that we conceive of new developments, explore alternatives, and envision possible futures. By bringing the exotic to our doorstep and carrying us into foreign lands, imagination can make us consider our own position with new eyes. By taking us into the past and carrying us into the future, it can recast the present and show it as holding unsuspected possibilities.

Imagination, however, can also be disconnected and ineffective. It can be based on stereotypes that simply project onto the world the assumptions of specific practices. Conversely, it can be so removed from any lived form of membership that it detaches our identity and leaves us in a state of uprootedness. As a way of belonging, imagination is therefore a delicate act of identity because it plays with participation and non-participation, inside and outside, the actual and the possible, the doable and the unreachable, the meaningful and the meaningless. It thus runs the risk of losing touch with the sense of social efficacy by which our experience of the world can be interpreted as competence.

Alignment

Like imagination, alignment is a mode of belonging that is not confined to mutual engagement. The process of alignment bridges time and space to form broader enterprises so that participants become connected through the coordination of their energies, actions, and practices. Through alignment, we become part of something big because we do what it takes to play our part. What alignment brings into the picture is a scope of action writ large, of coordinated enterprises on a large scale, not inherent in engagement or in imagination.

- We may engage with others in a community of practice without managing or caring to align this practice with a broader enterprise, such as the demands of an institution in the context of which we live.
- We may be connected with others through imagination and yet not care or know what to do about it.

Indeed, imagination does not necessarily result in a coordination of action. One can imagine what it was like to be a knight, but one does not necessarily adopt the code of chivalry for oneself. Claims processors can easily imagine that a large number of people do similar work under similar conditions, but they do not translate this understanding into action. They are not unionized and express no interest in being so; their professional identity does not congeal into any kind of global or political activism beyond their local engagement in work. On the other hand, they do not feel close to their own managers – especially upper management, whose work they express difficulty in imagining:

For one thing, I don't really know [them]. Sure I say "hi" to them, but they don't really make themselves, you know, known to us. Like we just know their names, we don't know what kind of a person they are, we don't, we don't know anything, they just, they're just there. We don't really know what they do, we don't really know anything about them.

Even so, processors do align their practices with the directives they receive and work hard to maintain that alignment. They even clean their desks and dress up whenever a visit is announced. This alignment with the expectations of their employer is an expression of their belonging to the broader social system in which their industry operates.

Neither engagement in shared practice nor imagination entails alignment and, in turn, alignment does not entail mutual engagement or imagination.

- Following the law of the land, complying with reified institutional requirements, buying the right kind of shoes to follow the latest fashion, or contributing to the monthly sales target – none of these forms of alignment requires engagement with the practices that generate such standards or definitions of competence. If we send a check to support a cause then we are aligning our energies with that cause to some extent, but in the process we are not necessarily engaged in any community of practice.

• Even though alignment can be broad in scope, it does not entail imagination. When they fill out forms of the type described in Vignette II, claims processors are aligning their actions with the demands of the institution. However, they do not (for a complex set of reasons) apply a corresponding amount of imagination to build a picture of why specific steps in procedures are the right thing to do. Similarly, each of the two stonecutters can follow a foreman's instructions and cut the right kinds of stones into the correct shapes. Of course, imagination can change both our understanding of alignment and our ability to control it – because imagination helps build a picture of how our part fits – but this is different from viewing alignment and imagination as equivalent, or as implying or subsuming each other.

In connecting and thus magnifying the effects of our actions, alignment is an important aspect of belonging. For instance, governmental institutions, scientific methods, artistic genres, religious faiths, fashions, political and social movements, educational standards, and business enterprises all propose broad systems of styles and discourses through which we can belong by aligning, for certain purposes, our ability to direct our energy and affect the world.

Because alignment concerns directing and controlling energy, it likewise concerns power: the power over one's own energy to exercise alignment and the power to inspire or demand alignment. The concept of power often has evil connotations, especially when it is used to characterize social relations. In the sense of directing and aligning energy, however, power is neither inherently evil nor necessarily conflictual (though it can be both in specific cases).[1] It is a condition for the possibility of socially organized action.

Trade-offs of alignment

Alignment amplifies the ramifications of our actions by coordinating multiple localities, competencies, and viewpoints. It expands the scope of our effects on the world. We can contribute to producing actions and artifacts that no specialized practice can produce. We can manage levels of scale and complexity that give new dimensions to our belonging. Alignment can thus amplify our power and our sense of the possible.

Alignment, however, can also be blind and disempowering. It can be an unquestioning allegiance that makes us vulnerable to all kinds of delusion and abuse. It can be coerced via threat or violence, thereby separating as much as it coordinates. It can be a process of coordination based on a literal interpretation of instructions and so open no vista into the perspectives it connects. It can be a prescriptive process that removes from communities their ability to act on their own understanding and to negotiate their place in the larger scheme of things. It can be a confrontation of conflicting interests that leaves some all-powerful and others powerless. It can be a violation of our sense of self that crushes our identity.

Belonging and communities

Engagement, imagination, and alignment each create relations of belonging that expand identity through space and time in different ways.

1) I have argued that *engagement* has a bounded character.
2) Because *imagination* involves unconstrained assumptions of relatedness, it can create relations of identity anywhere, throughout history, and in unrestricted number. Of course, not all of these relations are significant.
3) *Alignment* can also span vast distances, both socially and physically. It will tend to be more focused than imagination since it entails an investment of personal energy, which cannot be split indefinitely.

With engagement, imagination, and alignment as distinct modes of belonging, communities of practice are not the only kind of community to consider when exploring the formation of identities. Indeed, calling the viewers of a television program a community of practice, for instance, would be pushing the concept beyond its usefulness. Viewers know that there are others – perhaps millions – who watch the same show, but it is only through their imagination that they can conceive of their viewing as membership in such a collectivity. And if, for a given time, a number of people tune to a certain channel, gaze at the screen, and watch the same show, this kind of alignment derives only from the distribution of television sets and programs, not from the mutual relations involved in the negotiation of a shared practice.

Imagination creates a kind of community. Two readers of a given newspaper who happened to be traveling on the same train would be able to imagine a common history of reading the same kinds of articles. They might even assume that they are each the kind of person who typically reads that kind of publication, or that they have stores of characteristics and experiences in common. They could be wrong of course, but the point is that their mutual link to a common readership creates a kind of community to which they see themselves as belonging.[2] Similar scenarios could be compiled for the users of a computer system, the adepts of a sport, the successful, the overweight, people who stutter, those who hate fluorescent lights, or those who listen to the same kind of music. The inhabitants of a city, people who are disabled, immigrants from a certain region, people born as twins, lovers of Celtic music – each of these groups shares something that creates a kind of community. Belonging to such a community can contribute to the identities of those involved, even if it does not involve the joint development of a shared practice.

Alignment also creates a kind of community. Allegiance to a creed, a movement, the environment, a nation, a religion, a star performer, or a sports team can rally the energies of unlikely bedfellows. The commitments that unite them often have little to do with personal commonality or differences. The forms that such commitments take, and their root in specific experiences, may be unimaginable from one situation to another; it is their alignment that matters. A movement like environmentalism, for instance, is constituted by a collection of motivations, beliefs, and passions that may have very different origins for different participants. Yet, the alignment behind the idea of preserving the environment does create a vast community united by a common purpose. A positivist biologist and a new-age worshiper of the planet-being may not agree about very much, but they will show up at the same rally anyway, ready to forget all their differences and join forces in order to save a piece of marshland. This kind of allegiance can galvanize energies in ways that create a strong community.

One could endeavor to list the types of communities: of practice, of affinity, of taste, of interest, of economic status, of profession, of geographical proximity, of experience, of allegiance, of standardization, and so on. Each of these may have relevance to specific contexts. But such a list goes on and on. Rather than classifying communities under fixed categories, the modes of belonging introduced in this chapter provide a framework for understanding how these communities are constituted.

Though engagement, imagination, and alignment are distinct modes of belonging, they are not mutually exclusive. A given community can be constituted by all three in various proportions, and the variety of these combinations results in communities with distinct qualities. Given a community, one might wonder what the possibilities for mutual engagement are, what material supports imagination, and how alignment is secured. Such questions focus not on classification but on mechanisms of community formation, as well as on the trade-offs and kinds of work involved.

When the dominance moves from one mode of belonging to another, a community changes its character. For example, a nation under threat can shift from imagination to alignment to the extent that its citizens are ready to forget their individual differences and to kill and die for their nation.

One mode of belonging may affect another. Having to join the ranks of the unemployed, finding that your own child is homosexual, being promoted, or winning the lottery opens new ways of seeing yourself that can redirect your political orientation. Leaders often make appeals to imagination in an effort to justify alignment by claiming the existence of a "natural" community. The rise of nationalism in the nineteenth century is an example in point, when nationalist leaders made appeals to (often spurious) ties of common origins and linguistic unity in order to support their struggles for national alignment.[3]

The role of rituals, for instance, can be understood in terms of community formation. Rituals connect local practices and identities to other locations across time and space. They are a form of engagement that can bolster imagination – by cultivating the sense of others doing or having done the same thing – and alignment – by channeling an investment of the self into standardized activities, discourses, and styles.[4]

Because relations between engagement, imagination, and alignment are not fixed over time, these modes of belonging provide a framework for understanding the variety of community types, as well as for analyzing the transformations of these communities over time and appreciating the kinds of work of belonging that such transformations require.

The work of belonging

Because each mode involves trade-offs, it is not useful to think of one mode as better than the others in terms of potential for learning and identity. In fact, most of what we do involves a combination of engagement, imagination, and alignment, though more emphasis on one or the other gives a distinct quality to our actions and their meanings. One reason for distinguishing among engagement, imagination, and alignment is that they require different conditions and kinds of work. The alumni of a college or the listeners of a public broadcasting station may be aware that they belong to some kind of community, but getting them to pledge funds usually requires a substantial amount of alignment work. In fact, the demands of engagement, imagination, and alignment can conflict, even when they enhance the learning potential of each other. Taking the time to attend a conference to open one's horizon may conflict with the delivery schedule of a work team. To conclude this chapter, I will summarize the kind of "work of belonging" associated with each mode.

The work of engagement

The work of engagement is basically the work of forming communities of practice. As such, it requires the ability to take part in meaningful activities and interactions, in the production of sharable artifacts, in community-building conversations, and in the negotiation of new situations. It implies a sustained intensity and relations of mutuality. To recap, the work of engagement characteristically entails such processes as:

1) the definition of a common enterprise in the process of pursuing it in concert with others
2) mutual engagement in shared activities
3) the accumulation of a history of shared experiences
4) the production of a local regime of competence
5) the development of interpersonal relationships
6) a sense of interacting trajectories that shape identities in relation to one another
7) the management of boundaries
8) the opening of peripheries that allow for various degrees of engagement.

In order to support learning, engagement requires authentic access to both the participative and the reificative aspects of practice in concert. In terms of participation, engagement requires access to and interaction with other participants in the course of their own engagement. Engagement also requires the ability and the legitimacy to make contributions to the pursuit of an enterprise, to the negotiation of meaning, and to the development of a shared practice. In terms of reification, engagement requires access to the full reificative paraphernalia of practice in the course of its use: symbols, tools, language, documents, and the like. It is this dual access to participation and reification that makes engagement a special context for learning and identity. A lack of access to either participation or reification results in the inability to learn.

The work of imagination

Imagination requires the ability to disengage – to move back and look at our engagement through the eyes of an outsider. It requires the ability to explore, take risks, and create unlikely connections. It demands some degree of playfulness. Characteristically, the work of imagination entails such processes as:

1) recognizing our experience in others, knowing what others are doing, being in someone else's shoes
2) defining a trajectory that connects what we are doing to an extended identity, seeing ourselves in new ways
3) locating our engagement in broader systems in time and space, conceiving of the multiple constellations that are contexts for our practices
4) sharing stories, explanations, descriptions
5) opening access to distant practices through excursions and fleeting contacts – visiting, talking, observing, meeting
6) assuming the meaningfulness of foreign artifacts and actions
7) creating models, reifying patterns, producing representational artifacts
8) documenting historical developments, events, and transitions; reinterpreting histories and trajectories in new terms; using history to see the present as only one of many possibilities and the future as a number of possibilities
9) generating scenarios, exploring other ways of doing what we are doing, other possible worlds, and other identities.

Imagination requires the ability to dislocate participation and reification in order to reinvent ourselves, our enterprises, our practices, and our communities. New and perhaps incongruous mixes of participation and reification are one way of creating novel situations of learning.

In terms of participation, imagination requires an opening. It needs the willingness, freedom, energy, and time to expose ourselves to the exotic, move around, try new identities, and explore new relations. It requires the ability to proceed without being too quick with the constraints of a specific form of accountability, to accept non-participation as an adventure, and to suspend judgment. Participation can also serve imagination with visits, contacts, and travel that provide exposure to other ways of doing things, other enterprises, other practices, and other communities.

In terms of reification, imagination requires material to work with. Reification can provide tools of imagination – maps, visualization, stories, simulations – tools to see patterns in time and space that are not perceivable through local engagement. It can also provide a language: new words to talk about one's place in the world.

- On the one hand, imagination uses reification to create connections across boundaries and histories, beyond direct engagement. Reification thus feeds imagination through the ability of its forms to travel across time and space. It triggers imagination by causing interpretations with mismatched forms of participation.
- On the other hand, imagination plays with forms. It explores them as forms. It rearranges them, lets them propose their own combinations, builds on incongruity and serendipity. Reification thus affords an opportunity to step back and see situations in a different way. Reification can be detached from engagement and thrown around: it allows rearranging the world and dislocating experience.

With insufficient reification, there may not be enough material to play with, to bounce off from, and to shake free from time and place. It may be difficult for imagination to take off.

The work of alignment

Alignment requires the ability to coordinate perspectives and actions in order to direct energies to a common purpose. The challenge of alignment is to connect local efforts to broader styles and discourses in ways that allow learners to invest their energy in them. Whether it is about a scientific method, an artistic or a social movement, a moral commitment, or the charter of an organization, alignment requires the ability to communicate purpose, needs, methods, and criteria. Characteristically, the work of alignment entails such processes as:

1) investing energy in a directed way and creating a focus to coordinate this investment of energy
2) negotiating perspectives, finding common ground
3) imposing one's view, using power and authority
4) convincing, inspiring, uniting

5) defining broad visions and aspirations, proposing stories of identity
6) devising proceduralization, quantification, and control structures that are portable (i.e., usable across boundaries)
7) walking boundaries, creating boundary practices, reconciling diverging perspectives.

Alignment requires specific forms of participation and reification to support the required coordination. It requires participation in the form of boundary practices and of people with multimembership who can straddle boundaries and do the work of translation. With insufficient participation, our relations to broader enterprises tend to remain literal and procedural: our coordination tends to be based on compliance rather than participation in meaning. Furthermore, our common terms and shared artifacts can have disconnecting as much as connecting effects.

In terms of reification, alignment requires sharable artifacts – boundary objects able to create fixed points around which to coordinate activities. It can also require the creation and adoption of broader discourses that help reify the enterprise and by which local actions can be interpreted as fitting within a broader framework. With insufficient reification, coordination across time and space may depend too much on the partiality of specific participants, or it may simply be too vague, illusory, or contentious to create alignment.

Because engagement, imagination and alignment each have different but complementary strengths and weaknesses, they work best in combination. In fact, I will argue in Coda II that by combining them effectively, a community of practice can become a learning community. But before doing so, I must specify in more detail the mechanisms by which engagement, imagination, and alignment become constituents of our identities.

Chapter 9
Identification and negotiability

The mix of participation and non-participation that shapes our identities has to do with communities in which we become invested, but it also has to do with our ability to shape the meanings that define these communities. Each member of a couple, for instance, may identify very deeply with their being a couple. They may also be viewed and identified as a couple by all their friends and relatives. It may be an unquestionable part of who they are. Yet there may still be substantial argument about what it means to be a couple as a way of living together, and who can determine at any given time how being a couple is to be implemented. The fact that they care enough about being a couple to argue about it reflects the degree to which they identify with the relationship. Their identification holds them together enough to debate the question, but the question is not resolved by identification itself. Working out what it means to be together and how to go about living as a couple is an additional dimension of their relationship that contributes in its own right to shaping the kinds of identity that belonging to that couple will produce.

More generally, our identities form in this kind of tension between our investment in various forms of belonging and our ability to negotiate the meanings that matter in those contexts. Identity formation is thus a dual process.

1) *Identification* is one half of it, providing experiences and material for building identities through an investment of the self in relations of association and differentiation.

2) *Negotiability,* the other half, is just as fundamental, because it determines the degree to which we have control over the meanings in which we are invested.

The interaction of these two components of identity will be the central theme of this chapter. For this discussion, I will bring together the

188

themes introduced so far in Part II. Combining all these concepts will result in a kind of "social ecology of identity," which is summarized in Figure 9.1. This figure is in fact a wrap-up of the chapter, but I show it now because having an advance overall view of its structure may facilitate the reading of the chapter. Very briefly, here is how to interpret the figure (I will go from top to bottom, but the figure works both ways).

- The top shows identity as being constituted by two components.
- The next level down states that identification and negotiability can each give rise to participation as well as to non-participation, resulting in four combinations.
- Then I list familiar examples to illustrate these four possibilities for each mode of belonging as introduced in the last chapter. Indeed, each mode can be a source of identification and a source of negotiability:

  1) *engagement* – through our direct experience of the world, the ways we engage with others, and the ways these relations reflect who we are
  2) *imagination* – through our images of the world, both personal and collective, that locate us in various contexts
  3) *alignment* – through our power to direct energy, our own and that of others.

- The next layer shows the kinds of structural relations that shape processes of identification and negotiability. Identification congeals into forms of membership, and negotiability into forms of "ownership of meaning."
- The bottom layer shows the types of social structures that correspond to the two processes at the top.

Talking about identities in terms of an interplay of identification and negotiability will bring issues of power to the fore. As I specified in Chapter 8, power is not construed exclusively in terms of conflict or domination, but primarily as the ability to act in line with the enterprises we pursue and only secondarily in terms of competing interests. I will treat issues of power not so much in terms of political institutions or economic systems, which are the traditional focus of theories of power, but in terms of the negotiation of meaning and the formation of identities – that is, as a property of social communities. My focus on community, meaning, and identity is not to deny the importance of broader political and economic issues. The marginality of claims

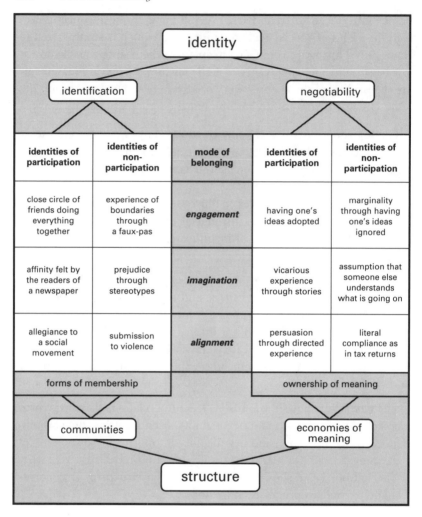

Figure 9.1. Social ecology of identity.

processors is certainly a function of a specific political and economic system, in which Alinsu represents a concentration of power.[1] But what struck me was the extent to which such a system affects the lives of people through the communities and identities they construct. Here, I will focus on just one aspect of power as an element of social life by arguing that a social concept of identity entails a social concept of power and, conversely, that a discussion of power must include considerations of community, negotiation of meaning, and identity. Note that issues of power of the kind I am discussing are inherent in social life, and will not disappear even if we are so lucky and wise to devise an ideal economic and political system.

Identification

By identification, I mean the process through which modes of belonging become constitutive of our identities by creating bonds or distinctions in which we become invested.[2] Nationality, for instance, is a common source of identification. The process of identification may include: reifying the group of inhabitants of a region into a nation; being identified as a national of that country; acquiring identification papers to prove it; and identifying with that nationality in a personal way, with a deep experience of allegiance. I will incorporate all these aspects of identification in my use of the term. In this sense, identification has the following characteristics.

- It is both participative and reificative. On the one hand, it is a reificative process of "identifying as" (and being identified as) something or someone – a category, a description, a role, or other kinds of reificative characterization. On the other hand, it is a participative process of "identifying with" something or someone – that is, developing an association whose experience is constitutive of who we are.
- It is both something we do to ourselves and something we do to each other. We identify with a community and, conversely, are recognized as a member of a community. We think of ourselves in terms of labels – I am a grown-up, an introvert, an opera lover – and, conversely, we are labeled by others as a good or bad pupil, a terrific or a terrible teacher, a popular student or a weirdo. So identification is a process that is at once both relational and experiential, subjective and collective.
- Identification can be both positive and negative in the sense that it includes relations that shape what we are and what we are not. It includes what we enjoy being and what we dread. It engenders identities of both participation and non-participation. We can be included in a community or excluded, and still identify with the situation in both cases. We can pride ourselves on being a mathematician and we can pride ourselves on not being a nerd. We can be ashamed of being a drug user and we can be ashamed of not understanding mathematics.

The concept of identification is commonly used in psychology to refer to relationships between specific people. My use of the term is not basically different, but I associate it more broadly with each of the modes of belonging introduced in the previous chapter. In this context, it refers to the constitutive character of our communities and our forms of membership (and non-membership) for our identities, as illustrated in the following diagram.

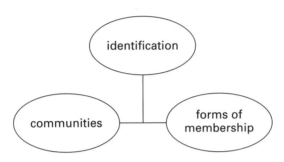

Identification is not merely a relation between people, but between participants and the constituents of their social existence, which includes other participants, social configurations, categories, enterprises, actions, artifacts, and so forth. Identification is not merely a subjective experience; it is socially organized. It is not merely a static relation; it is a dynamic, generative process. Because it represents an investment of the self, identification generates the social energy that sustains both our identities and our communities in their mutual constitution.[3]

In order to explore this concept of identification in its various facets, it is useful to consider it in the context of each mode of belonging.

Identification through engagement

I have already discussed many of the processes by which engagement is a source of identification, so I need only highlight a few main points here. Engagement in practice is a double source of identification: we invest ourselves in what we do and at the same time we invest ourselves in our relations with other people. As we build communities of practice through this process, we work out our relations with each other and with the world, and we gain a lived sense of who we are.

Through engagement in practice, we see first-hand the effects we have on the world and discover how the world treats the likes of us. We explore our ability to engage with one another, how we can participate in activities, what we can and cannot do. But all this takes place in the doing. Our enterprises and our definition of competence shape our identities through our very engagement in activities and social interactions.

In the context of engagement, identification takes place in the doing; hence, the development of competence, the negotiation of a trajectory, and the work of reconciliation across boundaries are not necessarily self-conscious. Identification through engagement does not require a reification of the relations it is based on. As a result, engagement may not be perceived as an obvious source of identification by those involved. The process of identity formation can remain largely transparent because our identities can develop by being engaged in action without being themselves the focus of attention.

However, engagement can also throw us off and disrupt the transparency of the identities that it creates. An unexpected success gives rise to a heightened sense of power; someone yells at us and we feel worthless. Through these disruptions of transparency and their resolution, identification involves the kind of layering of participation and reification described at the beginning of Chapter 6.

In the same chapter I argued that identity in practice is an experience of the familiar and the unfamiliar. In this context, boundaries are experienced very participatively but concretely through our inability to engage fully in an activity, participate in a conversation, perform a demanding task, notice a subtle cue, or respond to an unspoken expectation. Boundaries are met in that brief look of disapprobation or incomprehension when we have just put our foot in our mouth, the sensation of which can then linger as an indelible part of our identity.

At the core of processes of identification through engagement is the direct experience of mutuality characteristic of communities of practice. By recognizing each other as participants, we give life to our respective social selves. Within the bounds of engagement, our identities constitute each other through direct interactions so that identification is a two-way process. The mutuality of this process of giving and receiving can be very fulfilling. It can make a community of practice the source of great social energy. For that very reason, however, we can become hostage to this experience and fail to move on. And for that reason also, a lack of mutuality in the course of engagement creates relations of marginality that can reach deeply into our identities.

Identification through imagination

I have argued that identifying with a label like "claims processor" is not only a matter of engagement in practice, but also a matter of seeing the label as referring to a widespread kind of profession. Identifying with this kind of broad category, or using categories to characterize large groups of people, requires the work of imagination. In addition to the use of categories, imagination also allows a certain playfulness by which the process of identification can include the ability to try things, take liberties, reflect, assume the existence of relations of mutuality, and position ourselves in a completely different context.

Imagination is thus an important source of identification, one that takes the process beyond engagement in a variety of ways. Indeed, beyond engagement, identification depends on the kind of picture of the world and of ourselves we can build. It depends on the connections we can envision across history and across the social landscape. Through these connections, identification expands through time and space, and our identities take on new dimensions.

Postindustrial societies are almost dizzying in their frantic production of material for imagination. As a result, there are endless potential topics for identification and thus an infinite variety of potential communities.

- The expansion of consumer markets has generated countless ways of identifying with consumable products and putative communities defined by styles, fashions, brands, exotic gourmet foods, and so on.
- Entertainment and news industries have disseminated images and information that are fodder for imagination. More generally, communication technologies have changed the time and space constraints of identification.[4] The success of worldwide computer networks, for instance, is due not only to the access to information that they afford but also to the possibility of connecting with people who share an interest – developing, in the process, relations of identification with people all over the world. Thus our identities are expanded, spreading (so to speak) along the tentacles of all these wires and taking, through imagination, planetary dimensions.[5]
- The social sciences and related institutionalized discourses have contributed to the process by generating analytical social categories in terms of ethnicity, gender, class, age, and so on, all of which can become material for identification.[6]

In expanding identification beyond engagement, imagination can work by both association and opposition, defining our identities both by connecting us and by distancing us. If two Parisians meet while visiting the Grand Canyon, they are likely to engage in a lively conversation, recognizing in the midst of this foreign wilderness the bond of living in the same city, speaking the same language, driving down the same boulevards, and basking in the same sense of municipal grandeur – now temporarily dwarfed by the timeless cliffs of the canyon. Their identification with their city and their sense of mutual affinity are given a fleeting salience by the rocky vastness of the Arizona landscape. In Paris, however, these two Parisians may have little to do with one another – beyond swearing at each other's driving while complaining about traffic, smog, and the weather.

Imagination can yield a sense of affinity, and thus an identity of participation, but it can also result in a reaction of dissociation and a consequent identity of non-participation. We can imagine differences as well as commonalities. Parents forbid their children to befriend "those" neighbors. Leaders paint barbaric pictures of the enemy. Passing each other on the street, the artist and the businessperson, the adolescent and the elderly, the homeless and the police officer – each takes one look at the other and imagines an ocean of differences. There may indeed be an ocean of differences between them, but at the same time they may be wrong; they may be using irrelevant or misleading stereotypes. For that moment, however, it does not matter. Their imagination builds their selves by dissociation. They move on, refining in those imagined differences their sense of who they are.

Note that even when this kind of identification is instantaneous, it still involves the work of imagination – again not in the sense that it is less real than identification based on mutual engagement, but that it brings about relations of identification established through a picture of the world into which the self can be projected. Not only is building that picture of the world and locating ourselves in it as much part of identification as engaging in practice, but the two processes also feed each other. Our practices provide resources for building that picture, and that picture in turn determines how we understand our engagement in practice.

Identification through alignment

Through alignment, the identity and enterprise of large groups can become part of the identities of participants. Demanding or inspiring alignment is a form of identification because the power, individual or collective, to generate alignment extends our identity to the energy of those who align themselves. An inspiring leader or an authoritarian parent will incorporate the effects of their inspiration or control into their own identities. Members of a dedicated professional group will identify with the actions of their colleagues.

Similarly, "going along" – through willing allegiance or mere submission – is a form of identification because it shapes the way we experience our own power and thus contributes to defining our identity. Going to the ball game, rooting for the home team, entering in unison with a crowd of thousands into a big shout when a point is scored, hugging everyone after a victory, joining in the disappointment or the rage of a defeat – all this alignment of energy creates a way of taking part in something big. Identification through alignment does not have to be so sensational, however. It can take the form of concentration on a task, attention to details, or unwillingness to compromise.

As noted in Chapter 8, aligning our efforts with the styles and discourses of certain institutions, movements, or systems of thought can be a very profound aspect of how we define ourselves. Allegiance to a scientific method, to a political cause, or to a family tradition can become an essential part of our identity. Because alignment affords the ability to invest our energy in terms of broadly defined enterprises, it can make us "larger" by placing our actions in larger context.

Because alignment involves power, it often combines allegiance and compliance and thus results in the kind of subtle mix of participation and non-participation discussed in Chapter 7. I described the claims processors' experience of alignment with the institutional requirements of work as such a mixture. They begrudge the strictures and status of their positions, but they mostly subscribe to the political system that places them there. Their interpretations of their working conditions are indeed complex and somewhat contradictory. They tend to agree that it is crucial for them to fulfill the requirements of their employer in order to be paid and to keep their jobs. They even agree that they should try to serve Alinsu's customers as well as they can. Yet complaining is always considered appropriate, and getting away with small infractions is condoned as long as it is not done at the expense of someone else in the office. Hard work is admired, but it is also essential to try to have some fun: joining in, telling and hearing stories, eating snacks, gossiping, or learning astonishing facts about the world. The job is to be taken seriously, but it is proper to control carefully how much effort one invests in work, in learning, or in other displays of allegiance to the job and the corporation.

Even in this kind of mix of allegiance and compliance, alignment subtly becomes part of who we are. For instance, claims processors end up taking the company's measures of production and quality quite seriously. Meeting production requirements goes beyond a mere financial concern to become a yardstick of one's individual capacities. If they have difficulty maintaining their production and quality at the required level, they will take it very personally.

It is perhaps less clear that alignment is a form of identification when it manifests through pure relations of authority and submission. Yet, to the degree that such alignment directs our actions, it inevitably affects our identities. Indeed, even when alignment is achieved at gunpoint, it expresses a relation of power that seeps into the identities of those involved. Victims of abuse and tyranny must fight this invasion of their identities with efforts to dissociate themselves from their oppressors.

Negotiability

Identification, I have argued, is not the whole story. Processes of identification define which meanings matter to us, but do not in themselves determine our ability to negotiate these meanings. Another aspect of identity, therefore, is the issue of negotiability. Returning to the example of the couple, many people are deeply invested in relationships that do not afford them much say. And conversely, being able to control a relationship does not necessarily entail more identification with it. Sometimes identification and negotiability go together and sometimes they do not. But they cannot be reduced to each other.

Negotiability refers to the ability, facility, and legitimacy to contribute to, take responsibility for, and shape the meanings that matter within a social configuration. Negotiability allows us to make meanings applicable to new circumstances, to enlist the collaboration of others, to make sense of events, or to assert our membership. Just as identification is defined with respect to communities and forms of membership in them, negotiability is defined with respect to social configurations and our positions in them. Within these *economies of meaning*, negotiability among individuals and among communities is shaped by structural relations of *ownership of meaning*. This can be illustrated schematically by a diagram (see page 198) that parallels the one for identification. Unlike communities and membership in the earlier diagram, the concepts of economies and ownership of meaning are not commonly used and have not

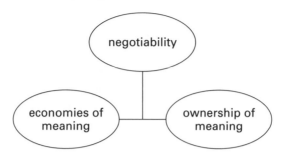

been introduced yet. I need to focus on them first before turning to negotiability. For this introduction, I will use the COB worksheet of Vignette II as a running example. Claims processors have rather limited control over the institutional conditions in which they work, and this worksheet stands as a symbol of their relations to their job and their employer.

Economies of meaning

The COB worksheet was not produced by claims processors in an effort to simplify their own work. Rather, it was designed by specialists and merely adopted by claims processors as part of their own practice. It is thus given meaning in at least two communities of practice:

1) the specialists who designed it give it meaning in the context of their own practice
2) claims processors produce their own meanings for it in the course of using it.

The meanings produced in the technical communities are not only different from those produced among claims processors, they also carry a very different status. When disgruntled customers pick up the phone and call Alinsu, they are not interested in the processors' own meanings – for instance, in their insecurity at not being able to assess the plausibility of their results. The processors who answer the phone know that. They know they cannot just tell a dismayed customer that they followed the worksheet carefully. They cannot say that they added lines A and B and lines D and E, and then subtracted line F from line C, even though this is just what they did. They are well aware that others have other meanings for the procedure and the worksheet, and that those other meanings have more value than their own. That is why they feel embarrassed on the phone. When talking among themselves about this issue, they are not embarrassed. Even when talking with me they were not embarrassed, because through the relationships we had established they had come to trust that I was, somewhat to their surprise, genuinely interested in their own meanings. Assuming that their local meanings are irrelevant to outsiders and have little currency in the broader scheme of things is an important factor influencing the way they construe these local meanings as a lack of understanding.

The meanings that the claims processors produce for the worksheet are not only local meanings; they are also part of a broader "economy of meaning" in which different meanings are produced in different locations and compete for the definition of certain events, actions, or artifacts. The notion of an economy of meaning is not relativistic in any simple sense of implying that all meanings should have the same value. On the contrary, an economy of meaning suggests precisely that some meanings do achieve special status. There may be, one could argue, good reasons that the technical meanings of the procedure have more currency than the processors' local meanings. But acknowledging this asymmetry is different from talking about a linear scale of understanding, by whose measure one could simply say that claims processors do not understand the worksheet. Indeed, as I argued in Coda 0, claims processors understand the worksheet either very insufficiently or all too well, depending on how one looks at the situation. In other words, saying – without qualifying the statement – that claims processors "do not understand" the worksheet is a tacit endorsement of the status of their own meanings within the economy of meaning in which they define their relations with the artifact.

The relations of claims processors to the COB worksheet must therefore be viewed not as a direct relation between people and an artifact, but rather as defined in the context of a broader economy of meaning in which the value of the meanings they produce is determined. Calling such social configurations "economies of meaning" makes sense because the notion of economy emphasizes:

1) a social system of relative values
2) the negotiated character of these relative values
3) the possibility of accumulating "ownership of meaning"[7]
4) the constant possibility of such positions being contested
5) systems of legitimation that to some extent regulate processes of negotiation.

An economy of meaning is not just a matter of official status. A parent, boss, or teacher may hold a position of authority, but in practice the actual ability to define the meaning of any situation must still submit to negotiation. So while an economy of meaning does reflect relations of legitimacy and power, it also captures the inherent fluidity of these relations, which are themselves shaped through the negotiation of meaning.

Ownership of meaning

Claims processors are unable to answer the phone confidently, or even to feel confident about the results of their own calculation, because the ownership of the meaning of the COB procedure is concentrated elsewhere in the economy of meaning. They have a local form of ownership: their own meanings reflect the struggle of their community and thus have a local kind of validity. But they do not have enough access to knowledgeable people to "appropriate" the technical meanings of the procedure into their own practice.

Negotiability is thus shaped by relations of "ownership of meaning" – that is, the degree to which we can make use of, affect, control, modify, or in general, assert as ours the meanings that we negotiate. By using the term "ownership," I do not want to suggest that meaning is somehow objectified and commodified, or that it becomes an object (like a piece of land) that someone owns to the exclusion of everyone else and with the legal right to decide what is done with it. But I do want to suggest that:

1) meanings have various degrees of currency
2) participants can have various degrees of control over the meanings that a community produces, and thus differential abilities to make use of them and modify them
3) the negotiation of meaning involves bids for ownership, so that the social nature of meaning includes its contestable character as an inherent feature.

Ownership of meaning, however, is neither an intrinsically antagonistic nor a particularly individualistic concept. Ownership of meaning can be shared and it can have degrees. In fact, it does not diminish from being shared.[8] On the contrary, because meanings are socially negotiated, shared ownership can widen participation in their production and thus increase ownership for all participants.[9] As a result, an economy of meaning is not necessarily divisive, aggressive, or contentious.

This notion of ownership does not imply that there is a single meaning attached to an event, action, or artifact. On the contrary, the notion of an economy of meaning implies the plurality of perspectives that are involved in the negotiation of meaning. Having a claim to owning the meaning of a piece of text, a knowing smile, a tool, or an idea is being able to come up with a recognizably competent interpretation of it. Such interpretation need not – in order to constitute ownership of meaning – be that of the author of the text, the producer of the smile, the builder of the tool, or the spokesperson of the idea; but it must have currency within an economy of meaning where it is recognized as a legitimate contender.[10]

Using the term "ownership" to refer to our ability to take responsibility for negotiating meaning, and thus to make some meanings our own, is not new. Teachers talk about students gaining ownership of the curricular material, and by this they refer to their achieving not only perfunctory mastery but personal meaning as well. In the world of work, too, people talk about having or not having ownership of their task or mission. In this sense, the notion of ownership refers both to an experience of holding some meanings as our own and to social relations of ownership with respect to others who might also claim some say in the matter. Ownership involves control over meaning, but the notion of control is not quite appropriate because it is too externalized. What I call ownership of meaning is more intimate; it is deeper than just control. It refers to the ways meanings, and our ability to negotiate them, become part of who we are.

Ownership of meaning is defined within economies of meaning where the values of meanings are interdependent. Thus, appropriation by some can entail alienation from others. For instance, the appropriation by professional communities of such concepts as health and justice is meant to generate practices and artifacts in the service of these public issues. But the technical discourses of such professional communities often end up constituting claims of ownership of the issues themselves. Such claims devalue the nontechnical understanding of these issues by the rest of the population, even though the definitions of issues like health and justice are in the end not primarily technical.

Similarly, because of differences in position within an economy of meaning, appropriation can cause alienation by overshadowing or displacing original meanings. Thus, the politician's interpretation of an opinion poll becomes the will of the people. In public discourses that favor the authority of the written text, the anthropologist's voice can come to displace those of the natives. In a broader economy of meaning, appropriation by outsiders can thus alienate the producers of the original meanings: they become unable to reclaim their own meanings, which they no longer recognize but which have gained, in the process, new currency in the economy of meaning at large.

Belonging to an economy of meaning can involve engagement, imagination, and alignment. For instance, the economy of meaning of a community of practice is primarily based on engagement, the economy of meaning of a cultural heritage involves imagination, and the economy of meaning of an institutional discourse is primarily a matter of alignment. I will now explore the notion of negotiability through each of these modes of belonging.

Negotiability through engagement

Mutual engagement in the negotiation of meaning involves both the production of proposals for meaning and the adoption of these proposals. In the pursuit a joint enterprise, these processes of production and adoption must go together. New meanings contribute to a joint enterprise to the extent that they are adopted; only then do they become effective in the community. Adoption is a necessary part of production.[11]

This kind of interweaving of production and adoption of meaning is familiar to those who take part in brainstorming sessions. In such a process of negotiation, production and adoption of meaning are so closely and dynamically intertwined that it is often difficult to distinguish between them. Adopting a meaning is contributing to its interactive production. For all practical purposes, it is largely unnecessary in such a setting to know exactly who is producing and who is adopting. In fact, if issues of ownership start to distinguish the production from the adoption of meaning, such issues are likely to come in the way of the joint activity. A brainstorming session works because production is no more of a contribution to the activity than adoption.

As I argued in Chapter 3, it is this interactional characteristic of practice that allows newcomers to appropriate the meanings of a community and develop an identity of participation. When learning how to speak, for instance, it is through an interplay of production and adoption of meaning that the child becomes a participant in conversations and acquires the language. It is not pure production, because the language already exists; but neither is it mere adoption, because the child is involved in the practice in which the language is used. Very early on, the child becomes engaged in producing meaningful utterances and, through this production, is able to explore the meanings of words in practice and develop an increasing ability to negotiate these meanings productively. Through such an interplay of production and adoption, mutual engagement supports the appropriation of the language by the child.

Although mutual engagement can be a vehicle for sharing ownership of meaning, it can also be a vehicle for denying negotiability and can thus result in non-participation. If production and adoption become consistently separable, the distinction between them becomes an issue of marginality. Members whose contributions are never adopted develop an identity of non-participation that progressively marginalizes them. Their experience becomes irrelevant because it cannot be asserted and recognized as a form of competence. I argued in Coda I that learning requires an interplay of experience and competence. A split between production and adoption of meaning thus compromises learning because it presents it as a choice between experience and competence: you must choose between your own experience as a resource for the production of meaning and your membership in a community where your competence is determined by your adoption of other's proposals for meaning. In other words, learning depends on our ability to contribute to the collective production of meaning because it is by this process that experience and competence pull each other.

When, in a community of practice, the distinction between the production and adoption of meaning reflects enduring patterns of engagement among members – that is, when some always produce and some always adopt – the local economy of meaning yields very uneven ownership of meaning. This situation, when it persists, results in a mutually reinforcing condition of both marginality and inability to learn.

Negotiability through imagination

Imagination, too, can be a way to appropriate meanings. Stories, for instance, can be appropriated easily because they allow us to enter the events, the characters, and their plights by calling upon our imagination. Stories can transport our experience into the situations they relate and involve us in producing the meanings of those events as though we were participants. As a result, they can be integrated into our identities and remembered as personal experience, rather than as

mere reification. It is this ability to enable negotiability through imagination that makes stories, parables, and fables powerful communication
devices. Play is another process of imagination by which we can achieve
a vicarious kind of negotiability, as when children appropriate meanings from the adult world.

For claims processors to get a sense of what the COB procedure
means beyond their own practice, it is therefore not necessary for them
to join the community of technicians who designed it. They could have
some conversations with the right people, they could read some explanations, they could spend some time as a group using their collective
imagination to refine a picture of the procedure. For such purposes, the
worksheet itself could be used without modification as an explanation
tool. The strictly procedural interpretation that trainees are taught is
not inherent in the worksheet. The same artifact can also be integrated
into conversations that trigger imagination and open access to meanings from other practices.

Here again, imagination is not to be construed in purely individualistic terms. Children at play, claims processors exchanging stories,
groups of students trying to make sense of a piece of text – all these are
social events. Disciplines like history or anthropology are entire social
institutions organized around the enterprise of understanding other
times and cultures and appropriating their meanings in a vicarious way,
whether this process of appropriation through imagination does justice
to the original meanings or betrays them.

When we cannot appropriate meanings because we do not have
enough access to a practice, it is still through a process of imagination
that we construe our exclusion as non-participation. Unlike computers
that merely follow instructions, claims processors assume that there is
some meaning to what they are told to do. But they assume that a large
portion of these meanings lie beyond their own engagement in the process. These meanings must belong to someone, to be sure, but not to
them: they are not theirs to access, let alone to own. In fact, becoming
experienced at claims processing is in part a matter of learning merely
to assume the meaningfulness of what you do. As I mentioned, the old-
timer who helped her less experienced peers with the worksheet had
not acquired a much better idea of what the procedure was about. She
had simply learned to trust the results she obtained and to assume they
made sense to someone.

The processes of imagination involved in assuming that meanings
we cannot appropriate belong to someone else can contribute to mar-

ginalization. For claims processors, the COB worksheet functions not only as a guide for computations but also as a subtle reification of their role within the organization. This local interpretation of the worksheet is not one that claims processors discuss or articulate very explicitly, probably because it does not seem relevant. Yet it transpires clearly in remarks like those of Maureen, at the end of the dialogue shown in Vignette II, when she concludes: "So I guess that's all you need to know: there is an aggregate." The meanings claims processors produce are about themselves as much as about the worksheet. Indeed, the impossibility of appropriating alien meanings turns the alien character of meaning back onto the identity of the interpreter. They become meanings of non-participation.

Assuming that meanings belong elsewhere does not always result in marginality. For newcomers, for instance, it is often a condition of entry into a community. For full members, it can be a way to focus on their own partiality within the whole. Thus I am not suggesting that it is necessarily bad merely to assume the existence of meanings without attempting to share in their ownership. We do so all the time because our lives would be unbearably complicated otherwise. We are aware of our limitations and we recognize that we cannot pretend to understand everything; we must focus our attention and our efforts on the meanings that really matter to us. In fact, people with an overwhelming sense of entitlement – people who imagine they can appropriate the meaning of everything – are usually blind to their own limitations, probably superficial, and apt to become extremely obnoxious.

Negotiability through alignment

Alignment requires the ability to affect the negotiation of meaning over a given social configuration. It is the mode of belonging that most clearly gives rise to economies of meaning, because it requires the coordination of actions and therefore the encounter of various perspectives and meanings. But different processes of alignment among the parties involved give rise to very different relations of negotiability.

1) Negotiating, persuading, inspiring, trusting, and delegating are all processes by which alignment can be reached through shared ownership of meaning.
2) Literal compliance, proceduralization, violence, conformity, and submission can all generate alignment with little regard to negotiability.

Demanding alignment can be a way to expand the scope of one's ownership of meaning without sharing it. For instance, the COB worksheet was meant to align the activities of claims processors with the procedural requirements of the company without sharing ownership of meaning. The technique Alinsu used for this purpose was to define actions in terms of a few predefined operations, such as arithmetic operators or entering a piece of data. It is no coincidence that the COB worksheet looks very much like a computer program. In fact, transforming it into a simple computer program would require little more than a literal translation into a programming language. A computer program is an extreme example of a reification designed to generate alignment without negotiability. It is designed for interpretation by a machine that can perform only a restricted, well-defined set of operations. Given a program that assumes only the availability of these basic operations, a computer can fulfill very useful functions without any access to or responsibility for the broader meanings of its digital feats.

As a source of alignment, this kind of literal compliance can be efficient, since it does not require the complex processes of negotiation by which ownership of meaning can be shared. But for the same reasons, it is brittle in that it makes alignment dependent on an environment that is specifically organized, conforming, and free of unforeseen situations. Such lack of negotiability can only engender either strict alignment in terms of the reification or no alignment at all, which results in an inability to adapt to new circumstances, a lack of flexibility, and a propensity to breakdowns. The applicability of such literal compliance is thus narrow. In particular, it does not support phone conversations in which customers expect to be invited – and indeed enabled – to negotiate, in their own terms, the meaning of their business with a company.

It is important, however, not to associate alignment exclusively with the lack of negotiability that results from such a one-sided process. Demanding alignment itself can be a means of sharing ownership of meaning. This can happen, for instance, when demanding alignment is a way of demonstrating a possibility and of providing initial guidance in order to hand over control. The reluctant compliance of students with the directives of a demanding teacher can take these students beyond their own limitations, likes, and dislikes, and may result in their reaching new understandings of their own. As I will argue in Chapter 12, the critical issue in such a case is negotiability, not authority.

The dual nature of identity

As my earlier example of a couple illustrates, there is a complex relation between identification and negotiability (and thus between communities and economies of meaning). On the one hand, we tend to identify most strongly with the communities in which we develop the most ownership of meaning. On the other hand, there is also an inherent tension between identification and negotiability. This tension takes two forms.

- Internally, a focus of common identification can itself become the object of struggles for ownership of its meaning. Civil wars and family disputes are often the fiercest, at least in part because such conflicts concern objects of strong identification for all the parties involved.
- With respect to the outside, the very process of identification constrains negotiability. Cults and other forms of totalizing membership are extreme examples, but less intense forms of identification also shape what is negotiable and to what extent it is so. Membership is therefore both enabling and limiting of identity; it is both a resource and a cost.

This tension is intrinsic to a social conception of identity. Theorizing about identity thus entails theorizing also about power and belonging.

The dual nature of power

Identity is a locus of social selfhood and by the same token a locus of social power. On the one hand, it is the power to belong, to be a certain person, to claim a place with the legitimacy of membership; and on the other it is the vulnerability of belonging to, identifying with, and being part of some communities that contribute to defining who we are and thus have a hold on us. Rooted in our identities, power derives from belonging as well as from exercising control over what we belong to. It includes both conflictual and coalescing aspects – it requires or creates some form of consensus in order to become socially effective, but the meaning of the consensus is something whose ownership always remains open to negotiation. Power thus has a dual structure that reflects the interplay between identification and negotiability.

This view takes power to involve a tension – a kind of inherent double bind, as it were – between identification and negotiability.[12] Consider, for example, the situation of one politician accusing another of a lack of patriotism. It is instructive to cast the processes at play in this familiar scene in terms of identification and negotiability. On the one hand, there is nationality, which is expected to engender identification. On the other hand, there is a struggle to define what that means in the particular circumstance – what kinds of behavior qualify as the shared "patriotism" that everyone is supposed to identify with. An accusation of lack of patriotism works only because it creates a tension between identification and negotiability. It appropriates the meaning of a national identity, with which people generally resonate, in order to score a point in a struggle for power.

Using patriotism to grab the moral high ground in a political contest is a visible and public example that involves a rather open struggle for power, but processes of the same kind pervade our everyday life. Among claims processors, being a "nice" person is a point of identification, but who can define what being nice means in specific circumstances? To say "You are not being very nice today" is a matter of appropriating the notion of niceness, and using identification with that notion in order to convince someone to change behavior. In this interplay of identification and negotiability, there is a discipline of belonging, which we apply to ourselves and to each other in a very fine-grained process.[13]

This view of power is rich and complex because it takes into account both our ability to get things done and our ability to live meaningfully. Identification without negotiability is powerlessness – vulnerability, narrowness, marginality. Conversely, negotiability without identification is empty – it is meaningless power, freedom as isolation and cynicism. Identification gives us material to define our identities; negotiability enables us to use this material to assert our identities as productive of meaning; and we weave these two threads into the social fabric of our identities.

The dual nature of belonging

The duality of identification and negotiability is reflected in the coexistence of communities and economies of meaning. As the interaction of identification and negotiability cuts across relations of engagement, imagination, and alignment, each of these modes gives rise to interwoven communities and economies of meaning at various levels of aggregation.

A community of practice, for instance, is at once both a community and an economy of meaning. The definition of a joint enterprise brings the community together through the collective development of a shared practice. But the definition of that enterprise – and therefore the meanings of the shared practice – are to be negotiated among the participants through what I have called, in Chapter 3, the politics of participation and reification. In other words, the very process that pulls the community together also creates an economy of meaning by generating something to negotiate; the focus of identification becomes the very object whose meaning is contested.

Such interactions of identification and negotiability can also take place at different levels. When a style or a discourse spreads through a vast community or constellation, claiming ownership of its meaning becomes a source of power by the very fact that such style or discourse is a source of widespread identification. These kinds of dual processes are at work, for instance, in methodological arguments in scientific discourses, in efforts to claim the moral high ground with respect to contentious decisions, or in setting trends by appropriating the meaning of such highly regarded achievements as "being cool."[14]

The interweaving of communities and economies of meaning must be understood across various levels of aggregation and through various modes of belonging. These different levels interact. Claims processors define their interpretation of the COB worksheet in an economy of meaning that overlaps but is not congruent with their community of practice. It is congruent with a broader community of alignment organized around the business process of claims processing, but this broader community is less a focus of identification than their local practice. In other cases, identification may be with a broad community of alignment yet find an intense economy of meaning at the level of engagement, as when outside political or religious convictions become contested within a community of practice. As our nexus of multimembership crosses these levels, the work of reconciliation must address issues of negotiability as well as identification. It is not impossible to be a feminist in a Catholic household and identify with both, but the level of negotiability required will demand some work.

The dual work of identity

Communities and economies of meaning tend to cover over-lapping territories in the social landscape, but they emphasize different aspects of social configurations.

1) Communities emphasize the ability of social configurations to constitute our identities through relations of belonging or not belonging.
2) Economies of meaning emphasize the social production and adoption of meaning, and thus the possibility of uneven negotiability and contested ownership among participants.

As a result, they require and reflect different kinds of work of the self. It might be useful to characterize this work in general terms, keeping in mind that these terms take on different meanings in different contexts.

- The work of *identification* can be described with concepts such as focusing social energy, inclusion and exclusion, commitment, affinity, differentiation, allegiance, solidarity, togetherness, stereotypes, paradigmatic trajectories, trust, shared histories, forgiveness, defining boundaries, acceptance, inspiration, stories of identity, and so on.
- The work of *negotiability* can be described with phrases like opening access to information, listening to other perspectives, explaining the reason why, making organizational policies and processes more transparent, seeking control, inviting contributions, defining individual rights, centralizing or distributing authority, negotiating and enforcing shared standards, opening decision processes, argumentation, sharing responsibilities, confrontation, voting, challenging boundaries, and so forth.

I should insist that it can be misleading to define the work of identification and negotiability by categorizing their elements so abstractly. A particular action can often be construed as an act of one or the other depending on the context. For instance, claiming to be a "collaborative team" can be a way to generate allegiance by proposing something that people can identify with; or, in the context of requesting the specific collaboration of someone, it can be a way to appropriate the definition of the community in order to push an agenda.

Indeed, the work of identification and the work of negotiability are accomplished through each other because each process is necessary to the other.

- Working the economy of meaning can be a way to preserve the community by sharing ownership of meaning. For instance, involving everyone in a decision complicates the process of arriving at that decision and may bring into the open all kinds of disagreements. Yet this sharing of ownership of meaning may well result in a deeper commitment to the community.
- Conversely, focusing on identification may keep a community together enough to go through a period of controversy and dissension. For instance, many communities surround difficult debates with rituals that affirm a shared identification and thus a commitment to working things out.

Although the two kinds of work can reinforce each other, they are not substitutes for each other. Both are needed, and one cannot replace the other. The reason that family disputes or the disputes of a couple can sometimes seem so pointless is that arguments threaten the mutual identification, while the identification necessary to sustain togetherness is not likely to emerge out of competing for the right to define what being together means. The work of community building is not done merely by attempting to define or enforce standards, or to appropriate righteousness. The work of identification takes more than laws and policing: it takes the mutuality that shared histories produce, a sense of connected past and future that creates bonds. Conversely, identification does not by itself preclude or resolve differences, though it may give people the will to work through their differences.

Social ecologies of identity

Adding the duality of identification and negotiability to the themes introduced so far in Part II yields the basic constituents of a social ecology of identity:

1) dimensions of practice as dimensions of identity
2) relations of participation versus non-participation
3) modes of belonging – providing for various forms of social configurations at various levels of aggregation
4) dual processes of identity formation – identification and negotiability
5) dual aspects of social structure – communities and economies of meaning
6) dual aspects of social status – membership and ownership of meaning.

By incorporating both power and belonging into an ecology of identity, the duality of identification and negotiability provides a sophisticated way of talking about the social construction of the person. It does not simply create an opposition between individuality and collectivity, but neither does it simply assimilate them. Instead, it takes a different cut at the individuality–collectivity dichotomy by recasting it in terms of processes of identity formation. Neither identification nor negotiability is inherently collective or individual. Yet their interplay in specific settings is what defines the meaning of the collective and the individual as an experience of identity.

Because identification and negotiability are not simple opposites, it is important *not* to assume that one is good and the other bad. Even though the term "community" has a positive aura about it, it does not always refer to a positive process. For instance, the formation of strong ties of identification at one level of aggregation may prevent the formation of communities at another. It may even drive people apart. Racism is not resolved – and is in fact exacerbated – by the sense of community that specific segregated neighborhoods may have developed. Certainly, in the case of wars, processes of identification at work inside each nation contribute to the breakdown of a broader community among nations.

I have argued that a community is not necessarily peaceful, and that an economy of meaning is not inherently antagonistic. Yet even when an economy of meaning is abrasive, intense, or cut-throat, it is important to consider the processes of identification that keep it together and prevent it from blowing apart or degenerating into outright violence. Similarly, a community may be harmonious, but it is nevertheless important to consider issues of negotiability and ownership of meaning and not simply assume a stable, self-sustaining unity.

In speaking of identification and negotiability, I am not referring to a choice between collaboration and competition, between agreement and struggle, or between solidarity and individual rights. Rather, I am trying to describe a dual process that is more fundamental than these moral choices.

- On the one hand, we form communities not because we fall short of an ideal of individualism or freedom, but because identification is at the very core of the social nature of our identities and so we define even our individualism and our freedom in that context.
- On the other hand, our communities give rise to economies of meaning not because we are evil, self-interested, or short-sighted, but be-

cause negotiability – and thus contestability – is at the very core of the social nature of our meanings and so we construct even our shared values in that context.

The resulting view of human nature is not reductionist, either in terms of individual utilitarianism or in terms of primordial communal togetherness. Because our identities are fundamentally constituted by processes of both identification and negotiability, our communities and our economies of meaning are inherent aspects of the social fabric in which we define who we are. Overlooking one process or the other, and especially thinking that one or the other could or should disappear to enable the other, is a misleading oversimplification of the social character of human nature.[15]

Coda II

Learning communities

I have argued in Coda I that learning involves an interaction between experience and competence. In communities of practice, the definition of competence and the production of experience are in very close interaction. Mutual engagement in a shared practice can thus be an intricate process of constant fine tuning between experience and competence. Because this process goes both ways, communities of practice are not only a context for the learning of newcomers but also, and for the same reasons, a context for new insights to be transformed into knowledge.[1]

- On the one hand, a community of practice is a living context that can give newcomers access to competence and also invite a personal experience of engagement by which to incorporate that competence into an identity of participation. When these conditions are in place, communities of practice are a privileged locus for the *acquisition* of knowledge.
- On the other hand, a well-functioning community of practice is a good context to explore radically new insights without becoming fools or stuck in some dead end. A history of mutual engagement around a joint enterprise is an ideal context for this kind of leading-edge learning, which requires a strong bond of communal competence along with a deep respect for the particularity of experience. When these conditions are in place, communities of practice are a privileged locus for the *creation* of knowledge.

This close interaction of experience and competence is a fertile ground for learning, but I have insisted that the two must remain in tension. If they settle down into a state of locked-in congruence, then learning slows down, and practice becomes stale. The concepts introduced in Part II can help describe the means by which a community of practice may keep this tension alive and thus be a learning community. Such a community includes learning, not only as a matter of course in

214

the history of its practice, but at the very core of its enterprise. As a way to build a characterization of a learning community, I will briefly rehearse the themes of each chapter in Part II.

Learning and identity in practice

Because learning transforms who we are and what we can do, it is an experience of identity. It is not just an accumulation of skills and information, but a process of becoming – to become a certain person or, conversely, to avoid becoming a certain person. Even the learning that we do entirely by ourselves eventually contributes to making us into a specific kind of person. We accumulate skills and information, not in the abstract as ends in themselves, but in the service of an identity. It is in that formation of an identity that learning can become a source of meaningfulness and of personal and social energy.

Viewed as an experience of identity, learning entails both a process and a place. It entails a process of transforming knowledge as well as a context in which to define an identity of participation. As a consequence, to support learning is not only to support the process of acquiring knowledge, but also to offer a place where new ways of knowing can be realized in the form of such an identity. If someone fails to learn as expected, it may therefore be necessary to consider, in addition to possible problems with the process, the lack of such a place as well as the competition of other places. In order to redirect learning, it may be necessary to offer learners alternative forms of participation that are as much a source of identity as they are finding elsewhere. The transformative practice of a learning community offers an ideal context for developing new understandings because the community sustains change as part of an identity of participation.

As a trajectory, an identity must incorporate a past and a future. Learning communities will become places of identity to the extent they make trajectories possible – that is, to the extent they offer a past and a future that can be experienced as a personal trajectory. In this regard, a community can strengthen the identity of participation of its members in two related ways:

1) by incorporating its members' pasts into its history – that is, by letting what they have been, what they have done, and what they know contribute to the constitution of its practice
2) by opening trajectories of participation that place engagement in its practice in the context of a valued future.

Similarly, I have argued that the experience of multimembership can become so private that it no longer fits within the enterprise of any community. The potentially difficult work of reconciliation can be facilitated by communities that endeavor to encompass, within their own practice, an increasing portion of the nexus of multimembership of their members. For instance, some workplaces are taking steps to reduce the chasm between family and work responsibilities. In other words, the work of reconciliation can be integrated in the community's enterprise and thus, to some extent, become part of a shared learning practice. Such communities will not only gain the allegiance of their members, they will also enrich their own practices.

Participation and non-participation: peripherality and marginality

When a community makes learning a central part of its enterprise, useful wisdom is not concentrated at the core of its practice. There is a wisdom of peripherality – a view of the community that can be lost to full participants. It includes paths not taken, connections overlooked, choices taken for granted. But this kind of wisdom often remains invisible even to those who hold its potential, because it can easily become marginalized within established regimes of competence. Note that there are two kinds of marginality involved here, reflecting the community–identity duality:

1) marginalities of *competence* – certain members are not full participants
2) marginalities of *experience* – certain experiences are not fully accountable to the regime of competence because they are repressed, despised, feared, or simply ignored.

Of course, these two kinds of marginality often overlap, but not always. Full participants are not immune to marginal experience.

Turning marginalities into peripheral wisdom requires identities that can play with participation and non-participation. When learning communities make such experiments a part of their regime of competence, the risks associated with exploration are not a threat to one's membership: taking risks at the margins does not imply exclusion. Note that this process does not imply weakening the core of the practice, which would leave little difference between exploration and floundering. The solidity of a shared history of practice is a social resource for further learning that must be put to work rather than dismissed. Learning communities do have a strong core, but they let peripheral and core activities interact, because it is in these interactions that they are likely to find the new experiences and new forms of competence necessary to create new knowledge. When a learning community – secure in its history of participation but encouraged and humbled by its excursions of non-participation – turns its searching gaze upon itself, it is mostly in the potential of its marginalities that it must look for the promise of its unrealized wisdoms.

Combining modes of belonging

Engagement, imagination, and alignment are all important ingredients of learning – they anchor it in practice yet make it broad, creative, and effective in the wider world. Since each mode of belonging involves trade-offs, combining them enables them to compensate for each other's shortcomings. Such combinations allow a learning community to move in various ways between participation and non-participation in order to create a richer context for learning.

The combination of engagement and imagination results in a *reflective* practice.[2] Such a practice combines the ability both to engage and to distance – to identify with an enterprise as well as to view it in context, with the eyes of an outsider. Imagination enables us to adopt other perspectives across boundaries and time, to visit "otherness" and let it speak its own language. It also allows us to include history in our sense of the present and to explore possible futures. It can produce representations and models that trigger new interpretations. In turn, engagement provides a place for imagination to land, to be negotiated in practice and realized into identities of participation. This process requires an opening of participation that allows imagination to have effects beyond itself so we may learn from it by bringing it back into a form of engagement. Otherwise, imagination is just an escape or a phantasm that merely reproduces current limitations and patterns of engagement. For instance, there is no point going on a retreat, a visit, or a sabbatical unless the new perspectives we gain in the process can find a realization in a new form of engagement upon our return. The required opening of participation is both personal and communal. Our identities must be able to absorb our new perspectives and make them part of who we are. And our communities must have a place for us that does justice to the transformations of identity that reflection and excursions can produce.

The combination of imagination and alignment produces the ability to act with respect to a broad and rich picture of the world. We align our activities and we understand why. We have a vision and it helps us situate what we are doing and make it effective. We have a big picture and we do something about it in concert with others. We can therefore embrace that big picture as part of our identity because it reflects the scope of our imagination as well as the scope of effects of our actions. In this process, our alignment can become more robust because it is part of a broad understanding of what it is about. Imagination thus helps us direct our alignment in terms of its broader effects, adapt it under shifting circumstances, and fine tune it intelligently, especially when things like instructions are unclear or inapplicable. This is the power of imagination when it is anchored in a process of alignment.

The combination of engagement and alignment brings various perspectives together in the process of creating some coordination between them. There is something unique that we can come to understand when our diverse perspectives converge in our attempts to align them for some purpose. The need to coordinate practices through mutual engagement translates into an exploration of boundaries that can serve to expand the possibilities for learning and identity on both sides. In negotiating alignment across discontinuities, we can be forced to perceive our own positions in new ways, to have new questions, to see things we had never seen before, and to derive new criteria of competence that reflect the alignment of practices. We may have to redefine our enterprises and see our own participation in a broader context. From our misunderstandings we may come to comprehend, in striking and expanded ways, the historical particularities and the ambiguities of our own actions and artifacts. In the process our views bounce back, reinterpreted. In this regard, I have argued that multimembership is a critical source of learning because it forces an alignment of perspectives in the negotiation of an engaged identity. Identity then becomes a living bridge – the dynamic locus of alignment – the subject and the object of the work of reconciliation necessary to bring diverging perspectives together, understand them through each other, and find a way to engage them with one another.

Combining these modes of belonging is not only a matter of finding ways in which they overlap; it is also a matter of timing. There are seasons for various combinations of each, and part of a learning community's task is to understand the rhythms of its own learning in order to find optimal opportunities for combining these modes.[3]

Reconfiguring identification and negotiability

If learning involves the ability to negotiate new meanings and become a new person, then it also involves new relations of identification and negotiability, new forms of membership and ownership of meaning, and thus changing positions within communities and economies of meaning. In this context, a learning community must pay attention to the cost of membership and to the blinders it creates, remembering that letting go of one's identity is both a loss and a liberation.

Identification and negotiability are structural issues. They cannot be manipulated in a vacuum because they are defined within systems of social relations with structural interdependencies. They are not just issues of motivation that can be addressed independently of content. From this standpoint, learning is a process of social reconfiguration. It transforms communities and economies of meaning. For instance, enabling children to grow up in the context of a family involves a structural transformation of that family as much as developmental changes in the members involved.

A learning community confronts structural issues of identification and negotiability both internally and externally.

- *Internally,* learning is a reconfiguration of its own structure as community and economy of meaning. For instance, differences in ownership of meaning distinguish newcomers and old-timers. Newcomers may identify with a community as much as old-timers do, and they may engage in many of the same activities. Nonetheless, their ability – both in terms of capability and legitimacy – to determine for themselves the value and appropriateness of their actions and the artifacts they produce does not belong to them yet. For newcomers to become full members they must gain new positions in the economy of meaning. Similarly, many of the characteristics of a learning community described in this coda (opening trajectories, core–periphery interactions, exploring marginalities) require processes of reconfiguration.

- *Externally,* a learning community confronts issues of identification and negotiability through its position in broader configurations. For claims processors to gain increased ownership of the meanings of their activities and artifacts would involve a reconfiguration not only of their own community, but also of their relations with other practices and of the economies of meaning in which they are to take new responsibilities for the meanings of what they do. Indeed, learning within a community does not necessarily lead to an increased level of negotiability in a broader context. An internal reconfiguration may reflect our new identities, understandings, perspectives, and skills. Yet, once we see our own practices as located in broader economies of meaning, we may come to the conclusion that the meanings we learn to produce locally have little currency in the wider scheme of things. It is therefore incumbent on a learning community to deal with its position in various communities and economies and with respect to various enterprises, styles, and discourses. It must seek the reconfigurations necessary to make its learning empowering – locally and in other relevant contexts.

A learning community is therefore fundamentally involved in social reconfiguration: its own internally as well as its position within broader configurations.

Reconfiguring relations of identification and negotiability is as significant for learning as is access to specific pieces of information. Issues like the acquisition of specific subject matters, involvement in civic concerns, and people's relations to their jobs are actually implicated in the structure of economies of meaning, even though they are often cast in terms of personal choices and abilities. Hence a notion like "information society" does not displace, but indeed begs the question of, identity. Of course, availability of information is important in supporting learning. But information by itself, removed from forms of participation, is not knowledge; it can actually be disempowering, overwhelming, and alienating. Looking at a very technical article full of indecipherable formulas can confirm in a very stark fashion our lack of negotiability. Access to information without negotiability serves only to intensify the alienating effects of non-participation.

What makes information knowledge – what makes it empowering – is the way in which it can be integrated within an identity of participation. When information does not build up to an identity of participation, it remains alien, literal, fragmented, unnegotiable. It is not just that it is disconnected from other pieces of relevant information, but that it fails to translate into a way of being in the world coherent enough to be enacted in practice. Therefore, to know in practice is to have a certain identity so that information gains the coherence of a form of participation. In making information more widely available, what the technological advances of a so-called information society really do is create wider, more complex, and more diversified economies of meaning and communities. With respect to the potential for learning communities, issues of identification and negotiability are then heightened, not transcended.

Epilogue
Design

Synopsis
Design for learning

Learning cannot be designed. Ultimately, it belongs to the realm of experience and practice. It follows the negotiation of meaning; it moves on its own terms. It slips through the cracks; it creates its own cracks. Learning happens, design or no design.

And yet there are few more urgent tasks than to design social infrastructures that foster learning. This is true not only of schools and universities, but also of all sorts of organizations in the public and private sectors, and even of entities usually not called organizations, like states and nations. In fact, the whole human world is itself fast becoming one large organization, which is the object of design and which must support the learning we need in order to ensure there is to be a tomorrow. Those who can understand the informal yet structured, experiential yet social, character of learning – and can translate their insight into designs in the service of learning – will be the architects of our tomorrow.

By way of conclusion, I will use the concepts introduced in this book to discuss some issues of design as they relate to learning and practice, and by extension to community and identity. This discussion will do two things. It will provide a summary of the main themes and, at the same time, illustrate the use that can be made of the conceptual framework I have outlined.

A perspective on learning

I have argued that the perspectives we bring to our endeavors are important because they shape both what we perceive and what we do. As a prelude to talking about design, I will start with a quick review of the perspective on learning inherent in this book. Although my examples were drawn mostly from the workplace, the relevance of the concepts I introduced is not limited to work settings; it extends to all kinds of settings, including the school, the playground, the street, and

225

the home. In fact, seen from the perspective of this book, learning in all these settings is more similar than different.

What claims processors learn is clearly the practice of a specific, easily identifiable community, one whose history is a response to the explicit demands of an institutionalized corporation. But what about the learning we do while reading newspapers or watching television, resolving a conflict among our children, learning how to cook Chinese food or how to use a new program on our personal computer? Indeed, we often learn without having any intention of becoming full members in any specifiable community of practice, or for that matter in any other kind of community.

Yet, the relevance of a social perspective is not limited to special situations of learning, because all learning eventually gains its significance in the kind of person we become – whether we are in a school, on a job, at a rally, among our kin, or watching television. This does not mean that all learning is best done in interaction with others. Just as there are tasks that are best done in groups and others that are best done by oneself, some learning is best done in groups and some learning is best done by oneself. At issue is what defines learning as learning. For instance, is reading a mystery novel an act of learning? What about a serious novel? What about a casual conversation at a party? What about a formal meeting? The difference between mere doing and learning, or between mere entertainment and learning, is not a difference in kind of activity. It is not that one is mindless and the other thoughtful, that one is hard and the other easy, or that one is fun and the other arduous. It is that learning – whatever form it takes – changes who we are by changing our ability to participate, to belong, to negotiate meaning. And this ability is configured socially with respect to practices, communities, and economies of meaning where it shapes our identities.

This social perspective on learning may be summarized succinctly by the following principles.

- ♦ *Learning is inherent in human nature:* it is an ongoing and integral part of our lives, not a special kind of activity separable from the rest of our lives (Introduction).

- ♦ *Learning is first and foremost the ability to negotiate new meanings:* it involves our whole person in a dynamic interplay of participation and reification. It is not reducible to its mechanics (information, skills, behavior), and focusing on the mechanics at the expense of meaning tends to render learning problematic (Chapter 1).

♦ *Learning creates emergent structures:* it requires enough structure and continuity to accumulate experience and enough perturbation and discontinuity to continually renegotiate meaning. In this regard, communities of practice constitute elemental social learning structures (Chapter 3).

♦ *Learning is fundamentally experiential and fundamentally social:* it involves our own experience of participation and reification as well as forms of competence defined in our communities (Chapter 2). In fact, learning can be defined as a realignment of experience and competence, whichever pulls the other. It is therefore impaired when the two are either too distant or too closely congruent to produce the necessary generative tension (Coda I).

♦ *Learning transforms our identities:* it transforms our ability to participate in the world by changing all at once who we are, our practices, and our communities (Chapter 3).

♦ *Learning constitutes trajectories of participation:* it builds personal histories in relation to the histories of our communities, thus connecting our past and our future in a process of individual and collective becoming (Chapters 3 and 6).

♦ *Learning means dealing with boundaries:* it creates and bridges boundaries; it involves multimembership in the constitution of our identities, thus connecting – through the work of reconciliation – our multiple forms of participation as well as our various communities (Chapters 4 and 6).

♦ *Learning is a matter of social energy and power:* it thrives on identification and depends on negotiability; it shapes and is shaped by evolving forms of membership and of ownership of meaning – structural relations that combine participation and nonparticipation in communities and economies of meaning (Chapters 7 and 9).

♦ *Learning is a matter of engagement:* it depends on opportunities to contribute actively to the practices of communities that we value and that value us, to integrate their enterprises into our understanding of the world, and to make creative use of their respective repertoires (Chapters 2 and 8).

♦ *Learning is a matter of imagination:* it depends on processes of orientation, reflection, and exploration to place our identities and practices in a broader context (Chapter 8).

♦ *Learning is a matter of alignment:* it depends on our connection to frameworks of convergence, coordination, and conflict resolution that determine the social effectiveness of our actions (Chapter 8).

♦ *Learning involves an interplay between the local and the global:* it takes place in practice, but it defines a global context for its own locality. The creation of learning communities thus depends on a dynamic combination of engagement, imagination, and alignment to make this interplay between the local and the global an engine of new learning (Chapter 5, Coda II).

Design and practice

By "design" I mean a systematic, planned, and reflexive colonization of time and space in the service of an undertaking.[1] This perspective includes not only the production of artifacts, but also the design of social processes such as organizations or instruction. Indeed, organizational design and instructional design have become disciplines in their own right.

In any discussion of design for learning, it is important to reiterate that communities of practice have been around for a very long time. They are as old as humankind and existed long before we started to concern ourselves with systematic design for learning. Communities of practice already exist throughout our societies – inside and across organizations, schools, and families – in both realized and unrealized forms.

1) Some are *potential.* They are possible communities among people who are related somehow, and who would gain from sharing and developing a practice together.

2) Some are *active.* They function as communities of practice, actively pursuing an enterprise, negotiating their forms of participation, and developing their own histories.

3) Some are *latent.* They exist as a kind of "diaspora" among people who share past histories and can use these histories as resources.

Communities of practice are thus not a novelty. They are not a new solution to existing problems; in fact, they are just as likely to have been involved in the development of these problems. In particular, they are not a design fad, a new kind of organizational unit or pedagogical device to be implemented.

Communities of practice are about content – about learning as a living experience of negotiating meaning – not about form. In this sense, they cannot be legislated into existence or defined by decree. They can be recognized, supported, encouraged, and nurtured, but they are not reified, designable units. Practice itself is not amenable to design. In other words, one can articulate patterns or define procedures, but neither the patterns nor the procedures produce the practice as it unfolds. One can design systems of accountability and policies for communities of practice to live by, but one cannot design the practices that will emerge in response to such institutional systems. One can design roles, but one cannot design the identities that will be constructed through these roles. One can design visions, but one cannot design the allegiance necessary to align energies behind those visions. One can produce affordances[2] for the negotiation of meaning, but not meaning itself. One can design work processes but not work practices; one can design a curriculum but not learning. One can attempt to institutionalize a community of practice, but the community of practice itself will slip through the cracks and remain distinct from its institutionalization.

This perspective suggests an addition to the list of principles just presented:

> ♦ *Learning cannot be designed:* it can only be designed *for* – that is, facilitated or frustrated.

Structure of the Epilogue

The Epilogue contains three chapters.

- Chapter 10 outlines a skeletal "architecture" for learning derived from the argument of this book. By this I mean that I will recast the conceptual framework developed so far into a design framework, laying out basic questions that must be addressed and basic components that must be provided by a design for learning.
- Chapters 11 and 12 apply this design framework in discussing two kinds of design that involve learning in a crucial way: organizations and education. There are many ways in which these two kinds of endeavor differ, but both must provide institutional support for learning and, in this respect, have much in common. These two domains of application are only examples. There are many other potential domains of application, including technology, facilities, marketing, and government.

Chapter 10
Learning architectures

When designing houses, architects frame their design according to conceptual architectures that capture the physiological and cultural aspects of human life relevant to the construction of dwellings. Architects know about sizes, shapes, colors, temperatures, and lighting. They think about issues such as open versus divided spaces or functionality versus aesthetics. They include basic components of living quarters such as facilities for physiological functions (eating, resting, bathing), social activities (congregating, playing, working), and storage (food, clothing, vehicles). When designing an office space, however, they frame their design according to a different architecture.

In other fields as well, designers usually have at their disposal some conceptual architectures reflecting the theories and perspectives that their professional communities have developed through conceptual analyses of their domain of design. The purpose of a conceptual architecture is to lay down the general elements of design. It is not a recipe; it does not tell a designer how to perform a specific design. But it does state what needs to be in place. It is a tool that can guide a design by outlining:

1) the general questions, choices, and trade-offs to address – these define the dimensions of a design "space"
2) the general shape of what needs to be achieved – the basic components and facilities to provide.

Conceptual architectures can exist at different levels of analysis. For instance, designers of computer systems base their designs on conceptual architectures at different levels, with different components and trade-offs. At the level of information processing, the basic elements include receiving, transforming, storing, displaying, and transmitting information. At the level of user interface, however, basic elements include facilities such as windows management, document management, network services, and help systems.

230

There are analogs for learning. For instance, a physiological analysis would address issues such as span of attention, retention, short-term and long-term memory, modes of perception, and fatigue.[1] In this chapter, I will show how my analysis of learning in terms of practice and identity can translate – at that level of analysis – into a conceptual architecture for learning. I will do this in two steps:

1) extracting from earlier chapters four issues that constitute basic dimensions of the "space" of design for learning
2) using the modes of belonging (Chapter 8) as basic components of a learning design.

In order to provide a synoptic picture quickly, I will merely list the basic issues and components here. The main concepts have already been discussed, and illustrations will be provided in the next two chapters, where I will apply this conceptual architecture to issues of organizational and educational design.

Dimensions

When it concerns practice and identity, design inevitably confronts fundamental issues of meaning, time, space, and power. These aspects can be captured with four dualities (as summarized in Figure 10.1.), which represent four basic dimensions of the challenge of designing for learning.

The idea behind these dualities is not a choice between two poles but the need to address the tension inherent in their interaction. Designing for learning is not a matter of chaos versus order or narrow locality versus abstract globality, but a matter of combining them productively.

Participation and reification

I have argued that participation and reification are dimensions of both practice and identity. As such they are two avenues for influencing the future – whether the direction of a practice or the trajectory of a person. In this sense, participation and reification are two complementary aspects of design that create two kinds of affordance for negotiating meaning.

1) One can make sure that some artifacts are in place – tools, plans, procedures, schedules, curriculums – so that the future will have to be organized around them.

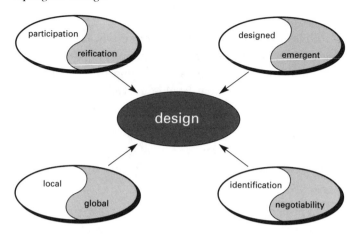

Figure 10.1. Four dimensions of design for learning.

2) One can also make sure that the right people are at the right place in the right kind of relation to make something happen.

Of course, participation and reification come as a pair. As a result, design cannot simply involve a choice between the two. One cannot assume that reification is unproblematically translated into practice; and participation is not necessarily coordinated enough to constitute a design. This suggests the following principle.

♦ *Design for practice is always distributed between participation and reification – and its realization depends on how these two sides fit together.*

As a consequence, the process of design involves decisions about how to distribute a design between participation and reification – what to reify, when, and with respect to what forms of participation; whom to involve, when, and with respect to what forms of reification. It is through these choices that design becomes a resource for the negotiation of meaning. These choices entail all the trade-offs of participation and reification I have discussed: rigidity versus adaptability, partiality of people versus ambiguity of artifacts, limited scope and mobility versus limited relevance and stability of interpretation, and so on.

The designed and the emergent

Practice and identity have their own logic – the logic of engagement, of mutual accountability, of trajectories and boundaries – of which design is only one structuring element. I have argued that the structure of practice is emergent, both highly perturbable and highly resilient, always reconstituting itself in the face of new events. Similarly, the structure of identity emerges out of the process of building a trajectory. It is this emergent character that gives practice and identity their ability to negotiate meaning anew. In a world that is not predictable, improvisation and innovation are more than desirable, they are essential.

The relation of design to practice is therefore always indirect. It takes place through the ongoing definition of an enterprise by the community pursuing it. In other words, practice cannot be the result of design, but instead constitutes a response to design.

- A piece of software, for instance, is the *result* of design. If it does not execute as expected then there is a bug. This bug indicates a faulty design stemming from an incomplete or inaccurate specification, or from a lack of detailed analysis.
- By contrast, practice is (among other things) a *response* to design. Unexpected adaptations of the design are inherent in the process. They do not necessarily indicate a lack of specification. In fact, they may very well indicate a healthy response, which allows a design to be realized meaningfully in specific – but always underspecified – situations.

In this context, increasingly detailed prescriptions of practice carry increasing risks of being turned around, especially when a form of institutional accountability is tied to them. Indeed, the response of satisfying (or giving the appearance of satisfying) the prescription may be at odds in fundamental ways with its design intents, as when students focus on test taking instead of the subject matter, or when managers push their quota instead of taking care of business. This suggests the following principle.

- *There is an inherent uncertainty between design and its realization in practice, since practice is not the result of design but rather a response to it.*

As a consequence, the challenge of design is not a matter of getting rid of the emergent, but rather of including it and making it an opportunity. It is to balance the benefits and costs of prescription and understand the trade-offs involved in specifying in advance. When it comes to design for learning, more is not necessarily better. In this regard, a robust design always has an opportunistic side: it is always – in a sense to be defined carefully for each case – a minimalist design.

The local and the global

I have argued that, owing to the inherently limited scope of our engagement, no practice is itself global. Even when it deals directly with global issues (I gave the example of an office at the UN), a practice remains local in terms of engagement. From this standpoint design will create relations, not between the global and the local, but among localities in their constitution of the global. No practice has the full picture. No practice subsumes another.

Designing for learning, therefore, cannot be based on a division of labor between learners and nonlearners, between those who organize learning and those who realize it, or between those who create meaning and those who execute. It cannot be fully assumed by a separate management, educational, or training community. Communities of practice are already involved in the design of their own learning because ultimately they will decide what they need to learn, what it takes to be a full participant, and how newcomers should be introduced into the community (no matter what other training these newcomers receive elsewhere). Whenever a process, course, or system is being designed, it is thus essential to involve the affected communities of practice.

To say that communities of practice must be involved in the design of their own learning is not to suggest that a local perspective is inherently superior. Recognizing that communities of practice will generate their own response to design does not imply that they must be left to their own devices. Indeed, communities of practice are only part of the broader constellations in which their learning is relevant. Every practice is hostage to its own past and its own locality. In the process of organizing its learning, a community must have access to other practices. Designing for learning always requires new connections among localities, connections that do justice to the inherent knowledgeability of engagement in practice while at the same time recognizing its inherent locality.

This complex relation between the local and the global can be expressed by the following paradox of design:

♦ *No community can fully design the learning of another.*

And at the same time:

♦ *No community can fully design its own learning.*

As a consequence, design for learning cannot cleanly separate between conception and realization, between planning and implementation; it must instead aim to combine different kinds of knowledgeability so they inform each other. A design, then, is not primarily a specification (or even an underspecification) but a boundary object that functions as a communication artifact around which communities of practice can negotiate their contribution, their position, and their alignment.

Identification and negotiability

As a process of colonizing time and space, design requires the power to influence the negotiation of meaning. In order to have an effect, it must shape (or form) communities and economies of meaning. Inherent in the process of design is the question of how the power to define, adapt, or interpret the design is distributed. Design represents a perspective, which may be more or less shared by those affected. The process of design does not inherently entail the privileging of certain perspectives at the expense of others, but such privileging is rarely completely avoidable. There is a cost to privileging in that it curtails negotiation and creates fragmentation among constituencies.

Design is a stake in the ground, something on which to take a stand. In this regard, it is a proposal of identity:

1) it creates a focus for identification – and possibly for non-identification
2) it is a bid for ownership of meaning – and possibly for sharing this ownership.

Design for learning must generate social energy at the same time it seeks to direct this energy. It must set up a framework, but it depends on this framework being negotiable in practice. This dilemma can be summarized as follows.

♦ *Design creates fields of identification and negotiability that orient the practices and identities of those involved to various forms of participation and non-participation.*

As a consequence, design can invite allegiance or be satisfied with mere compliance; it can thrive on participation or impose itself through non-participation. It can seek enough identification to focus energy on its realization; or it may prefer to be less dependent on widely shared inspiration. It may seek a realization by restricting negotiability and refusing to share the ownership of its meaning; or, on the contrary, it may endeavor to share this ownership and endow all involved with enough negotiability to decide how to participate in the process meaningfully.

A design space

These dimensions are fundamental because they reflect the inevitable confrontation of design with issues of meaning, time, space, and power, and also because they cannot be reduced to one another. Emergence can be local (improvisation) or global (patterns). Localizing decision making can involve sharing ownership of meaning, or preventing such sharing. Dealing with one dimension may help with the others, but it does not obviate the need to face all of them. Making choices between participation and reification does not in itself resolve issues of authority, connect the local and the global, or balance the designed and the emergent, though it is an aspect of addressing each of these challenges.

Each of these dimensions involves distinct – but interrelated – trade-offs and challenges: they present their own opportunities and obstacles and their own resources and constraints. A given design entails choices, inventions, and solutions along each dimension. These dimensions thus define a "space" of possible approaches to design problems, in which a given design is located by the way it addresses each dimension. For example, a meeting combines a group of people with a reified agenda; it can be run with more or less strict adherence to the agenda; it can depend on local expertise or invite external contributions; it can rely more or less on the leadership of one person.

The benefit of such a multiplicity of related but distinct dimensions is that it opens up the space of design by decoupling the issues involved. For instance, discussions of organizations in terms of the formal versus the informal often conflate these dimensions. What is simply local is often called informal, even though the local can be extremely formalized in its own ways – for instance, an after-hours softball team, a playground clique, or a reading group. Similarly, what reflects the purview of positions of authority is often called formal, even when it bypasses reified institutional channels. Having a richer space of design possibilities allows for more innovative approaches to problems. For example, decoupling issues of locality and globality from issues of authority can suggest new solutions by which connections between localities can bypass hierarchical channels.

Components

In addressing these dimensions of design, a learning architecture must offer facilities for each of the modes of belonging introduced

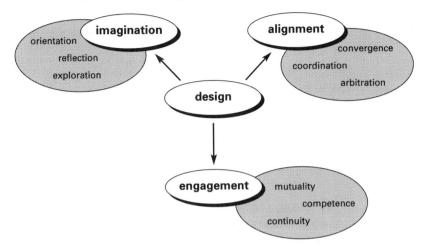

Figure 10.2. Three infrastructures of learning.

in Chapter 8. Indeed, it is by combining these three modes that we can form learning communities as discussed in Coda II. The challenge of design, then, is to support the work of engagement, imagination, and alignment. Here, I will use these modes as the main infrastructural components of a learning architecture. For each, I will list some examples of facilities, as summarized in Figure 10.2. (Note that the following lists are intended to be illustrative rather than exhaustive.)

Facilities of engagement

Supporting engagement is supporting the formation of communities of practice, with all the caveats previously mentioned about the ability of design interventions to do so. As a context for learning, engagement is not just a matter of activity, but of community building, inventiveness, social energy, and emergent knowledgeability. To support these processes, an infrastructure of engagement should include facilities of mutuality, competence, and continuity.

- *Mutuality*
    1) *interactional facilities:* physical (and virtual) spaces; interactive technologies and communication facilities that extend mutual access in time and space; time for interaction and travel budgets
    2) *joint tasks:* things to do together; availability for help
    3) *peripherality:* boundary encounters; ways of belonging to various degrees, peripheral participation, entry points; observation, casual encounters, open houses

- *Competence*
    1) *initiative and knowledgeability:* activities that bring about the knowledgeability of engagement; occasions for applying skills, devising solutions, and making decisions; problems that engage energy, creativity, and inventiveness
    2) *accountability:* occasions for exercising judgment and for mutual evaluation; recognizable style; negotiation of joint enterprises
    3) *tools:* artifacts that support competence; discourses, terms and concepts; delegation facilities (e.g., automation that allows practitioners to focus on more meaningful tasks)
- *Continuity*
    1) *reificative memory:* repositories of information, documentation, and tracking; retrieval mechanisms
    2) *participative memory:* generational encounters, apprenticeship systems; paradigmatic trajectories; storytelling

Facilities of imagination

The possibility of engagement is critical to learning, but it can be narrow. Although communities of practice are places of learning, the learning they enable does not necessarily include expansive images of history, of possibilities, or of complex systems writ large. It takes imagination in order for learning to encompass and deal with a broader context. Toward this end, an infrastructure of imagination should include facilities of orientation, reflection, and exploration.

- *Orientation*
    1) *location in space:* reification of constellations, maps and other visualization tools, open spaces
    2) *location in time:* long-term trajectories, lore, museums
    3) *location in meaning:* explanations, stories, examples
    4) *location in power:* organizational charts, process transparency
- *Reflection* – models and representations of patterns; facilities for comparisons with other practices; retreats, time off, conversations, sabbaticals, and other breaks in rhythm
- *Exploration* – opportunities and tools for trying things out; envisioning possible futures and possible trajectories; creating alternative scenarios, pushing boundaries, prototypes; play and simulations

Facilities of alignment

Imagination can open up practices and identities beyond engagement, but it is not necessarily effective in connecting learning to broader enterprises. Through alignment, we can learn to have effects and contribute to tasks that are defined beyond our engagement. In order to make this possible, an infrastructure of alignment should include facilities of convergence, coordination, and jurisdiction.

- *Convergence*
  1) common focus, cause, or interest; direction, vision; shared understanding, creed, values, principles
  2) allegiance, leadership, sources of inspiration, persuasion
- *Coordination*
  1) *standards and methods:* processes, procedures, plans, deadlines, and schedules; division of labor; styles and discourses
  2) *communication:* information transmission, spread of novelty, renegotiation
  3) *boundary facilities:* boundary practices, brokers, boundary objects, support for multimembership
  4) *feedback facilities:* data collection, accounting, measurements
- *Jurisdiction* – policies, contracts, due processes; mediation, arbitration, conflict resolution; enforcement, distribution of authority

A design framework

A learning architecture is not a new classification system for existing facilities. The point is not to wonder, say, under which heading technical databases fit. The point is rather to provide a framework to ask how a specific design – including combinations of traditional facilities such as real estate, information technology, and organizational structure – serves the different requirements of the learning architecture. So, given a spatial arrangement, a network system, or a curriculum, the idea is to be able to ask how such a design addresses the four dimensions and provides facilities that support engagement, imagination, and alignment. As I argued in Coda II, engagement, imagination, and alignment work best in combination, even though their respective demands may at times conflict. The challenge, then, is to enable a combination of all three without letting the need for one be fulfilled at the expense of the other two.

To illustrate how the components articulate with the dimensions, the matrix shown in Figure 10.3 lists various ways in which engagement, imagination, and alignment facilities address each of the four dimensions.[2] For instance, the local–global issue can be addressed through multimembership, maps, and standards, respectively.

	engagement	imagination	alignment
participation/ reification	combining them meaningfully in actions, interactions and the creation of shared histories	stories, playing with forms, recombinations, assumptions	styles and discourses
designed/ emergent	situated improvisation within a regime of accountability	scenarios, possible worlds, simulations, perceiving new broad patterns	communication, feedback, coordination, renegotiation, realignment
local/global	multimembership, brokering, peripherality, conversations	models, maps, representations, visits, tours	standards, shared infrastructures, centers of authority
identification/ negotiability	mutuality through shared action, situated negotiation, marginalization	new trajectories, empathy, stereotypes, explanations	inspiration, fields of influence, reciprocity of power relations

Figure 10.3. Articulating components and dimensions.

In Chapters 11 and 12, I will use the framework of a learning architecture to discuss issues of organizational and educational design. Note that my purpose is not to propose organizational or educational theories. I do not cover the topics exhaustively or systematically, and many of the points I make are not all that original. What is of interest here is to couch some organizational and educational issues in terms of a coherent conceptual framework that provides new ways to think about them. The exercise is meant to illustrate the kinds of questions and perspectives that can be derived from this learning theory.

Chapter 11
Organizations

Organizations are social designs directed at practice. Indeed, it is through the practices they bring together that organizations can do what they do, know what they know, and learn what they learn. Communities of practice are thus key to an organization's competence and to the evolution of that competence. I have argued, however, that communities of practice differ from institutional entities along three dimensions.

1) They negotiate their own enterprise, though they may at times construct a conforming response to institutional prescriptions (Chapter 2).
2) They arise, evolve, and dissolve according to their own learning, though they may do so in response to institutional events (Chapter 3).
3) They shape their own boundaries, though their boundaries may at times happen to be congruent with institutional boundaries (Chapter 4).

The contrast detailed here is one between organizational design and lived practice. From this perspective, there are two views of an organization like Alinsu:

1) the *designed organization,* which I will often call the "institution" to distinguish it from the organization as lived in practice
2) the *practice* (or, more accurately, the constellation of practices), which gives life to the organization and is often a response to the designed organization.

Both aspects contribute to making the organization what it is. Indeed, the organization itself could be defined as the interaction of these two aspects. Besides corporations like Alinsu, this characterization applies to nonprofit organizations and even subunits such as agencies, departments, or business units. It would also apply to many scientific fields,

241

professional organizations, religions, and political parties that have institutionalized their existence.

In exploring the relations of learning, design, and practice in organizations, I will use the framework introduced in Chapter 10 in order to

1) revisit the four dimensions of design in the context of organizational design

2) look at some aspects of organizational design from the perspective of an architecture of learning based on engagement,
imagination, and alignment.

Note that my discussion focuses on design and learning, without assuming a specific organizational form. It is often specialized communities of practice that deal with the design of an organization, and in this
sense it may appear that I am speaking of management. But my discussion does not assume this specific division of labor. It assumes a design
directed at a constellation of practices, but not the existence of a separate management community from which decisions and power ema-
nate. Organizations that were configured differently would still face the
issues I discuss.

Moreover, these issues are inherent in organizational design, whether
organizational politics are benign or acrimonious. Even if we had
achieved peace on earth or were angels in heaven, the organization of
practices would still face these challenges. That we are no angels – that
our organizational experience includes fear, jealousy, greed, control,
hoarding, deception, and the entire range of human relations in organizational politics – may well exacerbate the issues I will address, but is
not their primary cause.

Dimensions of organizational design

In the next four sections, I discuss issues of organizational practice in terms of the four dimensions of design introduced in Chapter 10:

1) participation and reification – trade-offs of institutionalization

2) the designed and the emergent – two sources of structure in
organizations

3) the local and the global – combining local forms of knowledgeability

4) fields of identification and negotiability – institutional identities as key to organizational learning.

Participation and reification: challenges of institutionalization

Organizational design requires the judicious use of institutionalization, that is, of the production of reflexive reifications such as policies, curriculums, standards, roles, job descriptions, laws, histories, affiliations, and the like. What is institutionalized becomes public, easier to pay attention to, and better able to cross boundaries, but there are costs to institutionalization.

- Institutionalization creates fixed points around which to negotiate alignment – but it tends to become frozen in reification and create a momentum of its own as diverse practices become invested in it for their own reasons.
- It offers opportunities for drastic change because it can reflect radically new perspectives – but it has a limited ability to mobilize the power of practice.
- By traveling across constellations, it can provide material for imagination and bring a sense of the global to various localities – but it can also engender alienation to the extent that it represents foreign viewpoints without allowing negotiability.
- In opening up a public economy of meaning and creating reified commitments that participants can refer to, it can restrain domination by specific interest groups – but it can also become the instrument of such domination.
- Processes, relations, and shared definitions that are institutionalized become more amenable to design, to management, and to measurement – but institutionalization consumes energy. It requires continual maintenance. It takes practices to produce it, sustain it, interpret it, enforce it, and keep it relevant.

Institutionalization must be in the service of practice. Practice is where policies, procedures, authority relations, and other institutional structures become effective. Institutionalization in itself cannot make anything happen. Communities of practice are the locus of "real work." Their practices are where the formal rests on the informal, where the visible counts on the invisible, where the official meets the everyday. Designing processes and policies is important, but in the end it is practice that produces results, not the processes and policies. The challenge is to support rather than displace the knowledgeability of practice. With a lack of institutionalization there may not be enough material to hold the organization together. Conversely, excessive institutionalization stalls the organization insofar as the practices end up serving the institutional apparatus, rather than the other way around.

Questions of the kind derived from this dimension of organizational design include the following.

1) What should be institutionalized and when should participation be relied upon?

2) What forms of participation are required to give meaning to institutional reification?

3) At what point is institutionalization a distraction or a misplaced use of resources?

4) Where are the points of leverage at which organizational interventions can support learning in practice?

The designed and the emergent: organizations as dual structures

Within an organization with its charter, its vision, its strategies, and its institutional structure, each community of practice has its own indigenous enterprise, its own vision, its own strategies. I have insisted that viewing practice as a response to but not a direct result of design does not belittle the influence of the institutional context on communities of practice. Many communities of practice do indeed arise in the process of giving existence to an institutional design; they may even owe their existence to the institutional context in which they arise. It may often seem, as it does for the claims processors, that the institutional setting causes the production of the practice and drives its history. Yet even when the existence of a community of practice is a response to an institutional mandate, it is not the mandate that produces the practice, it is the community.

Institutional design and practice are both sources of structuring in their own right. They interact and influence each other, but they maintain their own integrity as sources of structure. The informal is not without form, but its form is emergent, reflecting the logic of improvisation inherent in the negotiation of meaning. An organization is therefore the meeting of two sources of structure: the designed structure of the institution and the emergent structure of practice.

• Institutions define roles, qualifications, and the distribution of authority – but unless institutional roles can find a realization as identities in practice, they are unlikely to connect with the conduct of everyday affairs.

- Institutions establish relations of accountability through charters, targets, and systems of measurements – but each community of practice also defines its own regime of accountability. In fact, an institutional system of accountability is unlikely to be very effective unless it is integrated into the definition of competence of the communities of practice it is meant to align.

- Institutions provide a repertoire of procedures, contracts, rules, processes, and policies – but communities must incorporate these institutional artifacts into their own practices in order to decide in specific situations what they mean in practice, when to comply with them and when to ignore them.

The tension between practice and institution cannot be resolved once and for all. In fact, there must be a certain amount of free play between them. If the practice of claims processing was not distinct from the institution, the job would be impossible. I always remember a story I heard as a child about Swiss customs officers who wanted to protest their working conditions but could not legally engage in a traditional strike for reasons of national security. So they decided simply to work "by the book." Their clever but irreproachable protest of impeccable institutional compliance brought the whole system to a halt, with growing lines of exasperated vacationers, outraged commuters, and furious truck drivers.

The point of design for learning is to make organizations ready for the emergent by serving the inventiveness of practice and the potential for innovation inherent in its emergent structure. Institution and practice cannot merge because they are different entities. The relation between them is not one of congruence, but one of negotiated alignment. And the alignment is never secured; it must constantly be negotiated anew, because it is by being of different natures that they complement each other as sources of structure.

Questions of the kind derived from this dimension of organizational design include the following.

1) How can the design be kept minimal and still ensure continuity and coherence?
2) What are the obstacles to responsiveness to the emergent?
3) What are the provisions for renegotiating the design under new circumstances?

4) What are the mechanisms by which emergent patterns can be perceived?

5) How can communities of practice that take care of emergent issues feed their learning back into the organization?

The local and the global: constellations of knowledgeabilities

Most organizations are beyond the scope of engagement of their members. We belong to an organization by engaging in some of its constituent practices. It is therefore necessary to understand organizations in terms of relations among localities with their own perspectives on how they belong to the organization, their own interpretation of its charter, and their own forms of knowledgeability.

I have argued that practices never subsume each other. Because the scope of mutual engagement is essentially bounded, extending our purview always involves trade-offs between kinds of complexity. A global overview surrenders details of texture in order to highlight broader connections. These kinds of trade-off are inherent in the process of re-framing one practice in terms of another, as when claims processors fill out production reports for accounting.

Even when practices take responsibility for the organization as such, they remain local in the way they pursue that enterprise. In other words, practices like management are forms of locality as is any other practice. They must take the institution, not the constellation of practices, as their purview. No one's purview is the constellation itself, because no one has that scope of engagement. As a consequence, a constellation, even from the inside, is always known with respect to specific forms of engagement, and therefore always known partially. There is no global view of a constellation that can be achieved at the level of practice.

Of course, certain views can have more currency than others. In corporations like Alinsu, the perspective of management is definitely privileged with respect to the definition of the organization. But it is important not to confuse the institutional privileges certain perspectives obtain within an economy of meaning with intrinsic qualities putatively possessed by these perspectives. Having clout within an economy of meaning merely expands the scope of influence of a perspective; it does not make that perspective inherently global.

It may be tempting to picture the design of an organization as a kind of umbrella: an overarching structure on top, with practices underneath unified by virtue of being under the same umbrella. Indeed, diagrams of the formal versus the informal almost always place the formal on top and the informal below. Yet, it is more accurate to view organizational design as a method by which a set of practices manages itself as a constellation. In this sense, the design of an organization is not so much an overarching structure as it is a boundary object. It connects communities of practice into an organization by crossing boundaries. It does not sit on top; it moves in between. It does not unify by transcending; it connects and disconnects. It does not reign; it travels, to be shaped and appropriated in the context of specific practices.

In this regard, it is as important for the design to create channels of communication among practices as it is to create institutional abstractions for them to live by. The fundamental principle is to connect and combine the diverse knowledgeabilities that exist in a constellation of practices. The challenge of organizational design is thus not to find the one kind of knowledgeability that subsumes all others, but on the contrary to coordinate multiple kinds of knowledgeability into a process of organizational learning. Sharing a vision, then, is being able to see each other as well as envisioning common goals.

Questions of the kind derived from this dimension of organizational design include the following.

1) Does the organizational design serve as a communication tool?
2) Does it help the various forms of knowledgeability involved in a constellation to recognize each other?
3) Are information flows reciprocal?
4) Are there forms of multimembership that connect the local and the global?
5) Which perspectives are privileged and which are marginalized or made invisible?

Fields of identification and negotiability

An organization gives rise to fields of both identification and negotiability. Even in the most competitive, aggressive, and ruthless organizational environment, there must somehow be enough identification that people argue and machinate rather than kill each other. And even in the most benign organizations, there are enough perspectives, diverging interests, and points of contention that issues of negotiability and ownership of meaning must be dealt with.

The field of identification of a community of practice includes the ways it organizes membership internally as well as the ways it can assert its belonging to the organization. Its field of negotiability includes the control it has over its own activities as well as its ability to affect the institutional environment with the meanings that it produces. For instance, the field of negotiability of claims processors is internally rather invasive in the sense that institutional prescriptions reach quite deep within their practice. But it is not completely proceduralized in the sense that claims processors can organize their own work flow during the day, something they value highly. Outwardly, their field of negotiability is fairly restricted and closed in the sense that the local meanings they produce have hardly any effect on the organization and its institutional relation with them.

The fields of identification and negotiability are not necessarily congruent. In organizations, many people belong where they have little say and many have a say where they do not belong. Yet the two fields are related. The field of negotiability will affect how communities of practice direct their allegiance. It will affect how their members perceive the scope of their influence and the purview of their contributions. It will therefore affect what they attempt to understand, what problems they try to address, and how they direct their inventiveness. It will affect what they do with the information and resources that are available and what information and resources they seek. Most of all, the field of negotiability will affect what they care about because they can have an effect on it. It will therefore affect how they define their own enterprise in relation to the stated charter of the organization.

Changing the field of negotiability – that is, rendering negotiable things that were not or had not been perceived as negotiable (and vice versa) – changes what we consider to be within our purview. Once something has become negotiable, it expands our identities because it enters the realm of what we can do something about. As a transformation of identity, the learning involved in such changes is profound and cannot easily be undone. Opening and closing, shrinking and expanding, or tightening and loosening a field of negotiability can have more effect on learning than most other kinds of change or program. This is true whether the initiative to modify a field comes from within or outside a given community. Establishing and fine tuning fields of identification and negotiability is therefore a crucial aspect of organizational development.

Questions of the kind derived from this dimension of organizational design include the following.

1) What are the sources of identification that keep an organization together?

2) What are the obstacles to expanding fields of identification?
3) How can an organizational design promote and distribute ownership of meaning?
4) By what processes can a community modify its field of negotiability?

Organization, learning, and practice

In many organizations, learning is the province of the training department, which is often considered an auxiliary function. For the most part, such training functions focus on the delivery of courses that are separated from the communities in which their subject matter is relevant. It is not uncommon for newcomers to spend weeks or months in training classrooms.

In this regard, one would do well to be suspicious of any training scheme that is purely *extractive* in nature. By this I mean schemes that "extract" requirements, descriptions, artifacts, and other elements out of practice, transform them into institutional artifacts (courses, manuals, procedures, and the like), and then redeploy them in reified form, as if they could be uprooted from the specificities and meaningfulness of practice. This kind of extractive training ignores an organization's most valuable learning resource: practice itself.

By contrast, an *integrative* training scheme focuses on practice and seeks "points of leverage" at which design can support learning. Building learning communities and training newcomers are twin goals – not merely compatible, but complementary. When the formation of newcomers is an integral part of the learning of a community of practice, generational encounters engender a process of reflection that serves both newcomers and the community. This approach suggests the following set of general guidelines.

1) Construe learning as a process of participation, whether for newcomers or old-timers.
2) Place the emphasis on learning, rather than teaching, by finding leverage points to build on learning opportunities offered by practice.
3) Engage communities in the design of their practice as a place of learning.
4) Give communities access to the resources they need to negotiate their connections with other practices and their relation with the organization.

Note that the problem does not lie in the use of instructional material, designated settings (like classrooms) for learning, or specialists who focus on training issues. A learning community needs resources to create a rhythm of engagement, imagination, and alignment. For example, if such a community goes into a classroom for a period of intensified reflection, a separate institutionalized setting can create just the discontinuity that is needed for exploring new relations and new possibilities.

Similarly, coming together from a variety of locations for a training session can be an occasion for creating a community among people who might not otherwise have much opportunity to meet. This expanded community, the relationships that are created, and the exchange of experiences may well end up being more significant than the content of any instructional program. The value of an institutionalized setting for learning often resides as much in its community-building potential as in the pedagogical intentions of its curriculum.

The point is not that classroom instruction is to be avoided or that a training function is useless, but that both are to supplement, not substitute for, the learning potential inherent in practice. There is a big difference between organizing classroom training that is supposed to be the totality of the learning event versus seeing classroom time as a resource for the practice of learning communities that are in charge of their learning. With respect to newcomers, it may be better to intersperse moments of information sharing and reflection with moments of peripheral engagement in practice than to "front-load" all the classroom training and call that "learning." The former approach grounds classroom learning in practice as well as involves the community in integrating the growing understanding of newcomers into its practice.

Unlike a training focus, the notion of a learning architecture makes learning concerns into issues of organizational design. It elevates learning from relegation as a secondary function to being the central organizational principle. The purpose, then, is not primarily to design and deliver courses but rather to develop the learning potential of an organization. Toward this end, a learning architecture combines infrastructures of engagement, imagination, and alignment in support of learning communities as defined in Coda II.

Organizational engagement

In terms of organizational engagement, communities of practice are fundamental elements of an architecture of learning.

- First, as people build histories of doing things together, any organization will spawn some communities of practice, even if it makes a habit of indiscriminately tearing them apart. Communities of practice will be there, recognized or not.
- Second, and more importantly, communities of practice are organizational assets that represent investments in mutual engagement. The learning that they embody constitutes the competence of the organization, and the development of communities of practice is essential to developing this competence.[1]

Note that, since they are by nature self-organizing, communities of practice usually have rather modest organizational needs. Encouraging and nurturing them does not require very much in terms of institutional apparatus and organizational resources – places and occasions to congregate, a bit of traveling money, time to do things together, institutional room to take initiatives. That is not to say that they do not require energy, commitment, work, or financial wherewithal to pursue their enterprise; nor is it to say that they are best ignored or left to themselves.[2] But it is to say that they are driven by doing and learning rather than by institutional politics.

Communities of practice: the social fabric of learning

Communities of practice address all four dimensions of design introduced in Chapter 10. With respect to the challenges of organizational design, their importance can be summarized as follows.

- *Negotiation of meaning.* In communities of practice, participation and reification are deeply interwoven into a sustained history of practice, which becomes a resource for continuing this history. Members are therefore particularly well-equipped to engage in the negotiation of meaning. Indeed, little said can signify much, and every action calls upon a wealth of past interpretation and negotiation.
- *Preservation and creation of knowledge.* Because communities of practice are sustained by the negotiation of meaning, they can be attuned to emerging needs and opportunities. They can preserve histories of learning as living practices, not just books and databases. For that reason, they are also the ideal context for ensuring that new generations of members are ready to carry a competence into the future. A characteristic of communities of practice, I argued, is that personal experience and regimes of competence interact closely, and the

tension of that close interaction, if kept alive, is productive of new knowledge.

I have also noted that this productivity can be lost in two ways. Marginalization often separates experience and competence by creating a choice between them (Chapter 9). Conversely, internally focused core membership tends to render them congruent. In either case, the creation of knowledge is impaired. By keeping the tension between experience and competence alive, communities of practice create a dynamic form of continuity that preserves knowledge while keeping it current. They can take care of problems before they are recognized institutionally. It is communities of practice, therefore, that can take responsibility for the preservation of old competencies and the development of new ones, for the continued relevance of artifacts, stories, and routines, for the renewal of concepts and techniques, and for the fine tuning of enterprises to new circumstances.

- *Spreading of information.* The mutual accountability derived from pursuing a joint enterprise and the interpersonal relations built over time together make the sharing of information necessary, relevant, and tailored. As a result, a new piece of information acquired by one member can quickly become everyone's.[3] In communities of practice, information entails communication because it is part of an ongoing process of negotiating meaning. Information travels through a community of practice at a rate, for reasons, and with effects that reflect this process. Communities of practice are thus nodes for the dissemination, interpretation, and use of information. They are nodes of communication. It is therefore often useful to have communities of practice that cut across other types of locality, such as product lines or specific functions, so that knowledge travels naturally across the landscape. For instance, I noted the usefulness of simultaneous membership in communities of practice of coworkers and peers – with complementary and overlapping forms of competence, respectively (Chapter 2). This idea requires multimembership to be elevated to an organizational principle.

- *Home for identities.* A focus on communities of practice does not entail paying less attention to individuals. On the contrary, it places a very specific focus on people, but not people in the abstract. It is commonplace to say that it is people who make the difference in an organization, but it is less commonplace to understand this truism in terms of focusing on what makes us human, on what enables us to make a difference – on the work of negotiating identities inherent in knowledgeability. What we learn with the greatest investment is what enables participation in the communities with which we identify. We function best when the depth of our knowing is steeped in an identity of participation, that is, when we can contribute to shaping the communities that define us as knowers.

Aligning learning with the goal of an organization depends critically on the allegiance of participants. This allegiance in turn depends on the communities of practice in which their engagement and their identities constitute each other. Indeed, the kind of personal investment and social energy required for creative work are not a matter of institutionalized compliance or abstract affiliation; they are a matter of engaging the identities of participants. Because developing an organizational competence has to do with practice, it has to do with communities and identities.[4] In this regard, treating people as members of communities of practice does not mean stereotyping them, but rather honoring the meaningfulness of their participation and valuing their membership as a key to their ability to contribute to the competence of the organization. By offering an institutional home to the communities of practice that are key to its competence, an organization helps sustain the kinds of identity that allow participants to take active responsibility for some aspect of organizational learning.

Communities of practice are organizational assets because they are the social fabric of the learning of organizations. Not being formal entities, however, they are a resource that is easily overlooked. They are important organizational assets whether they are contained within an organization or stretch beyond its boundaries, and whether it is fully or only partially in the context of the organization that they define their enterprises. In some cases, it is precisely their ability to cross institutional lines that makes them crucial. An organization's ability to deepen and renew its learning thus depends on fostering – or at the very least not impeding – the formation, development, and transformation of communities of practice, old and new.

Boundaries

Sustained engagement, I have argued, gives rise to boundaries. These boundaries are a sign that communities of practice are deepening, that their shared histories give rise to significant differences between inside and outside. This is what inevitably happens when serious learning is taking place. From that standpoint, boundaries are inevitable and useful. They define a texture for engaged identities, not vague identities that float at the level of an abstract, unfathomable organization. When communities of practice are considered in a broader context, their boundaries define them as much as their core. Boundaries reflect the fact that people and communities are always engaged in learning and that learning creates bonds. In this sense, boundaries are a sign of depth.

Within an architecture of organizational learning, boundaries of practice are regions worth paying attention to. By focusing on these discontinuities, one can anticipate problems of coordination, understand issues of miscommunication, and come to expect transformations as people and objects travel across the social landscape.

- Focusing on boundaries helps explain unusual events, connections that are and are not made (even when people are in close proximity), and unexpected interpretations of events, actions, statements, or documents.
- Boundaries confront newcomers and outsiders who seek entry into a community – for example, through as simple an experience as the inability to participate in a conversation or an activity.
- At boundaries, things can fall through the cracks – overlooked or devalued because they are not part of any established regime of accountability.
- For the same reason, boundaries can be difficult places to inhabit to the extent that practices focus on their own competence and there is (at the boundary) no regime of competence to assert one's experience as knowledge. They can be places of marginality where separation is maintained in spite of some mutual engagement.

Boundaries are important locations, but not just because they can cause problems. Discontinuities can be as productive as continuities for the negotiation of meaning. Boundaries are like fault lines: they are the locus of volcanic activity. They allow movement, they release tension; they create new mountains; they shake existing structures.

- Because boundaries create new interplays of experience and competence, they are a learning resource in their own right.
- For the same reason, they are the likely locus of the production of radically new knowledge. They are where the unexpected can be expected, where innovative or unorthodox solutions are found, where

serendipity is likely, and where old ideas find new life and new ideas propagate.

• I argued in Chapter 4 that boundaries are also places where new practices often start. Boundary processes create their own histories over time and, in due course, new practices emerge at the boundaries between old ones, and thus new communities take shape. Again, the value of these new practices is not always easy to recognize, because they are at the intersection of multiple regimes of competence yet not clearly within any of them.

As places of coordination and translation activity, boundaries play an important role in structuring the negotiation of meaning in an organization. Like communities of practice, boundaries are places to cultivate in order to foster learning – for instance, through the various types of boundary processes described in Chapter 4.

I have also argued that organizations must learn to recognize the value of people whose multimembership allows them to be brokers across boundaries. Because their usefulness can easily be overlooked – they may not contribute centrally to any specific practice – they are often the first casualties in processes of reorganization. Multimembership is a particularly interesting form of organizational participation because it incorporates boundaries into an identity, and the work of reconciliation involved produces a kind of lived resolution of the boundary. It is therefore a process by which engagement addresses issues of locality and globality.

Depth and fragmentation

It is fairly clear that organizations must be interested in practice in order to get anything done, but it is perhaps less clear why they should be interested in communities of practice. After all, the formation of communities of practice incurs a liability to the extent that their very depth may seem to fragment organizations and therefore be contrary to the goal of forming a broader, coherent configuration. And indeed, communities of practice do create distinct histories, which give rise to boundaries and can thus be a source of fragmentation.

In an organization, the challenge of engagement requires a balancing act between depth and fragmentation. As a learning architecture, an organization does not form by denying, avoiding, or proscribing boundaries. It does not gain coherence through the blending of communities of practice into one amorphous and abstract configuration. The opposite of fragmentation is not homogenization, which is a suspicious form of unity. Who wants blending, anyway? And for what purpose? Blending, somehow, always ends up privileging the perspective of the blade. Rather, organizations become learning architectures by putting boundaries to work and managing them as learning assets.

The notion of boundary does have negative connotations, because boundaries in organizations have traditionally been viewed as reflecting organizational politics that separate groups or pit them against one another. Communities of practice create localities and boundaries that do not primarily reflect organizational politics, but instead reflect and shape organizational learning.[5] When boundaries entail separation and disconnectedness, it may be a good idea to fight them, but when they reflect learning, it becomes necessary to understand their value.

From the perspective of learning, communities of practice and their boundaries are both organizational assets and organizational liabilities, but in complementary ways.

- On the one hand, communities of practice are learning assets through the depth of engagement they develop, but the locality of engagement entails the liability that useful connections beyond the boundaries of any given practice may not be apparent or sought.
- On the other hand, carefully managing boundaries by fostering boundary encounters helps prevent the deepening of communities from evolving into stale inbreeding or a source of excessive fragmentation. Instead, it allows that deepening to create new opportunities for learning.

At the level of engagement, then, the learning architecture of an organization is composed of both communities and boundaries. Enduring communities of practice are a sign of learning. The local depth they produce inevitably creates boundaries, which are therefore also a sign of learning. But then boundaries themselves become learning opportunities, and the richness of boundary processes becomes a sign of learning as well. Such an evolving constellation of practices defines a landscape of continuities and discontinuities that dynamically shape an organization's ability to negotiate meaning. In this landscape, both the continuities created by communities of practice and the discontinuities created by their boundaries are organizational assets – and, like all assets, potential liabilities.

Organizational imagination

When it comes to belonging to an organization, claims processors are rather isolated and focused on their local practice. They have very little to do with colleagues (even within the corporation) who perform the same job elsewhere or use the same computer system, and they do not belong to professional associations or unions. Claims processing is only one link in a broader service process, but claims processors have little connection with the constellation of practices that is defined by the process as a whole. They have very few contacts with other parts of the corporation (sales, underwriting) that serve the same clients, and can therefore show little concern for the total service the company provides to a given client. They know that claims processing is essential to Alinsu's business, but they have little sense of how, as communities of practice, they are part of a constellation that embodies and sustains that competence. They do not even have a sense that their competence, individual and communal, is valued, recognized, and managed as a corporate asset. As a result, they do not engage in a systematic reflection on the nature of the competence to which they contribute, on what is needed to ensure its future development, on what connections to seek inside and outside the company, and on what their own trajectories may be within this context. Because their job fails to capture their imagination, their relation to Alinsu remains mostly distant, passive, and uninspiring.

Because organizations are usually beyond the scope of our engagement, imagination plays an important part in transcending fragmentation, bringing the global into the local and making learning an aspect of organizational life. In fact, the very reification of an organization will trigger imagination, whether the process of building an image of the organization is an informed one or based merely on assumptions.

The decisions of what to reify publicly in an organizational design is therefore a decision about what material will be available for belonging through imagination. In this regard, good candidates are aspects of organizational life that communities of practice do not produce themselves (because such aspects are beyond their purview) but to which they need to have access in order to define their enterprise in an informed way. Their location in broader constellations is one such aspect.

Even in the context of one organization, most communities of practice are tied to a great number of constellations reflecting various connections to the organization and to the world. Part of the practice of a

example of constellation	example of effect on practice
organizational units	defining organizational affiliation, often via forms of institutional accountability
common function	coordinating and optimizing the function across an organization
common customer	understanding and addressing systematically the total service rendered
end-to-end process	improving a production process as a whole by interconnecting practices
critical organizational competence	nurturing and expanding competence, sharing knowledge, inducing newcomers
professional discipline	supporting professional membership and identity
geographical location	taking advantage of proximity and casual encounters
common historical roots	sharing styles and discourses
common interests	organizing the systematic pursuit of interests
use of facilities or tools	sharing tips, participating in design

Figure 11.1. Examples of organizational constellations.

community is to negotiate its place in this nexus of constellations, some of which are institutionalized and some of which are not. Figure 11.1 lists some examples of constellations potentially relevant to an organization and the effects on practice of focusing on such constellations.

Constellations such as those listed in Figure 11.1 represent aspects of organizational practices that demand various degrees of attention, depending on the circumstances. Some of these constellations are contained within an organization and some are not; some are clearly reified institutionally and some are not; but all are candidates for institutionalization if there is a perception that the organization must pay more attention to these aspects. The process of locating practice through institutionalization of constellations serves two purposes.

1) It allows the organization to pay attention to certain aspects of its structure. It is indeed difficult to channel substantial organizational support and resources toward a constellation (and the issue it represents) unless it is somehow reified in the institution.

2) Institutionalizing constellations also allows the constituent communities of practice to understand their part in the constel-

lation and to integrate some responsibility for those aspects into their practices.

Reifying constellations structures the fields of identification and negotiability because it provides new material to locate oneself and opens new issues to negotiation. For example, there are often conflicts and trade-offs between competing concerns; an emphasis on process may conflict with an emphasis on competence. The short-term demands of getting things done may conflict with the long-term requirement of developing competence and keeping the practices of the involved communities up-to-date. If neither process nor competence is institutionally managed in its own right as a constellation of practices, then it is very difficult for participants to resolve possible conflicts in any systematic way or to decide how much energy to invest in each. Again here, multimembership is an organizational principle, but it is construed in terms of constellations rather than single practices, that is, in terms of imagination rather than engagement.

Managing a concern as a constellation of practices – rather than simply a plan of action – involves processes of imagination by which communities can open their fields of identification and negotiability. This entails giving the constellation visibility by creating a social focus – a "downtown," so to speak – so that the communities involved can orient themselves toward the constellation and each other in that context. Not everybody lives downtown, but it is a place of activity and identity that stirs up the suburban imagination. This focus helps organize the ways people move around the constellation: doing things together, having conversations, developing boundary practices, and fashioning personal trajectories. The reification of the constellation then becomes a boundary object around which communities can use their imagination to orient their engagement, reflect on what they are doing, and explore new avenues for organizational participation.

I should reiterate here that by "managing" a concern I do not mean that there necessarily exist distinct structures, practices, and communities of management. I mean only that the concern of interest is reified institutionally by being identified with a constellation of practices and that resources and responsibilities become focused on it. The design of an appropriate managing structure for a given constellation – how much to centralize or specialize managing functions – will vary greatly depending on the nature of the constellation. In particular, institutionalized constellations that are large or dispersed have different requirements than small ones. Similarly, those whose main purpose is to accomplish or produce something specific may well have different management requirements than those whose main purpose is to sustain relations or competence. Whatever the designed structure, however, managing a concern as a constellation means that, through organizational imagination, "management" can become a feature of a whole constellation viewed as an interconnected system of practices, communities, and identities.

Organizational alignment

Institutionalizing constellations is a very different move than devising prescriptions of practice – for example, by proceduralizing a process like the calculation of the COB worksheet (Vignette II, Chapter 9). In fact, the COB worksheet was a facility of alignment in that it allowed claims processors to do what was expected of them; but it ended up squelching the inventiveness and knowledgeability of engagement and obviating the need for imagination. Proceduralized prescriptions align practice with the rest of the organization, but they do so by narrowing the scope of responsibility and localizing the activity. By contrast, the reification of constellations locates the actions of a community of practice in a broader context. Both locating and localizing can promote alignment, but in different ways:

1) *locating* nurtures imagination and expands fields of identification and negotiability in order to give actions a broader scope
2) *localizing* curtails imagination and ignores the knowledgeability of engagement in order to direct actions.

The purpose of localizing is to atomize practices so that each location can make independent decisions. Locating, by contrast, tends to create overlaps in purview among practices so that coordination requires communication and negotiation.

Suppose, for instance, that a company wants to improve the delivery of a service or product. Focusing on the entire process, all the way from order to completion, is a good heuristic. But if the various communities of practice involved are localized by the design and do not form a tight constellation, they can hardly take responsibility for inefficiencies and mistakes whose causes fall outside their narrow purview. Because of this disconnection, the process is very inefficient; and for the same reason, no one is in a position to do anything about it. In such a case, institutionalizing the constellation defined by the process – and supporting the formation of communities around and across it – is likely to yield a more effective way to improve it than reengineering it with yet another institutionally efficient system of localizing procedures.

Localizing decisions is a one-way process of alignment. It privileges the perspectives of those who define procedures and hides the knowledgeability of those who apply them. Privileging certain perspectives and certain forms of knowledgeability can simplify alignment by decreasing the need for negotiation. Yet even when such privileging is necessary, it has to be understood as a cost – it is a trade-off. By skewing the institutional apparatus, discourse, and style toward specific practices, what an organization gains in alignment it loses in engagement and imagination. It gives up some of its ability to combine institutional reification with local participation, to engage the designed with the emergent, to connect the global with the local, and to inspire identification with negotiability. This loss translates into losses in responsiveness to local events, sensitivity to changing conditions, reflectivity, richness of interactions, exchanges of meaningful information, and shared learning. An organization whose design reflects the privileging of certain perspectives and the marginalization of others is always less than itself. By contrast, an organization that functions in a sufficiently coordinated fashion, without excessive recourse to privileging, thrives on intensive negotiation of meaning and is thus likely to be more dynamic and more pervasively creative.

Note that my argument does not imply laissez-faire or an absence of leadership. It is important not to reduce the issue of privileged and marginalized perspectives to hierarchical relations defined through organizational design. Of course, institutional authority is a crucial aspect of negotiability, but the two should not be conflated. There is a difference between assigning institutional decision-making authority versus privileging some perspectives through a design while marginalizing others. For instance, there is a suggestion box in the office, but claims processors never use it – not because they fear or resent the authority of their managers, which they accept readily, but because they do not see the point. They have seen simple suggestions become complicated projects. For them, their knowledgeability as defined in their own terms has no place in the design of the organization. In fact, the suggestion box, in its squarish, lonely, and empty silence, stands as an enduring symbol of the very distance it is supposed to bridge.

A somewhat paradoxical implication of the distinction between the privileging of perspective and institutional authority is that it may not matter that much whether an organization is strongly hierarchical in terms of institutional authority, leadership, and well-defined chains of command. More important are the ways in which the institutional design, discourses, and styles provide resources for negotiating meaning across perspectives.[6] As instruments of alignment, leadership, authority, and policies all have the potential to become resources for negotiating meaning – as much as they can thwart the process. And therein lies the crucial difference.

Contrasting alignment as negotiation of meaning with alignment as institutional abstraction is not a simplistic moral argument against authority or institutionalization. Rather, it is a learning-based argument for participatory kinds of organizational designs focused on resources for the negotiation of meaning. In the end, it is in the opportunities for negotiating meaning creatively that the learning of an organization resides. Learning from this perspective is a very dynamic and systemic process in which mutual alignment continually plays the role of catalyst. This focus on the negotiation of meaning is a focus on the potential for new meanings embedded in an organization. It is a focus not on knowledge as an accumulated commodity – as the ability to repeat the past – but on learning as a social system productive of new meanings.

Chapter 12
Education

Education, in its deepest sense and at whatever age it takes place, concerns the opening of identities – exploring new ways of being that lie beyond our current state. Whereas training aims to create an inbound trajectory targeted at competence in a specific practice, education must strive to open new dimensions for the negotiation of the self. It places students on an outbound trajectory toward a broad field of possible identities. Education is not merely formative – it is transformative.

In this chapter, I will argue that issues of education should be addressed first and foremost in terms of identities and modes of belonging (as discussed in Part II), and only secondarily in terms of skills and information. To make this argument, I will adopt much the same structure as in the previous chapter. Again, I will have two main sections that apply the framework of Chapter 10.

1) I will first use the four dimensions of design introduced there to discuss issues of educational design.
2) I will then use the framework of the three modes of belonging and of learning communities to discuss education as a process of identity transformation.

This discussion assumes neither that education takes place in schools as we know them nor that education is for children. In fact, once education is understood in terms of identity, it may no longer seem such a good idea to front-load "education" at the beginning of a life. Identity formation is a lifelong process whose phases and rhythms change as the world changes. From this perspective, we need to think about education not merely in terms of an initial period of socialization into a culture, but more fundamentally in terms of rhythms by which communities and individuals continually renew themselves. Education thus becomes a mutual developmental process between communities and individuals, one that goes beyond mere socialization. It is an investment

263

of a community in its own future, not as a reproduction of the past through cultural transmission, but as the formation of new identities that can take its history of learning forward.

Dimensions of educational design

To the extent that education involves design, it involves the kinds of issues listed in Chapter 10:

1) *participation and reification* – how much to reify learning, its subject and its object
2) *the designed and the emergent* – the relation between teaching and learning is not one of simple cause and effect
3) *the local and the global* – educational experiences must connect to other experiences
4) *identification and negotiability* – there are multiple perspectives on what an educational design is about: its effect on learning depends on inviting identities of participation.

Each of the following sections introduces a set of trade-offs and questions related to the dimension under consideration, with illustrations drawn mainly from traditional issues of schooling.

Participation and reification: learning as negotiation

One activity traditionally associated with educational design is the codification of knowledge into a reified subject matter, for instance, in the form of a textbook or a curriculum. This kind of educational reification creates an intermediary stage between practices and learners. Common examples are the use of grammatical categories to teach language or the use of word problems to connect mathematics to everyday situations. Because of this additional step, making sense of the reification becomes an additional problem that may not exist in practice. Reification is therefore potentially a hurdle as well as a help to learning. In other words, there is a pedagogical cost to reifying in that it requires additional work – even, possibly, a new practice – to make sense of the reification.

Reifying knowledge for educational purposes offers something visible and fixed for newcomers to vie for in their quest for full membership, but it does not guarantee access to the relevant forms of participation. In fact, by reducing knowing to reified items, the codification of knowledge may create the illusion of a simple, direct, unproblematic relation between individual learners and elements of a subject matter. Reification may seem to lift knowledge out of practice, and thus to obviate the need for (and complexities of) participation. And yet, what the subject matter comes to mean in the lives of learners still depends on the forms of participation available to them.

To the extent that knowledge is reified, decontextualized, or proceduralized, learning can lead to a literal dependence on the reification of the subject matter, and thus (as I argued in Chapter 9) to a brittle kind of understanding with very narrow applicability. This is especially true if the delivery of codified knowledge takes place away from actual practice, with a focus on instructional structure and pedagogical authority that discourages negotiation. As a form of educational design, the reification of knowledge is thus not in itself a guarantee that relevant or applicable learning will take place. In fact, it can be misleading in that evaluation processes reflecting the structure of a reified curriculum are circular. Students with a literal relation to a subject matter can reproduce reified knowledge without attempting to gain some ownership of its meaning. An evaluation process will become more informative regarding the learning that has actually taken place to the extent that its structure does not parallel that of instruction too closely, but instead conforms to the structure of engagement in actual practice and the forms of competence inherent in it.

I am not claiming that the reification of knowledge is harmful. Codifying knowledge is a useful exercise, one whose value as a tool of reflection extends even beyond its pedagogical purpose. My point is that educational design is not primarily about such reification, but more fundamentally about pondering when to reify and when to rely on participation. It is about balancing the production of reificative material with the design of forms of participation that provide entry into a practice and let the practice itself be its own curriculum, as described in Chapter 3.

In this balancing act, the primary focus must be on the negotiation of meaning rather than on the mechanics of information transmission and acquisition. Of course, there are mechanics involved in learning – processes of perception and memory, development of automatisms and skills, accumulation and processing of information, structuring of activities, and changes in behavior. While the mechanics of learning do need to be in place, they need not take center stage or become the primary focus of educational design.

- Focusing on the mechanics of learning at the cost of meanings tends to render learning itself problematic by reifying learning as a process and participants as learners. Learning a new word, for instance, is much more difficult if the purpose is to memorize it in a list rather than include it in meaningful activities.
- In many cases, when the meanings of learning are properly attended to, the mechanics take care of themselves. We learn to speak a language so successfully by immersion in part because we are focused on the experience of meaning rather than on the mechanics of learning.

In practice, it is in the meanings we are able to negotiate through learning that we invest ourselves, and it is those meanings that are the source of the energy required for learning.

Questions of the kind derived from this dimension of educational design include the following.

1) To what degree should the subject matter be reified for educational purposes?
2) What forms of participation are required to give meaning to the subject matter?
3) How much should learning itself be reified as a process?
4) At what point is such reification more a distraction than a help?
5) What forms of participation can be designed that do not require reification of the subject matter beyond what is already part of the practice?

The designed and the emergent: teaching and learning

A focus on teaching is not equivalent to a focus on learning. The two are not even mirror images. In an instructional context, such as a school classroom or a training session, the reification of learning combined with institutional authority can easily create the impression that it is teaching that causes learning. Yet the learning that actually does take place is but a response to the pedagogical intentions of the setting. Instruction does not cause learning; it creates a context in which learning takes place, as do other contexts.

- Learning and teaching are not inherently linked. Much learning takes place without teaching, and indeed much teaching takes place without learning.
- To the extent that teaching and learning are linked in practice, the linkage is one not of cause and effect but of resources and negotiation.

In other words, teaching does not cause learning: what ends up being learned may or may not be what was taught, or more generally what the institutional organization of instruction intended. Learning is an emergent, ongoing process, which may use teaching as one of its many structuring resources. In this regard, teachers and instructional materials become resources for learning in much more complex ways than through their pedagogical intentions, an important theme to which I shall return shortly.[1]

Pedagogical debates traditionally focus on such choices as authority versus freedom, instruction versus discovery, individual versus collaborative learning, or lecturing versus hands-on experience. But the real issue underlying all these debates is the interaction of the planned and the emergent. Teaching must be opportunistic because it cannot control its own effects. Opportunism does not mean laissez-faire. At issue is not authority per se but the extent to which it thwarts the negotiation of meaning. For that matter, laissez-faire, too, can prevent negotiation by offering no proposals around which to organize it. What matters is the interaction of the planned and the emergent – that is, the ability of teaching and learning to interact so as to become structuring resources for each other.

Questions of the kind derived from this dimension of educational design include the following.

1) How can we honor the emergent character of learning?
2) How can we minimize teaching so as to maximize learning?
3) What kind of rhythm and shifts of focus will allow learning and teaching to inform each other?
4) How can we maximize the processes of negotiation of meaning enabled by that interaction?

The local and the global: from practice to practice

To the extent that educational design spawns its own practices, they will tend to have their own localism, their own regimes of competence, and even their own internal generational encounters. That a classroom, for instance, is the result of educational design does not guarantee a wider scope of relevance for what is learned there than what is learned anywhere else. In fact, as I argued in Chapter 4, if school practices become self-contained then they cease to point anywhere beyond themselves. School learning is just learning school.

From that perspective, applying what one has learned in a classroom becomes a matter of moving from one practice to another. In this respect, there is not that much difference between the schoolhouse and the claims processing center. Both are local practices that have specific relations to the rest of the world. That each setting gives rise to local practices does not mean that what both groups learn in their respective practices has no relevance anywhere else. Learning in practice is not necessarily parochial. On the contrary, what participants learn in both settings becomes part of their identities, and is thus carried into other parts of their lives. But what their learning will mean in the broader context of their lives – how it will become knowing that will shape their overall trajectories and their broader experience of the world – is in both cases the same open question.

I started by saying that while training focuses on specific practices, education has a broader scope. Educational design is thus caught in a tension between the local and the global. In this tension, the challenge is to balance the scope of educational experience with the locality of engagement, the need to be detached from practice with the need to be connected to it. The traditional approach to this conundrum is informational: to seek generality in more abstract formulations that have a wider range of applicability and subsume other practices under an overarching, self-contained educational program. But there is a problem with this approach: it confuses abstraction and generality. The ability to apply learning flexibly depends not on abstraction of formulation but on deepening the negotiation of meaning. This in turn depends on engaging identities in the complexity of lived situations. I would argue that the problem of generality is not just an informational question; it is more fundamentally a question of identity, because identity is the vehicle that carries our experiences from context to context.

From this perspective, schools gain relevance not just by the content of their teaching – much of which can be acquired just as well in other circumstances – but by the experiments of identity that students can engage in while there. Consequently, deep transformative experiences that involve new dimensions of identification and negotiability, new forms of membership, multimembership, and ownership of meaning – even in one specific or narrowly defined domain – are likely to be more widely significant in terms of the long-term ramifications of learning than extensive coverage of a broad, but abstractly general, curriculum.

Questions of the kind derived from this dimension of educational design include the following.

1) How can we broaden the scope of coverage without losing the depth of local engagement?

2) How can we create links to other practices so that education does not become self-contained?

3) How can we enable transformative experiences that change students' understanding of themselves as learners and thus their ability to move among practices and learn whatever they need to learn where they are?

Identification and negotiability: identities of participation

An educational design faces issues of identification and negotiability at multiple levels. To the extent that it is a process of colonizing learning, of claiming a territory, of deciding what matters, and of defining success and failure, it is a contested terrain. Like organizational design, it involves a whole constellation of practices, but can differentially privilege the various perspectives of specific communities.

In this context, an educational design competes with other sources of identification and negotiability. One problem of the traditional classroom format is that it is both too disconnected from the world and too uniform to support meaningful forms of identification. It offers unusually little texture to negotiate identities: a teacher sticking out and a flat group of students all learning the same thing at the same time. Competence, thus stripped of its social complexity, means pleasing the teacher, raising your hand first, getting good grades. There is little material with which to fashion identities that are locally differentiated and broadly connected. It is no surprise, then, that the playground tends to become the centerpiece of school life (and of school learning), that the classroom itself becomes a dual world where instruction must compete with message passing, and that some students either seek their identity in subversive behavior or simply refuse to participate.[2]

If an institutional setting for learning does not offer new forms of identification and negotiability – that is, meaningful forms of membership and empowering forms of ownership of meaning – then it will mostly reproduce the communities and economies of meaning outside of it. It will not open new trajectories of participation unless they are already opened somewhere else. Focusing on an institutionalized curriculum without addressing issues of identity thus runs the risk of serving only those who already have an identity of participation with respect to the material in other contexts. Others must be willing to abandon their claim to ownership of meaning, have but a literal relation to information, and live with that kind of identity. In fact, for many students, school presents a choice between a meaningful identity and learning – a choice that creates a conflict between their social and personal lives and their intellectual engagement in school.[3] What appears to be a lack of interest in learning may therefore not reflect a resistance to learning or an inability to learn. On the contrary, it may reflect a genuine thirst for learning of a kind that engages one's identity on a meaningful trajectory and affords some ownership of meaning. To an institution focused on instruction in terms of reified subject matters sequestered from actual practice, this attitude will simply appear as failure to learn.

In terms of learning, identification with or alienation from an institution of learning will have deeper effects than success or failure in acquiring elements of a curriculum. For instance, many claims processors report that their experience of schooling was one of institutional marginalization. But the institutional relations they find at work are not that different. When institutionally marginalized students leave school, taking institutionally marginalized jobs such as claims processing at Alinsu fits in with what they have learned in school. It merely extends the trajectory and institutional identity that schooling has offered them.[4]

Questions of the kind derived from this dimension of educational design include the following.

1) Which sources of identification does an educational design compete with and which does it offer?
2) What broader economies of meaning is it part of? What kinds of economies of meaning does it generate internally? And how are the two articulated?
3) For whom is the design an opportunity to build an identity of participation?
4) Who defines success and failure, and how is this definition negotiated among the parties involved?

Education and identity: a learning architecture

To talk about a learning architecture that addresses some of the issues just raised, I will use the framework introduced in Chapter 10 with infrastructures of engagement, imagination, and alignment. Talking about learning in terms of these modes of belonging makes it possible to consider educational designs not just in terms of the delivery of a curriculum, but more generally in terms of their effects on the formation of identities. Students need:

1) places of engagement
2) materials and experiences with which to build an image of the world and themselves
3) ways of having an effect on the world and making their actions matter.

From this perspective the purpose of educational design is not to appropriate learning and institutionalize it into an engineered process, but to support the formation of learning communities of the kind described in Coda II.

Once learning communities are truly functional and connected to the world in meaningful ways, teaching events can be designed around them as resources to their practices and as opportunities to open up their learning more broadly. Again, there is a profound difference between viewing educational design as the source or cause of learning and viewing it as a resource to a learning community.

Educational engagement

The first requirement of educational design is to offer opportunities for engagement. Learners must be able to invest themselves in communities of practice in the process of approaching a subject matter. Unlike in a classroom, where everyone is learning the same thing, participants in a community of practice contribute in a variety of interdependent ways that become material for building an identity. What they learn is what allows them to contribute to the enterprise of the community and to engage with others around that enterprise. In fact, this is how most learning takes place outside of school, where it is true not only of adults, but also of children: we are all engaged in the pursuit of a socially meaningful enterprise, and our learning is in the service of that engagement. Our communities of practice then become resources for organizing our learning as well as contexts in which to manifest our learning through an identity of participation. What is crucial about this kind of engagement as an educational experience is that identity and learning serve each other.

Rather than mistrusting social relationships and interests, as traditional learning institutions often do, a learning community incorporates them as essential ingredients of learning in order to maximize the engagement of its members. Building complex social relationships around meaningful activities requires genuine practices in which taking charge of learning becomes the enterprise of a community. In terms of infrastructure, this means:

1) activities requiring mutual engagement, both among students and with other people involved
2) challenges and responsibilities that call upon the knowledgeability of students yet encourage them to explore new territories
3) enough continuity for participants to develop shared practices and a long-term commitment to their enterprise and each other.

As stated previously, it is more important for students to have experiences that allow them to take charge of their own learning than to cover a lot of material. A curriculum would then look more like an itinerary of transformative experiences of participation than a list of subject matter. Given enough resources, the practice of a learning community can become rich and complex enough to be the driving force of a complete education.

Educational imagination

It is not enough for education to provide a locus of engagement. If the purpose of education is not simply to prepare students for a specific capability, but rather to give them a sense of the possible trajectories available in various communities, then education must involve imagination in a central way. Students must be enabled to explore who they are, who they are not, who they could be. They must be able to understand where they come from and where they can go. In terms of design, it is necessary to support all three aspects of imagination introduced in Chapter 10.

- *Orientation.* Educational imagination is about locating ourselves – getting a panoramic view of the landscape and of our place in it. It is about other meanings, other places, other times. It is about directions and trajectories. In this sense, it is about identity formation as an expanding image of the world.
- *Reflection.* Educational imagination is about looking at ourselves and our situations with new eyes. It is about taking a distance and seeing the obvious anew. It is about being aware of the multiple ways

we can interpret our lives. In this sense, it is about identity as self-consciousness.

- *Exploration.* Educational imagination is also about not accepting things the way they are, about experimenting and exploring possibilities, reinventing the self, and in the process reinventing the world. It is daring to try on something really different, to open new trajectories, to seek different experiences, and to conceive of different futures. In this sense, it is about identity as a creation.

Of course, television, magazines, books, and the media in general do offer endless material for imagination. It is perhaps precisely because they furnish material for identification through imagination that they are so successful in fascinating us, and that they compete so successfully with schools for the attention of students. But when imagination is anchored in a learning community, it can become part of a lived identity and so become an active rather than passive force. For a learning community, imagination is a way to expand the definition of its enterprise.

One cannot stress enough that these aspects of an infrastructure of imagination are matters of identity, not just of information. Information for its own sake is meaningless; it must capture our identities and expand them. Again – this time in terms of imagination – it is more important for the informational content of an educational experience to be identity-transforming than to be "complete" in some abstract way. This is especially true in a world where it is clearly impossible to know all there is to know, but where identity involves choosing what to know and becoming a person for whom such knowledge is meaningful. Learning is a lifelong process that is not limited to educational settings but *is* limited by the scope of our identities. In this regard, educational designs must aim to launch this broader learning process rather than substitute for it.

Educational alignment

Through local engagement and panoramic imagination, students may gain a good understanding of their situation and still not be able to take charge of their destiny with respect to a broader context. Toward this end, they must have first-hand experience of what it takes to accomplish something on a larger scale. How does one contribute to a broad enterprise? How can local actions add up to large-scale effects? What are the processes of coordination by which various contributors

converge on a joint goal? What are the demands of participation in the
world into which education is meant to lead? How does one have an
effect on such a world? What are the structures of power by which alignment is legislated and enforced? How can one gain some leverage in
that context? How can one enter the various economies of meaning
with a chance of finding a reasonable place in them?

Educational design must engage learning communities in activities
that have consequences beyond their boundaries, so that students may
learn what it takes to become effective in the world. A learning community offers opportunities to explore alignment in a variety of ways.

- *Boundary processes.* A learning community must push its boundaries
  and interact with other communities of practice. But in order to go
  beyond just imagination, these contacts must take place in the course
  of seeking alignment for some meaningful purpose.
- *Experiences of multimembership.* A learning community must articulate participation inside with participation outside. Bringing multiple forms of membership together entails including the necessary
  work of reconciliation into its own practice, and thus expanding its
  own horizon.
- *Styles and discourses of broader constellations.* A learning community
  must become self-conscious about appropriating the styles and discourses of the constellations in which it expects to have effects.
  Science or civic education is as much about discourses of alignment
  as it is about lists of facts or techniques.
- *Institutional participation.* A learning community must be given opportunities to become involved in the institutional arrangements in
  the context of which it defines its enterprise. As I mentioned earlier,
  a large part of institutionalized educational design consists in an apprenticeship in institutional identity.

Problems of alignment cover a range of educational concerns, from
issues of proper spelling to issues of political power. Today more than
ever, issues of alignment are fundamental to education because the
scope of our interdependencies expands at the same time as our societies remain fragmented. To be able to have effects on the world, students must learn to find ways of coordinating multiple perspectives.
This observation is rather commonplace. What is not so widely understood is that this ability is not just a matter of information and skill. It
is not an abstract technical question, nor merely learning the repertoires of multiple practices. Rather, it is a matter of identity – of strad-

dling across boundaries and finding ways of being in the world that can encompass multiple, conflicting perspectives in the course of addressing significant issues. Exercising this sort of identity is a result of participation in a learning community challenged by issues of alignment. It is one of the most critical aspects of education for the kind of world we live in.

Educational resources

I have argued that an educational design does not enable learning by attempting to substitute for the world and be the entire learning event. It cannot be a closed system that shelters a well-engineered but self-contained learning process. On the contrary, it must aim to offer dense connections to communities outside its setting.

If education is understood as fulfilling a different function than preparation for engagement in specific practices, then it may be useful to have specific settings dedicated to it. Such a specialized setting may need to be distinct from other forms of engagement, but it must not be sequestered from them. In order to combine engagement, imagination, and alignment, learning communities cannot be isolated. They must use the world around them as a learning resource and be a learning resource for the world.

There are all sorts of reasons to shelter newcomers from the intensity of actual practice, from the power struggles of full participation, and possibly from the abuses of established members. Similarly, there are all sorts of reasons to shelter old-timers from the naiveté of newcomers and spare them the time and trouble of going over the basics. Still, I argued in Chapter 6 that the generational encounter involves not the mere transmission of a cultural heritage, but the mutual negotiation of identities invested in different historical moments. When old-timers and newcomers are engaged in separate practices, they lose the benefit of their interaction.

This segregation, which is typical of the modern experience of youth, is doubly costly. The young are not given a chance to invest their fresh energy in pushing histories of practice forward, nor is their unbridled naiveté subjected to the accountability inherent in engagement in actual practice.

- On the one hand, newcomers are not directly exposed to the accountability of practice and the lived models of paradigmatic trajectories. Their educational experience is thus impoverished.

- On the other, practices do not benefit from the need for reflection introduced by the generational encounter. Communities are thus deprived of the contributions of potentially the most dynamic, albeit inexperienced, segment of their membership – the segment that has the greatest stake in their future.

In terms of identity, this segregation creates a vacuum. Generational issues of identification and negotiability become resolved in isolation. Local ownership of meaning is not exposed to broader economies. Identification finds material in relationships among newcomers; that is, newcomers are having to invent identities and meanings among themselves. In this context they can try some pretty wild things, but their attempts remain local, self-contained, and without much effect on history. Without mutual engagement and accountability across generations, new identities can be both erratically inventive and historically ineffective.

An important function of educational design is thus to maximize, rather than avoid, interactions among generations in ways that interlock their stakes in histories of practice. As I mentioned earlier, teachers, parents, and other educators constitute learning resources, not only through their pedagogical or institutional roles, but also (and perhaps primarily) through their own membership in relevant communities of practice. In other words, it is not so much by the specific content of their pedagogy as by their status as members that they take part in the generational encounter.

If the pedagogical and institutional functions of educators completely displace their ability to manifest their identities as participants in their communities of practice, they lose their most powerful teaching asset. For instance, in many schools, the separation from mature practice is exacerbated by the roles of teachers as managers of large classrooms. In such a role, teachers do not have much opportunity to act as themselves – as adults and thus as doorways into the adult world. Rather, they constantly have to act as teachers – that is, as representatives of the institution and upholders of curricular demands, with an identity defined by an institutional role. Hence, in terms of forming identities of participation, the organization of schooling tends to offer students very limited contacts with adulthood as a lived identity.

This observation prompts two strategic remarks. First, teachers need to "represent" their communities of practice in educational settings. This type of lived authenticity brings into the subject matter the concerns, sense of purpose, identification, and emotion of participation. It is not, however, something that I have seen emphasized in our schools. Yet for students, it is the kind of access to experience they need in order to feel connected to a subject matter. This principle suggests that being an active practitioner with an authentic form of participation might be one of the most deeply essential requirements for teaching.

Second, it is desirable to increase opportunities for relationships with adults just being adults, while downplaying the institutional aspects of their role as educators. What students need in developing their own identities is contact with a variety of adults who are willing to invite them into their adulthood. By this I do not mean that adults must be role models in a dramatic fashion. The main point is not to be exemplary in any idealized sense – though some authentic ideals can be helpful – but rather to act as members and engage in the learning that membership entails, and then to open forms of mutual engagement that can become an invitation to participation.

Indeed, the mutuality of engagement is a mutuality of learning. I argued in Chapter 3 that it is because practice is a process of interactive learning to start with that it enables newcomers to insert themselves into existing communities. It is the learning of mature members and of their communities that invites the learning of newcomers. As a consequence, it is as learners that we become educators.

If learning is a matter of identity, then identity is itself an educational resource. It can be brought to bear through relations of mutuality to address a paradox of learning: if one needs an identity of participation in order to learn, yet needs to learn in order to acquire an identity of participation, then there seems to be no way to start. Addressing this most fundamental paradox is what, in the last analysis, education is about. In the life-giving power of mutuality lies the miracle of parenthood, the essence of apprenticeship, the secret to the generational encounter, the key to the creation of connections across boundaries of practice: a frail bridge across the abyss, a slight breach of the law, a small gift of undeserved trust – it is almost a theorem of love that we can open our practices and communities to others (newcomers, outsiders), invite them into our own identities of participation, let them be what they are not, and thus start what cannot be started.

Notes

Introduction

1. I am not claiming that a social perspective of the sort proposed here says everything there is to say about learning. It takes for granted the biological, neurophysiological, cultural, linguistic, and historical developments that have made our human experience possible. Nor do I make any sweeping claim that the assumptions that underlie my approach are incompatible with those of other theories. There is no room here to go into very much detail, but for contrast it is useful to mention the themes and pedagogical focus of some other theories in order to sketch the landscape in which this book is situated.

   Learning is a natural concern for students of *neurological* functions.

   - Neurophysiological theories focus on the biological mechanisms of learning. They are informative about physiological limits and rhythms and about issues of stimulation and optimization of memory processes (Edelman 1993; Sylwester 1995).

   Learning has traditionally been the province of *psychological* theories.

   - *Behaviorist* theories focus on behavior modification via stimulus–response pairs and selective reinforcement. Their pedagogical focus is on control and adaptive response. Because they completely ignore issues of meaning, their usefulness lies in cases where addressing issues of social meaning is made impossible or is not relevant, such as automatisms, severe social dysfunctionality, or animal training (Skinner 1974).
   - *Cognitive* theories focus on internal cognitive structures and view learning as transformations in these cognitive structures. Their pedagogical focus is on the processing and transmission of information through communication, explanation, recombination, contrast, inference, and problem solving. They are useful for designing sequences of conceptual material that build upon existing information structures (J. R. Anderson 1983; Wenger 1987; Hutchins 1995).
   - *Constructivist* theories focus on the processes by which learners build their own mental structures when interacting with an environment. Their pedagogical focus is task-oriented. They favor hands-on, self-directed activities oriented toward design and discovery. They are useful for structuring learning environments, such as simulated worlds, so as to afford the construction

of certain conceptual structures through engagement in self-directed tasks (Piaget 1954; Papert 1980).

- *Social learning* theories take social interactions into account, but still from a primarily psychological perspective. They place the emphasis on interpersonal relations involving imitation and modeling, and thus focus on the study of cognitive processes by which observation can become a source of learning. They are useful for understanding the detailed information-processing mechanisms by which social interactions affect behavior (Bandura 1977).

Some theories are moving away from an exclusively psychological approach, but with a different focus from mine.

- *Activity* theories focus on the structure of activities as historically constituted entities. Their pedagogical focus is on bridging the gap between the historical state of an activity and the developmental stage of a person with respect to that activity – for instance, the gap between the current state of a language and a child's ability to speak that language. The purpose is to define a "zone of proximal development" in which learners who receive help can perform an activity they would not be able to perform by themselves (Vygotsky 1934; Wertsch 1985; Engeström 1987).
- *Socialization* theories focus on the acquisition of membership by newcomers within a functionalist framework where acquiring membership is defined as internalizing the norms of a social group (Parsons 1962). As I will argue, there is a subtle difference between imitation or the internalization of norms by individuals and the construction of identities within communities of practice.
- *Organizational* theories concern themselves both with the ways individuals learn in organizational contexts and with the ways in which organizations can be said to learn as organizations. Their pedagogical focus is on organizational systems, structures, and politics and on institutional forms of memory (Argyris and Schön 1978; Senge 1990; Brown 1991; Brown and Duguid 1991; Hock 1995; Leonard-Barton 1995; Nonaka and Takeuchi 1995; Snyder 1996).

2. Lave and Wenger (1991).
3. The roots of social theory go all the way back to Plato's arguments on the nature of a republic. The tradition was continued by European political philosophy. According to sociologist Anthony Giddens, who has done much to establish social theory as a legitimate and coherent intellectual tradition, the roots of the modern version of social theory are to be found in the work of political economist Karl Marx and sociologists Emile Durkheim and Max Weber (Giddens 1971). But social theory is broader than just theoretical sociology. It includes contributions from such other fields as anthropology, geography, history, linguistics, literary criticism, philosophy, political economy, and psychology.
4. Giving primacy to structure yields great analytical power because it seeks to account for a wide variety of instances through a unifying underlying structure. This is, of course, the methodological approach of structuralism (Lévi-Strauss 1958), but a focus on structure over specific actions and actors is also a characteristic of many

approaches that claim no specific allegiance to structuralism (Blau 1975). Even historian Michel Foucault (1966), who distances himself very forcefully from structuralism, ends up giving primacy to historical discourses to the point of questioning the very relevance of individual subjects. Resolving the dichotomy between structure and action is the motivation for Giddens's "structuration" theory, which is based on the idea that structure is both input to and output of human actions, that actions have both intended and unintended consequences, and that actors know a great deal but not everything about the structural ramifications of their actions (Giddens 1984). Though my purpose is not to address directly the theoretical issue of the structure–action controversy, I will work within assumptions similar to Giddens's.

5. Concerns with the situatedness of experience are characteristic of a number of disciplines.

   - In *philosophy*, they are rooted in the phenomenological philosophy of Martin Heidegger (1927), whose writings have been brought to broader audiences through the work of philosopher Hubert Dreyfus (1972, 1991), computer scientists Terry Winograd and Fernando Flores (1986), and psychologist Martin Packer (1985).
   - In *psychology*, ecological approaches explore the implications of a close coupling between organism and environment (Maturana and Varela 1980; Winograd and Flores 1986). From this perspective, the environment is viewed as offering specific "affordances" (i.e., possibilities for actions) for specific organisms (Gibson 1979). Situated in this context, cognition is understood as a process of conceptually mediated and coordinated perception (Clancey 1997).
   - In *education*, John Dewey (1922) views thinking as engagement in action, and Donald Schön (1983) views problem solving as a conversation with the situation.
   - In *sociology*, two schools of thought concern themselves with this issue. One is symbolic interactionism (Blumer 1962), and I would include under this category interactional theories of identity (Mead 1934; Goffman 1959). The other school is ethnomethodology (Garfinkel 1967), which has influenced my theorizing mostly through the work of anthropologists Lucy Suchman (1987), on activity as situated improvisation with plans as resources, and Gitti Jordan (1989), on apprenticeship and interactional analysis, and of sociologist Jack Whalen (1992) on the choreography of conversations.

6. Concerns with issues of practice go all the way back to Karl Marx's use of the notion of "praxis" as the sociohistorical context for a materialist account of consciousness and the making of history (Marx 1844). Since then, concerns with practice have come in a variety of guises as a way to address the constitution of both culture writ large and local activities. My own interest in the concept of practice originated in my work with anthropologist Jean Lave, who had used it as a central argument in her critique of cognitive approaches and her contention that social practice is the key to grasping the actual complexity of human thought as it takes place in real life (Lave 1988; Lave, in preparation). Sociologist/anthropologist Pierre Bourdieu is perhaps the most prominent practice theorist. He uses the concept of practice to counter

purely structuralist or functionalist accounts of culture and to emphasize the generative character of structure by which cultural practices embody class relations (Bourdieu 1972, 1979, 1980). Social critic Michel De Certeau (1984) uses the concept of practice to theorize the everyday as resistance to hegemonic structures, and consumption as carving spaces of local production. Literary critic Stanley Fish (1989) uses the concept of practice to account for the authoritative interpretation of texts in the context of what he calls "interpretive communities." (See also Ortner 1984 for an overview of uses of the concept of practice in anthropology as a way to talk about structure and system without assuming that they have a deterministic effect on action; Chaiklin and Lave 1996 for a collection of perspectives on practice; as well as Turner 1994 for a critique of the use of the concept.) In addition, my understanding of the concept of practice has been influenced by authors who are not avowed practice theorists but whose theories do address related issues. These authors include (in alphabetical order):

1) computer scientist Pelle Ehn (1988) – computer-system design as providing tools for professional practices
2) activity theorist Yrjo Engeström (1987) – developmental perspective on historically constituted activities
3) social critic Jürgen Habermas (1984) – lifeworld as opposed to system as background for a rationality of communication
4) urban geographer Jane Jacobs (1992) – different moral systems governing economic and political practices
5) sociologist of science Bruno Latour (Latour and Woolgar 1979) – science as practice, factuality as mobilization
6) anthropologist Julian Orr (1996) – practice as communal memory through the sharing of stories
7) sociologist of science Leigh Star (1989) – boundary issues, translation, marginality
8) psychologist Lev Vygotsky (1934, 1978) – engagement in social activity as the foundation for high-level cognitive functions
9) social critic Paul Willis (1977, 1981, 1990) – accounts of social reproduction (e.g., social classes) through local cultural production
10) philosopher Ludwig Wittgenstein (1953) – meaning as usage in the "language games" of specific "ways of life."

7. There is a vast literature on identity in the social sciences. While the concept has received much attention in psychology, it has also been explored in social theory as a way of placing the person in a context of mutual constitution between individuals and groups (Strauss 1959; Giddens 1991). Of special relevance to my understanding of issues of identity is the work of other members of the Learning and Identity Initiative at the Institute for Research on Learning. Linguist Penelope Eckert (1989) explores the practices developed by adolescents with respect to social categories as well as the styles by which they construct identities in the context of those practices, particularly regarding issues of class and gender. Linguist Charlotte Linde (1993) views identity as a narrative, a life story that is cast in terms of cultural systems of coherence and that is constantly and interactively reconstructed in the telling. Anthropologist Lindy Sullivan (1993) analyzes the multiple interpretations that

an ethnic community obtains – even internally – thus leading to complex and diverse identities.

8. Ever since the early days of social theory, defining basic types of social configuration and analyzing the source of their cohesion and boundaries have been a central concern. Examples include social classes (Marx 1867); societies and communities (Tönnies 1887); groups formed through mechanical solidarity based on similarity, versus organic solidarity based on complementarity; occupational groups (Durkheim 1893); open and closed groups; interest groups (Weber 1922). From a practice-theoretical tradition, the concept of community of practice focuses on what people do together and on the cultural resources they produce in the process. In different traditions, the following categories are closely related to mine, but with a different focus.

- In *social interactionism*, the theory of social worlds developed by sociologist Anselm Strauss and his colleagues (Strauss 1978; Star 1989) deals with social configurations created by a shared interest: the world of arts, the world of baseball, the world of business. This theory shares my concerns with perspectives, boundaries, and identity, though my emphasis on practice as a source of cohesion places learning at the center of the analysis and results in a more fine-grained approach. (Many social worlds are what I would call constellations of practices; see Chapter 5.) The tradition of social interactionism places its emphasis on social groups and on their interactions in forming societies and places of identities. Membership in social worlds is therefore a matter of affiliation and identity a matter of social categories. By contrast, theories of practice place the emphasis on what people do and how they give meaning to their actions and to the world through everyday engagement. Membership then is a matter of participation and learning, and identity involves ways of relating to the world. With the notion of practice as a point of departure, it becomes necessary to pay attention to mechanisms of belonging beyond affiliation, and salient social categories are only part of the story.
- In *social psychology*, network theory (Wellman and Berkowitz 1988) also addresses a level of informal structure defined in terms of interpersonal relationships. Communities of practice could in fact be viewed as nodes of "strong ties" in interpersonal networks, but again the emphasis is different. What is of interest for me is not so much the nature of interpersonal relationships through which information flows as the nature of what is shared and learned and becomes a source of cohesion – that is, the structure and content of practice.
- In *organizational research*, the perspective of occupational communities is contrasted with that of organizational structure as ways of accounting for the formation of identity in practice. While learning is surely a background concern, these studies focus primarily on issues of occupational self-control, deskilling, and career in relation to employment situations (Van Maanen and Barley 1984).

9. The relation of the subject to the object of its consciousness is an age-old question, which has traditionally been framed as a dyadic relation, but which social theory has endeavored to situate in a social context. The notion of the individual subject has

even been called into question by poststructuralist and feminist attempts to "decenter" the subject – that is, to move away from a self-standing subject as the source of agency and meaning. Poststructuralists decenter the person by giving primacy to historically constituted forms of discourse or semiotic structures, of which the "presence" of the individual is an epiphenomenon. Subjectivity is merely finding a "position" in such a discourse (Foucault 1966, 1971; Derrida 1972; but see Giddens 1979 and Lave et al. 1992 for some constructive critiques). Feminists decenter the person by proposing more encompassing notions of subjectivity (Gilligan 1982) and by reframing classical dichotomies such as public vs. private life and production vs. reproduction (Fraser 1984) or visible vs. invisible work (Daniels 1987; Star 1990b). Two interesting attempts to bring many of these views together are Henriques et al. (1984) and Benhabib (1992).

10. Any attempt to deal with the social world must confront issues of power (Giddens 1984). My attempt to develop a concept of power centered on the notion of identity (Chapter 9) does not directly address the concerns of traditional theories of institutionalized power in economic and political terms – for example, private ownership and class relations (Marx 1867), institutional rationalization (Weber 1922; Lukács 1922; Latour 1986), state apparatus with legitimation of authority and use of force (Parsons 1962; Althusser 1984; Giddens 1995). My own conception is more in line with theories that consider power relations in the symbolic realm: ideology and hegemony (Gramsci 1957); symbolic or cultural capital (Bourdieu 1972, 1979); pervasive forms of discipline sustained by discourses that define knowledge and truth (Foucault 1971, 1980). Of course, the different forms of power in a society interact, sometimes reinforcing each other and sometimes creating spaces of resistance.

11. The social constitution of meaning has been addressed from a variety of perspectives (Lévi-Strauss 1958; Berger and Luckman 1966; Bourdieu 1972; Lave 1988; Eckert and McConnell-Ginet 1992; Gee 1992; Weick 1995). There is also a substantial literature of resistance in anthropology that studies the strategies people use to produce their own meanings under conditions of oppression, especially under colonialism (Comaroff 1985; Ong 1987). A parallel line of work addresses similar issues under various institutional arrangements in capitalist societies – on the street (Whyte 1943; Hebdige 1979; De Certeau 1984), at work (Hochschild 1983; Van Maanen 1991; Orr 1996), and in schools (Willis 1977; Eckert 1989; Mendoza-Denton 1997).

12. All names used in my discussion of the claims processing center are pseudonyms. A more detailed ethnographic description and analysis of this setting can be found in Wenger (1990). My fieldwork lasted about one year. I started by attending training classes, including exams for new recruits and a mock job interview. I then followed my classmates "on the floor," and joined a processing unit as an observer-participant. I processed claims at my own desk and participated in the conversations and social events of the unit. In addition to this direct involvement, I interviewed a number of trainees and claims processors, some individually and some in small groups. Whenever possible, I tried to receive all my information from the same channels as the trainees and processors with whom I was working. Though I tried to have as authentic an experience as possible, I never hid my identity: it was always known to everyone involved that I was a researcher.

The center employed about 200 people, grouped in units of 15 to 25. Claims were submitted by mail. They were received by the clerical department, sorted, and sent down to the processing units to be processed. The claims processors never actually sent benefits to the customers. As they processed a claim, they entered all the information into a computer system. This information was then dispatched to a centralized location, from where checks were sent to customers or service providers. Alinsu's claims processors were not expected to question medical issues. The purpose of processing claims was not to reach a settlement, as in the more complex case of casualty insurance (fire and auto). Rather, the purpose was to assess reasonableness of the medical charges, verify coverage by the patient's plan, and calculate benefits — as quickly as possible.

Modern American practices of medical claims processing are the result of the specific history of health insurance in the United States. Their origins go back to the nineteenth century, when, in the wake of the transformation of the household economy into an economy based on wage labor, some European states initiated various social insurance programs in response to labor unrest and in order to court the allegiance of the working class. Yet, the United States took a different path that led to a largely privatized system. Commercial health insurance was attempted (unsuccessfully at first) as early as the middle of the nineteenth century. A number of fraternal societies and unions had also been offering some forms of coverage. It was not until the beginning of the twentieth century that the debate about how the nation should address the problem of health insurance became a significant public issue, but this debate never led to a national system of the kind adopted by some European countries. Commercial health insurance started to take shape in the 1930s when the success of the early Blue Cross experiments convinced commercial carriers to offer limited forms of medical coverage. From these early days, health insurance developed into a large industry, which — at the time of my study — had grown to provide extensive coverage, the bulk of it through employer-paid group plans of the type administrated by Alinsu. For an accessible account of the history of the medical insurance industry, see the book by sociologist Paul Starr (1982) on the social transformation of American medicine.

Vignette II

1. A government medical insurance plan for the elderly in the United States.

Coda 0

1. This is the distinction between "cultural" and "procedural" transparency I made earlier (Wenger 1990).

Intro I

1. See the end of Chapter 1 for further discussion of the contrast between the tacit and the explicit.
2. In fact, in his studies of professional practices, Donald Schön (1983) argues that a central characteristic of these practices is what he calls *reflection-in-action*.

Chapter 1

1. In this regard, this perspective is distinct from, although not incompatible with, neurological and cognitive approaches that focus on the mechanics underlying the human experience (Edelman 1993; Clancey 1997). For the same reasons, it is also distinct from the field known as "distributed cognition," which tends again to focus on the mechanics of group performance (Hutchins 1995).

2. By "world" I mean the context which is not itself our experience but within which we live and with respect to which our experience is achieved. When I want to emphasize the collective character of our experience, the world is defined in contrast to human beings, but when I refer to specific experiences or events, the world includes other people not directly involved. In this sense, the negotiation of meaning is a characterization of what philosopher Martin Heidegger describes as being-in-the-world (Heidegger 1927; Dreyfus 1991). However, my notion is different in that it is a fundamentally active, productive process. For that reason, it does not assume an abstract notion of being as its point of departure; on the contrary, it produces our being as an experience by making our living in the world meaningful.

3. I would argue that our actions do not achieve their meanings in and of themselves, but rather in the context of a broader process of negotiation. By starting with practice as a context for the negotiation of meaning, I do not assume that activities carry their own meanings. This is one reason that I will not take discrete activities, or even systems of activities, as a fundamental unit of analysis. In this regard, theories based on practice have a different ontological foundation than activity theory (Leont'ev 1981; Wertsch 1985).

4. Even an activity that may seem to be purely interpretive – like reading a book – is a process of negotiation of meaning in this sense: it involves constructing a situation, including imaginary dimensions, in which the reading makes sense. From this standpoint, there is no fundamental difference between an interpretive activity (like reading) and action in the world (like problem solving).

5. This distinction differentiates my approach from functional, cybernetic, or system-theoretical accounts, which might very well grant the status of participant very widely in order to see all actions as part of one total system in which the "actants" (to use Bruno Latour's term) can be either artifacts or people. The appeal of such a view is that the blurring affords a unified account of how the social world functions as a system. Indeed, mechanical artifacts can be made to have direct effects on the world, and in many cases artifacts can be designed to fulfill many of the same functions as human beings, without much practical difference in the final outcome. As long as you are made aware of a fire, so what if it is a smoke alarm that warns you; as long as you get your paycheck, so what if the process that puts the money in your bank account is a chain of actions in which more than half of the links are artifacts. From a functional perspective concerned with specific outcomes, the exact mix of reification and participation in a system may not be a crucial consideration – as long, of course, as the system functions properly, that is, as long as there is no need to renegotiate its design. My purpose is different. I am interested in meaning and in learning, not just in descriptions of functioning systems. Therefore, the mutual ability to negotiate meaning and to recognize an experience of meaning in each other makes a difference among "actants."

6. The concept of reification has been used in a variety of ways in social theory. Giddens (1984) distinguishes between three uses as follows.

   1) The attribution of personified characteristics to objects and social relations, as in animism.
   2) The process by which societies endow social phenomena with thinglike properties. This usage goes back to the work of Karl Marx, who theorized that the exchange value of commodities gives an objectified embodiment to social relations of labor (Marx 1867). (The use of the term "reification" in this sense was rendered systematic in the work of philosopher Georg Lukács 1922). More generally, for Giddens (1979), reification in this sense characterizes the process by which social phenomena appear factual in ways that hide their social production and reproduction.
   3) The ways in which social theorists treat their own concepts as though they were objects in the world.

   My own use of the term does not fall in any of these categories. It is closest to the second, though it is more general and taken not to be an exceptional illusion but rather to be fundamental to the very possibility of human meaning. (Of course, I cannot help acknowledging with a chuckle that in this book I am often guilty of the third usage.)
7. Thanks to Maryalice Jordan-Mash for suggesting this example.
8. In fact, dealing with reification that we have not initiated is typical of life in the modern world. The proliferation of institutional systems of reification is central to what Giddens (1990, 1991) describes as the "extreme reflexivity of late modernity." It is typified by the information-processing functions performed by such service organizations as Alinsu.
9. Thanks to Estee Solomon-Gray, who contributed to the initial conception of this diagram.
10. This is an example discussed by philosopher Michael Polanyi (1983), who has made the contrast between explicit and tacit knowledge a central theme of his work and with whom the contrast is mostly associated. But the distinction has appeared under other names, including propositional vs. nonpropositional knowledge (Johnson 1987), declarative vs. procedural knowledge (J. R. Anderson 1983), and know-how vs. know-that (Dewey 1922). See Coda I for a continuation of this discussion in terms of boundaries between practices.

Chapter 2

1. In this sense, it is related to the idea of a node of "strong ties" in network theory, but with a focus on the practice that is created in the process rather than on the network of relations and the flow of information (Wellman and Berkowitz 1988).
2. Although it would technically be possible for them to work at home, finding new forms of mutual engagement would present a serious organizational challenge.
3. In this sense, the bond of a community of practice is much more complex than what Emile Durkheim calls "mechanical solidarity," which is based on similarity and which, in the evolutionary spirit of his time, he associates with less "evolved" forms of community (Durkheim 1893).

4. In defining "community," Raymond Williams (1976) argues that it is the one term in social discourse that is consistently used with positive connotations.

5. In fact, in his classical studies of social cohesion, Emile Durkheim takes the very concept of crime as evidence of moral solidarity (Durkheim 1893).

6. In his study of flute making, philosopher Scott Cook describes how professional flute makers negotiate the quality of a piece as it passes from hand to hand, making judgments that combine technical and aesthetic criteria. He argues that the development of this shared accountability in their practice is what allows those firms to produce flutes that are consistently the best in the world (Cook 1982; Cook and Yanow 1993).

7. Anthropologist David Moore (1994) argues that the accountability inherent in practice implies an ability to give an account of what one does. But that would place too much emphasis on the reified. There is also a participative aspect to accountability by which the judgment of whether an action contributes to an enterprise does not involve an explicit account of why that is so.

8. A communal regime of accountability can be multilayered, even as it is shared in its full complexity. In his study of corporate management practices, sociologist Robert Jackall (1988) makes a point of showing how a standard of rationality is upheld as a discourse within a practice of expediency and competitiveness. The point is not that rationality is a ruse, but that invoking such standards while being expedient reflects the complex "moral mazes" that managers have to negotiate. In this context, expediency and internal competition are part of the enterprise and, at the same time, something that it is part of the enterprise to deny. Again, sharing a regime of accountability is not tantamount to peaceful collaboration.

9. Scott Cook and John Seely Brown use the word *genre* in this context to refer to anything that is both collective and tacit (Cook and Brown 1996). For myself, here, I stick to the common usage of referring to a class of artifacts or actions similar in style and form.

10. The notion of repertoire typically refers to performances rather than artifacts, but the distinction is not particularly relevant for the negotiation of meaning. The achievement of meaning is always a performance, and a repertoire thus construed certainly includes props.

11. In many versions of activity theory (Wertsch 1981, 1985) and critical psychology (Garner 1986; Holzkamp 1983, 1987), there is a basic distinction between tools and symbols. The argument is that a tool has a more direct relation to its use than a symbol, because the former's meaning derives from its shape and the latter's from convention. From this perspective, the physical sound of a word, for instance, has a more or less arbitrary relation to its meaning, whereas the shape of a tool has a nonarbitrary relation to its possible use(s). (Vygotsky 1934 even argues that a distinctive characteristic of symbols is that they are reversible and so can become instruments of self-control for the user.) Yet tools can be used for purposes other than those intended by the designers. A hammer can be a good paper weight. Moreover, tools (e.g., a powerful computer on one's desk) can also possess symbolic value beyond their instrumental purpose. More generally, the distinction between tool and symbol is not fundamental for my purpose here, because both are given meaning through the same process of negotiation in specific circumstances and within the context of specific practices. Both present a mix of history and ambiguity, of participation and reification.

12. The notion of shared discourse, for instance, is very different from that of belief or presupposition (Turner 1994) or "mental model" (Senge 1990). A discourse reflects an enterprise and the perspective of a community of practice, but it is neither a set belief nor a model of the world that individuals have in their heads. A discourse is a social, interactive resource for constructing statements about the world and coordinating engagement in practice. Here I use the notion of discourse very much in the sense defined by Michel Foucault (1971) and adopted by James Gee (1992) as a characterization of practice. However, as I will insist later, I do not equate discourse and practice.

Chapter 3

1. In her study of life stories, Charlotte Linde (1993) shows the length to which people will go to supply coherence to their life trajectory by reinterpreting past events within the continuity of a narrative of identity. At the same time, she documents the large extent to which the construction of this coherent narrative is an interactive social process, as people negotiate the coherence of their life in the very telling of their story.

2. The philosopher Stephen Turner (1994) proposes that individual *habituation* is a better concept than *practice* as a foundation for a social theory, because habituation can be located and thus taken to be causal with respect to human actions. I suspect that he is interested in a mechanistic explanation and is thus talking about a different enterprise. There is little doubt that habits play a central role in the learning that gives rise to practices. Yet this observation is either obvious but at the wrong level of explanation, or at the right level but uninformative: the level at which the concept of practice does some interesting work, I have claimed, is the negotiation of meaning.

3. In this regard, it is not just an instantiation of an underlying structure. Pierre Bourdieu (1972, 1980), for instance, argues that practices are generated from an underlying structure, which he calls the *habitus*. In my argument, the habitus would be an emerging property of interacting practices rather than their generative infrastructure, with an existence unto itself. This position is closer to Giddens's notion of structuration (Giddens 1984; see note 4 of the Introduction), but with practices as specific contexts for the knowledgeability of actors.

4. In this sense, practice could be said to exhibit "chaotic" characteristics (Goerner 1994). But as I will argue shortly, there are limits to the relevance of physical analogies because people do not merely react to events locally. Rather, they interpret these events in terms of their understanding of history, their picture of the world, and their identity.

5. Fish (1989) argues that continuity in practice arises because not everything changes at once. This is a good point, but not quite sufficient as an explanation. Continuity is not an entirely passive process; it is also a matter of constructing identities.

6. Students of self-organizing systems have noted the generative nature of the "edge of chaos" (Kauffman 1993; Wheatley 1995). The ability to include both structure and dynamism, to walk the line between chaos and order, is a characteristic that makes communities of practice a likely locus of creativity. In this sense, a community of practice has the characteristics of what organizational theorist Dee Hock (1995) calls a "chaordic" organization.

7. These are two assumptions that I have often met in various forms in my conversations with people, especially those who deal with practices other than their own because of management responsibilities or for theorizing purposes. Inherent resistance to change, for instance, is a common assumption in the business literature on organizational transformation. I would submit that communities of practice are more resistant to views of their evolution that are not based on a deep understanding of their practice than to change per se.

8. See Lave and Wenger (1991).

9. This is a subtle point. Stephen Turner, for instance, assumes that practice is a tacit object to be transmitted, and goes on to argue that the impossibility of transmission of such an object invalidates the concept of practice (Turner 1994). In my definition of practice, it is not necessary to account for the reproduction of practice with a separate mechanism, such as transmission, imitation, or even internalization (Vygotsky 1934; Parsons 1962; Bandura 1977). There is not a separate process for the transmission of practice. Because practice is from the start a social process of negotiation and renegotiation, what makes the transition between generations possible is already in the very nature of practice. From this perspective, generational encounters are never simply continuity and never simply discontinuity, but always an interplay of both. Neither are such encounters the mere transmission of a heritage, nor a mere replacement of the old by the new. Rather, they are always the reconstitution of a community of practice around a discontinuity.

Chapter 4

1. In using the term "boundary" I do not subscribe to the contemporary notion that boundaries are harmful and must be avoided. On the contrary, I will argue that boundaries are at once unavoidable, necessary, and useful, even though there may be specific cases when they need to be crossed, rearranged, or even dissolved altogether. (See Chapter 11 for further discussion of this issue in the context of organizations.)

2. See Star (1989) or Star and Griesemer (1989).

3. Bruno Latour sees such traveling by standardized reifications – representational devices he calls "immutable mobiles" – as designed and destined for "centers of calculation" where they are gathered, combined, and rearranged into patterns that afford new perspectives on the world, and thus new forms of power (Latour 1986). The power of codification goes beyond mere claims processing, for instance; once medical diagnoses and procedures are translated into codes, they can be combined through statistical methods to generate new information about diseases and treatments. (For a discussion of the codification of medical information, see Bowker and Star 1995.)

4. This perspective is fundamental to the approach known as "participatory design," as exemplified by the tool perspective of computer scientist Pelle Ehn (1988).

5. She observed interesting dynamics in the process of brokering among school kids. It is often those at the periphery of a group who can introduce outside elements (e.g., new style of music or clothing), since the leaders are too committed to what already holds the group together (Eckert, personal communication).

6. This was gleaned from personal conversations with Robin Karol of the DuPont

Corporation, which by virtue of its business in potentially dangerous chemicals has an extensive and pervasive safety program.

7. Leigh Star notes that many technical design projects succeed because of people she calls "tall thin people" who can follow the design across levels of successive delegation, from conception to implementation (Star 1990a).

8. Bruno Latour uses the term "mobilization" to describe the social processes by which scientific facts and theories become established in scientific circles. In this context, the translation of perspectives is not so much focused on brokering learning as it is on attempts to create broad alliances and mobilize allegiance to a fact or a theory (Latour 1986).

Chapter 5

1. In this respect, the concept of practice is different from that of culture, a concept that has long concerned anthropologists and social theorists – and, more recently, organizational theorists (Ortner 1984; Martin 1992). Practice is much more enterprise-specific and thus community-specific than is culture. If the scope of a community is too wide for mutual engagement in the pursuit of a joint enterprise, then all that is left is the repertoire. Culture then would be a composite repertoire created by the interaction, borrowing, imposing, and brokering among its constituent communities of practice in the context of what I will describe in Part II as an economy of meaning.

2. This geography of practice is what Anselm Strauss (1978) was trying to capture with his notion of "social world." Multiple practices belong to the same social world, and that creates special relations among them. What the notion of constellations of interlocking communities of practice brings into the picture is the structuring character of learning viewed as an engine of practice development.

3. This idea goes back to the concerns expressed by European social theorists regarding industrialization in the nineteenth century, most notably in the work of the German Ferdinand Tönnies and the French Emile Durkheim. Tönnies (1887) talked explicitly about a transition from community (*Gemeinschaft*) to society (*Gesellschaft*) and viewed that transition as threatening social decay. Although Durkheim (1893) did not view the move from "mechanical solidarity" to "organic solidarity" as a form of social disintegration, he did assume that one was progressively replacing the other. Even in the more recent interest in "communitarianism" there is an assumption that globalization inevitably implies a loss of community (Etzioni 1993).

4. Some authors have indeed adopted the position that local tradition is all that can be trusted (e.g., Oakeshott 1933; Lyotard 1984, quoted in Eagleton 1990). These authors share some of the intuitions I am trying to articulate in this book, but they arrive at different conclusions. As will become clearer in Part II, I place the locality of communities of practice within broader structures without assuming that the global or the local is better than the other or that history is a movement from one to the other. What is needed is not a choice between the two but rather a geographical approach to social theory – one that does justice to what David Harvey (1989) calls the "time/space compression" of modernity and to what Michel Foucault (1975) sees as the widening institutionalization of technologies of discipline, on the one hand, and, on the other, to the ability of social practices to carve new spaces, which

Paul Willis (1981) views as loci of cultural production and in which Michel De Certeau (1984) argues that even consumption is a form of production. As political philosopher Seyla Benhabib (1992) argues, the choice between naive absolute universalism and radical postmodern parochialism is a false dichotomy, which she resolves in terms of what she calls "interactive universalism." This resolution entails a search for new kinds of communicative ethics of the sort developed by Jürgen Habermas (1984).

Coda I

1. For myself, the question of what a computer knows was part of what led me to the inquiry that resulted in this book. I wanted to understand how informative computer models could be with respect to human knowledge in the context of instructional systems based on artificial intelligence. This quest led me to explore ideas way beyond my original community of practice in artificial intelligence. Such questions about computers are not so far-fetched, and computer scientists and philosophers do ask them. For instance, the philosopher Hubert Dreyfus has made quite a stir in artificial intelligence (AI) circles by asking questions of this kind and building an argument that the AI project was bound to fail (Dreyfus 1972). His argument is different from mine, based on Heideggerian phenomenology rather than social practice. In fact, I do not argue that the AI program is bound to fail. My point is that the philosophical questions we ask of it – questions about intelligence, knowledge, and learning – are often not well-defined to start with because we do not place them in the context of human practices.

2. Note here that a contrast between experience and competence is not simply parallel to a contrast between individuality and collectivity. An experience of meaning may be a joint experience, and competence is manifested by individual members.

3. Organizational theorists Ikujiro Nonaka and Hirotaka Takeuchi (1995) give, as an example of transformation between tacit and explicit knowledge, the case of an employee of a manufacturer of bread-making machines who had apprenticed herself to a baker in order to understand how good bread was made. She was able to develop concepts about kneading dough that were key to the success of the design of a machine. It is a beautiful analysis, but what it does not highlight is the importance of boundary crossing in bringing about a new view of a practice. As another example, in her study of the computerization of a paper mill, organizational theorist Shoshana Zuboff (1984) distinguishes between what she calls "action-oriented" skills and "intellective" skills. She defines the latter as the ability to give meaning to symbols outside the context of direct, action-oriented perception. And indeed the paper mill workers, who used to dip their hands in the vats to determine the quality of the paper mixture, had difficulty interpreting data about the same mixture on a computer screen. Again, I agree with most of her analysis, but I still think that she tends to overgeneralize the classification between types of knowledge, and thus to individualize capabilities excessively, because she does not focus enough on issues of practice boundaries. Like the COB worksheet for the claims processors, the computer system of the paper mill workers was designed outside their community of practice. Their difficulties thus had to do in a crucial way with straddling boundaries and with conforming procedurally to a view of their practice that they had not constructed.

4. See Cook and Brown (1996) for an argument about the distinction and productive interaction between knowledge and knowing.

5. This observation is common among ethnographers of schooling who venture outside the classroom (Willis 1977; Eckert 1989; Mendoza-Denton 1997).

Intro II

1. These assumptions are found in various, more or less subtle, forms throughout the literature in social theory and political philosophy, as well as in popular culture. They are so pervasive that it would take an entire book just to discuss them and argue each case. For instance, enlightenment philosopher Jean-Jacques Rousseau (1762) assumed that humans are born "good" but are then corrupted by society. Assumptions about the conflict between individual freedom and social constraints can also be found in early writing in social interactionism (Fisher and Strauss 1978). The reverse assumption underlies functionalist theories that conceive of the social in terms of norms to be internalized by individuals as constraints on their behavior, which would otherwise presumably be wild and dangerous (Parsons 1962). More recently, various forms of these assumptions are reflected in the debate between classical liberals (and libertarians) and communitarians, who build their respective political agendas around a polarization of the individual–collective dichotomy (see note 15 of Chapter 9).

Chapter 6

1. From this perspective, the fact that there is no competition for advancement among claims processors – that everybody can advance up to "level 8" without a selective mechanism of competition for a restricted number of positions – may well be a crucial aspect of the job. It creates a collaborative atmosphere in which there is no advantage to hoarding information.

2. Penelope Eckert has made similar observations among different communities of practice in high schools. She distinguishes between the "jocks" who are college-bound and participate in school activities, and the "burnouts" who feel alienated by the school. She notes that the two groups have developed different forms of individuality. When she asked a question like "Do you share your problems with your friends?" the jocks would reply that you would not want people to know you had a problem, whereas the burnouts would say that this is what friends are for. Similarly, burnout girls would find it natural to wear each other's clothes, whereas jock girls thought it was absurd because everybody would know (Eckert 1989). Many claims processors were "burnouts" in school, and there are intriguing parallels between school and work with respect to institutional and interpersonal relations (Eckert and Wenger 1994).

3. The internal logic of a trajectory is an important aspect of the construction of an identity. In her study of life stories, Charlotte Linde (1993) analyzes some of the "systems of coherence" used by people in creating the internal logic of their life narrative. Her study suggests that many of these systems of coherence are popular versions of analytical paradigms, such as psychodynamics, socioeconomic factors, etc. In his analysis of modernity, Anthony Giddens (1991) regards the trajectory of the

self as an increasingly reflexive project. By looking at texts about self-help and therapy, he shows how concerns with the self are becoming explicit, pervasive, institutionalized, and the object of techniques for self-development. The kind of trajectory I am talking about here includes these institutional and technical reifications of the self, but it is not inherently a reflexive project. Nor is identity through participation merely an outdated issue. As mentioned in Chapter 3, even the self-help industry – in its technical approach to the project of the self – has realized the importance of sustained support groups for transformations of identity that are durable and realized in practice.

4. This notion of temporality is close to the Heideggerian notion, but it does not take mortality as its background. Rather, it is defined in much closer relations of mutual engagement with others who are at different moments of their own trajectory. In fact, mortality itself is something we can only become aware of through the death of others. Of course, unlike Heidegger, I am trying neither to address an existential issue nor to place a value judgment on our involvement with the social world as "authentic" being or as a "falling" of our being (Dreyfus 1991).

5. A set of paradigmatic trajectories is different from a specific role model, or from the notion of the "generalized other" used by social theorist George Herbert Mead (1934). Indeed, it involves a community of mutual relations of engagement, and is therefore less specific than a role model but more specific than a generalized other.

6. The point is not, for instance, that continuity is more desirable than discontinuity for the evolution of a practice. Parents who project themselves onto their children and view them merely as a continuation of themselves do not serve their children well. Both continuity and discontinuity have a role to play in the definition of identities across generations and are fundamental to processes of social reproduction (Lave and Wenger 1991).

7. In fact, the inability to bring together various parts of our identities is considered pathological.

Chapter 8

1. The concept of power has been the topic of much interest and debate in social theory. Entering these controversies is beyond the scope of this book. For an explicit discussion of the concept of power in social theory, see Giddens (1984; 1995, Chap. 6).

2. Historian Benedict Anderson (1983) argues that the rise of the newspaper was instrumental in creating the possibility of the modern nation because it enabled readers to see themselves as part of "imagined communities." In fact, I was inspired to think about imagination as a source of community by his use of the term "imagined community" to account for the origins and spread of nationalism. Anderson argues that nations are best understood as imagined communities. Central to his historical account of the birth of these communities is the combination of the invention of print and the rise of capitalism: as printers looked for new markets, they created the production and distribution systems that delivered printed material across vast areas. This wide distribution of common reading material became fodder for imagination, created new connections among people, and gave rise to new possibilities for developing communities based on imagination.

3. See B. Anderson (1983).

4. The success of some organizations in supporting personal transformations can be understood in terms of processes of community formation. For instance, the effectiveness of Alcoholics Anonymous (AA) in promoting the discipline of sobriety can be analyzed in terms of engagement, imagination, and alignment work that link learning, practice, identity, and community. Newcomers spend weeks and months of regular meetings with a local community, rehearsing their life stories under close coaching by old-timers, with the explicit goal of understanding themselves as alcoholics. The purpose of this process is not just to introduce them to a local practice, but to bolster their imagination so they may conceive of their situation as fitting into the characteristics of a broader community. Belonging to a widespread community of recovering alcoholics is expected to give them the courage to align themselves with the organization and to apply its strict regimen of abstention to themselves. From this perspective, only membership in a community with a strong combination of engagement, imagination, and alignment work can sustain the delicate process of staying sober for years. See Cain (n.d.) and Lave and Wenger (1991).

Chapter 9

1. Analyzing this system is beyond the scope of this book. Relevant topics of analysis include: the development of the insurance industry (Starr 1982); automation and the deskilling controversy (Braverman 1974; Barley 1988; and, more specifically in the insurance industry, Attewell 1987); the "pink collar" work force (Kanter 1977; Valli 1985); power as the technology of discipline (Foucault 1975; Zuboff 1984).
2. Note that identification is not merely internalization (Vygotsky 1934; Parsons 1962). Even though identification suggests that we "take in" the world and make it part of our self, this relation remains neither fully internalized nor simply external but instead assumes the ongoing construction of an identity in a social context.
3. It is worth comparing the notion of identification with related notions such as solidarity (Durkheim 1893) or commitments (Farley 1986). Solidarity is a functional necessity of groups viewed as collections of individuals. It is a source of cohesion that reflects a moral choice. Similarly, the commitments that come with participation in communities are moral imperatives. Both solidarity and commitments are aspects of social life that make communities cohere. They may be critical to the success of a community or desirable for promoting harmonious relationships. But identification is a more fundamental process, one which reflects the mutual constitution of participants and social groups and out of which solidarity or commitments may arise. Identification is not a functional requirement of groups that demands a moral stand on the part of individuals. Rather, it is constitutive of our very self. It is not something we do or do not do out of a desire to make our social configurations cohere; it is essential to our very being.
4. Indeed, geographer David Harvey argues that modernity is characterized by a process of time and space compression that enables the development of new social relations and cultural forces (Harvey 1989).
5. On-line communities offer new venues for grass-roots connections (Rheingold 1993), as well as new fields for commercial ventures (Armstrong and Hagel 1996).
6. Giddens (1990, 1995) argues that the social sciences are part of what he calls the *reflexivity* of modernity. In this sense they are different from the natural sciences, because their products are integrated into their very subject of study.

7. Many social theorists use economic metaphors to talk about social relations beyond the production of marketable commodities. Pierre Bourdieu, for instance, talks about "symbolic capital" to describe the power that position, class, education and the resulting style and demeanor confer on a person (Bourdieu 1972, 1979). In general, however, Bourdieu is concerned with the power of elites on a large scale and not so much with localized distributions of power.

8. The distinction between sharing ownership of meaning and sharing meaning itself is important. Note that I have refrained from using the term "sharing" with respect to meaning. The reason is that I think the question of whether meaning is shared is neither decidable nor very interesting in practice. In fact, I would say that it is the wrong kind of question to start with, because it depends on a definition of sameness which is itself undecidable in the abstract. What can be shared is practice and ownership of meaning, that is, the ability to negotiate meaning in given circumstances.

9. In this regard, an economy of meaning may be somewhat different from an economy of goods, though the ownership of many goods also can be shared and collaborative.

10. This is how Stanley Fish defines interpretive authority with respect to literary and legal texts. The authority of an interpretation of such text does not derive from agreeing with the author's, but from having currency with respect to the practices of what he calls an interpretive community (Fish 1989). Ownership of meaning is thus a communal process that gives authority to some interpretations. The currency of these interpretations will change as the economy of meaning formed by this and other interpretive communities brings about new contenders.

11. In fact, organizational theorists Wilfred Drath and Charles Palus (1994) propose to construe leadership as such a process of producing meanings that can be adopted by a community of practice. They contrast this new "participative" definition with more traditional views of leadership as influence or domination. A leader, then, is not so much someone who can manipulate people's motivations or control their behavior as someone who can expand the potential of negotiability for other participants in a community of practice.

12. The use of anthropologist Gregory Bateson's specialized term *double bind* is a bit far-fetched in this very general context (Bateson 1968), but there is an important similarity. Indeed, the kind of identity-based theory of power that I propose views power not just as the use of force, but as the creation of an inescapable tension between what is shared and what is contested.

13. This view is reminiscent of Michel Foucault's view of power and institutional discipline as pervading human interactions (Foucault 1975). But I would say that what his theory misses is a notion of identity and identification to explain why the power of institutional discourses works in the first place. Without such a notion, power seems to be just an intrinsic feature of discourse itself.

14. Penelope Eckert has studied the economies of meaning that preadolescents construct around "being cool" and what she calls "the developmental imperative." The idea is that being more grown-up is a cool thing. As a result, members of preadolescent communities of practice gain popularity, and power, by introducing adolescent behaviors into their cohort. But interest in owning the definition of coolness is not limited to adolescent communities of practice; it is also appropriated by commercial enterprises that view these communities as their market (Eckert, forthcoming).

15. This clarification is important in light of the current debates between communitarians and classical liberals (Benhabib 1992; Etzioni 1993; Holmes 1993). My use of the concept of community is neither a nostalgia for the past nor the basis for a political agenda that is simplistically community-based. As argued by political scientist Stephen Holmes (1993), the social constitution of the individual is so fundamental that it cannot in itself differentiate between political systems. Because belonging and power go together, the political notion of individual rights is a critical construction as a protection against arbitrary exercise of power. In fact, to the extent that sharing ownership of meaning (e.g., distributing power and negotiability) generates community, there is less contradiction between classical liberals and communitarians than their polarized debates would suggest.

Coda II

1. I must again insist that viewing communities of practice as privileged places of learning does not imply that belonging to one is an unqualified boon. Membership is not necessarily a positive, elevating, or empowering process. The word "learning" has positive connotations; it is easier to say that a neighbor is successfully learning to be a physician than to say that a cousin is successfully learning a life of crime on the street. Successful membership in a community of practice implies learning, but whether it is good or bad is a different issue.
2. This kind of reflective practice is what educator Donald Schön (1983) sees as the main characteristic of professional creativity.
3. See for instance Darrouzet et al. (1995).

Synopsis

1. The use of the term "colonization" in this sense is due to Anthony Giddens (1990, 1991), who views modernity as characterized by an obsession with, and an optimism for, what he calls "the colonization of the future." This attempt at human control over both the natural environment and the social world is made systematic by three pervasive processes:

    1) *risk assessment* – an awareness and calculation of risk, which enables an interpretation of the future as manipulable through choices and actions
    2) *reflexivity* – the collection of information about our own situation and the institutionalization of this knowledge into organized systems of expertise and forms of action
    3) *historicity* – the use of history as a basis from which to influence the future and the making of further history.

    Under this definition, the concept of modernity could be construed as referring to "design societies," where devising systematic ways to control our environment has become a generalized concern. In this respect, my discussion of design with regard to learning and practice will highlight some limits of design as a modernist project of colonization and thus temper the project with some cautionary notes of a somewhat postmodernist sort, but without the radical pessimism typical of some forms of postmodernism.

2. The concept of affordance as used here is discussed in Cook and Brown (1996). The term "affordance" comes from ecological psychology, where it refers to the relation of an organism to its environment (Gibson 1979). The combination of the paws of a squirrel and of a tree afford climbing. Similarly, our legs and a staircase afford climbing; we may also be able to climb a steep incline, but with much more difficulty. Designing in practice is providing certain affordances for the negotiation of meaning.

Chapter 10

1. For examples of translations of neurological theories into learning design principles that are actually quite compatible with my conclusions, see the work of Renata and Geoffrey Caine (1994) and Robert Sylwester (1995).
2. Thanks to George Pòr for suggesting this exercise.

Chapter 11

1. If, as organizational theorists C. K. Prahalad and Gary Hamel (1990) suggest, an organization is defined in terms of its "core competencies," then the constellations of communities of practice that embody these competencies are what gives an organization its identity in terms of what it knows how to do as an organization (Snyder 1996).
2. In fact, community-development consultants Juanita Brown and David Isaacs (1995) claim that "celebrating community" is crucial for sustaining the commitments that build communities.
3. This is the aspect captured in network theory by the notion of "strong ties" (Wellman and Berkowitz 1988). A community of practice, however, is more than just a node of interpersonal ties; it reflects a shared history around which these ties are organized.
4. Note that this issue is made more acute by the move away from very stable forms of employment. If an organization cannot guarantee stable employment, it must create allegiance by guaranteeing learning as a path to employability. In this context, membership in some dynamic communities of practice of significance to an employee's professional trajectory may become one of the most important factors in making a job attractive. See Waterman et al. (1994).
5. For a discussion of various types of organizational boundaries in psychological terms, see Hirschhorn and Gilmore (1992).
6. The concept of negotiation used here should not be construed exclusively in terms of organizational machinations. Of course, learning in organizations is inevitably implicated in organizational politics (Argyris and Schön 1978; Senge 1990). But the significance of understanding organizational learning in terms of negotiation runs deeper than just the political climate. We fail to say what we mean not just because we intend to deceive, hide, or manipulate (though often enough we do indeed) and not just because we fear, mistrust or despise (though often enough we may well). But more fundamentally, we fail to say what we mean because what we mean must be negotiated – it is a social process, not just a statement. This is why learning in organizations depends so crucially on opportunities for the negotiation of meaning.

Chapter 12

1. Brown and Duguid (1996) use the evocative phrase "stolen knowledge" to refer to all the knowledge that learners glean from teachers beyond or in spite of their pedagogical intentions.
2. See Eckert (1989) and Willis (1977) for analyses of these complex relations between school learning and identity formation.
3. This choice is in sharp contrast with the lives of professionals and scientists for whom intellectual engagement and participation in social communities are synonymous (Eckert, Goldman, and Wenger 1997).
4. See Eckert and Wenger (1994) for an extended version of this argument.

Bibliography

Althuser, L. (1984). *Essays on Ideology*. London: Verso.

Anderson, B. (1983, reprinted 1991). *Imagined Communities*. London: Verso.

Anderson, J. R. (1983). *The Architecture of Cognition*. Cambridge, MA: Harvard University Press.

Anderson, J. R. (1984). Cognitive psychology and intelligent tutoring. *Proceedings of the Cognitive Science Society Conference* (Boulder, CO). Hillsdale, NJ: Erlbaum, pp. 37–43.

Argyris, C., and Schön, D. A. (1978). *Organization Learning: A Theory of Action Perspective*. Reading, MA: Addison-Wesley.

Armstrong, A., and Hagel, J. (1996). The real value of on-line communities. *Harvard Business Review*, May–June, pp. 134–7.

Attewell, P. (1987). The deskilling controversy. *Work and Occupations* 14: 327–46.

Bandura, A. (1977). *Social Learning Theory*. Englewood Cliffs, NJ: Prentice-Hall.

Barley, S. (1988). Technology, power, and the social organization of work: toward a pragmatic theory of skilling and deskilling. *Research in the Sociology of Organizations* 6: 33–80.

Bateson, G. (1968). A note on the double-bind – 1962. In D. Jackson (ed.), *Communication, Family and Marriage*. Palo Alto, CA: Science and Behavior Books.

Benhabib, S. (1992). *Situating the Self: Gender, Community, and Postmodernism in Contemporary Ethics*. New York: Routledge.

Berger, P., and Luckman, T. (1966). *The Social Construction of Reality*. Garden City, NY: Doubleday.

Blau, P. (ed.) (1975). *Approaches to the Study of Social Structure*. New York: Free Press.

Blumer, H. (1962). *Society as Symbolic Interaction in Human Behavior and Social Process*. Boston: Houghton Mifflin.

Bourdieu, P. (1972, translated 1977). *Outline of a Theory of Practice*. Cambridge University Press.

Bourdieu, P. (1979, translated 1984). *Distinction: A Social Critique of the Judgement of Taste*. Cambridge, MA: Harvard University Press.

Bourdieu, P. (1980, translated 1990). *The Logic of Practice*. Stanford University Press.

Bowker, G., and Star, L. (1995). Knowledge and infrastructure in international information management: problems of classification and coding. In L. Bud-Frierman (ed.), *Information Acumen: The Understanding and Use of Knowledge in Modern Business*. London: Routledge.

301

Braverman, H. (1974). *Labor and Monopoly Capital: The Degradation of Work in the Twentieth Century*. New York: Monthly Review Press.

Brown, J. S. (1991). Research that reinvents the corporation. *Harvard Business Review*, Jan.–Feb., pp. 102–11.

Brown, J. S., and Duguid, P. (1991). Organizational learning and communities of practice: toward a unified view of working, learning, and innovation. *Organization Science* 2: 40–57.

Brown, J. S., and Duguid, P. (1996). Stolen knowledge. In H. McLellan (ed.), *Situated Learning Perspectives*. Englewood Cliffs, NJ: Educational Technology Publications, pp. 47–56.

Brown, J., and Isaacs, D. (1995). Building corporations as communities: the best of both worlds. In K. Gozdz (ed.), *Community Building: Renewing Spirit and Learning in Business*. San Francisco: Sterling and Stone.

Cain, C. (n.d.). Becoming a non-drinking alcoholic: a case study in identity acquisition. Working paper, Department of Anthropology, University of North Carolina, Chapel Hill.

Caine, R., and Caine, G. (1994). *Making Connections: Teaching and the Human Brain*. Reading, MA: Addison-Wesley.

Chaiklin, S., and Lave, J. (eds.) (1996). *Understanding Practice: Perspectives on Activity and Context*. Cambridge University Press.

Clancey, W. (1997). *Situated Cognition: On Human Knowledge and Computer Representations*. Cambridge University Press.

Comaroff, J. (1985). *Body of Power, Spirit of Resistance: The Culture and History of a South African People*. University of Chicago Press.

Cook, S. N. (1982). Part of what judgment is. Doctoral dissertation, Massachusetts Institute of Technology, Cambridge.

Cook, S. N., and Brown, J. S. (1996). Bridging epistemologies: the generative dance between organizational knowledge and organizational knowing. Working paper, Xerox PARC, Palo Alto, CA.

Cook, S. N., and Yanow, D. (1993). Culture and organizational learning. *Journal of Management Inquiry* 2: 373–90.

Daniels, A. K. (1987). Invisible work. *Social Problems* 34: 403–15.

Darrouzet, C., et al. (1995). *Rethinking "Distance" in Distance Learning*. Menlo Park, CA: Institute for Research on Learning.

De Certeau, M. (1984). *The Practice of Everyday Life*. Berkeley: University of California Press.

Derrida, J. (1972). *Marges de la philosophie*. Paris: Editions de Minuit.

Dewey, J. (1922). *Human Nature and Conduct. An Introduction to Social Psychology*. London: Allen and Unwin.

Drath, W., and Palus, C. (1994). *Making Common Sense: Leadership as Meaning-Making in a Community of Practice*. Greensboro, NC: Center for Creative Leadership.

Dreyfus, H. L. (1972, reprinted 1992). *What Computers Still Can't Do: A Critique of Artificial Reason*. Cambridge, MA: MIT Press.

Dreyfus, H. L. (1991). *Being-in-the-World, A Commentary on Heidegger's Being and Time, Division I*. Cambridge, MA: MIT Press.

Durkheim, E. (1893, translated 1984). *The Division of Labor in Society*. New York: Free Press.

Eagleton, T. (1990). *The Ideology of the Aesthetic*. Oxford, UK: Blackwell.

Eckert, P. (1989). *Jocks and Burnouts: Social Categories and Identity in the High School.* New York: Teachers College Press.

Eckert, P. (forthcoming). *Variations as Social Practice.* Oxford, UK: Blackwell.

Eckert, P., and McConnell-Ginet, S. (1992). Think practically and act locally: language and gender as community-based practice. *Annual Review of Anthropology* 21: 461–90.

Eckert, P., and Wenger, E. (1994). Transition from school to work: an apprenticeship in institutional identity. Working paper, Learning and Identity Initiative, Institute for Research on Learning, Menlo Park, CA.

Eckert, P., Goldman, S., and Wenger, E. (1997). The school as a community of engaged learners. Report no. 17.101, Institute for Research on Learning, Menlo Park, CA.

Edelman, G. (1993). *Bright Air, Brilliant Fire: On the Matter of the Mind.* New York: Basic Books.

Ehn, P. (1988). *Work-Oriented Design of Computer Artifacts.* Stockholm: Arbetslivscentrum.

Engeström, Y. (1987). *Learning by Expanding.* Helsinki: Orienta-Konsultit.

Etzioni, A. (1993). *The Spirit of Community: The Reinvention of American Society.* New York: Crown.

Farley, M. (1986). *Personal Commitments.* San Francisco, CA: Harper & Row.

Fish, S. (1989). *Doing What Comes Naturally: Change, Rhetoric, and the Practice of Theory in Literary and Legal Studies.* Durham, NC: Duke University Press.

Fisher, B., and Strauss, A. (1978). Interactionism. In T. Bottomore and R. Nisbet (eds.), *A History of Sociology.* New York: Basic Books.

Foucault, M. (1966, translated 1970). *The Order of Things: An Archaeology of the Human Sciences.* New York: Vintage.

Foucault, M. (1971, translated 1972). *The Archaeology of Knowledge (and the Discourse on Language).* New York: Pantheon.

Foucault, M. (1975, translated 1979). *Discipline and Punish: The Birth of the Prison.* New York: Vintage.

Foucault, M. (1980). *Power/Knowledge: Selected Interviews and Other Writings.* New York: Pantheon.

Fraser, N. (1984). What's critical about critical theory? The case of Habermas and gender. In S. Benhabib and D. Cornell (eds.), *Feminism as Critique: On the Politics of Gender.* Minneapolis: University of Minnesota Press.

Garfinkel, H. (1967). *Studies in Ethnomethodology.* Englewood Cliffs, NJ: Prentice-Hall.

Garner, J. (1986). The political dimension of critical psychology: an elucidation of, and a German–English glossary of, the concepts in foundation of psychology. Diplomarbeit, Free University, Berlin.

Gee, J. P. (1992). *The Social Mind: Language, Ideology, and Social Practice.* New York: Bergin and Garvey.

Gibson, J. (1979). *The Ecological Approach to Visual Perception.* New York: Houghton Mifflin.

Giddens, A. (1971). *Capitalism and Modern Social Theory: An Analysis of the Writings of Marx, Durkheim and Max Weber.* Cambridge University Press.

Giddens, A. (1979). *Central Problems in Social Theory: Action, Structure, and Contradiction in Social Analysis.* Berkeley: University of California Press.

Giddens, A. (1984). *The Constitution of Society.* Berkeley: University of California Press.

Giddens, A. (1990). *The Consequences of Modernity*. Stanford University Press.

Giddens, A. (1991). *Modernity and Self-Identity: Self and Society in the Late Modern Age*. Stanford University Press.

Giddens, A. (1995). *Politics, Sociology and Social Theory: Encounters with Classical and Contemporary Social Thought*. Stanford University Press.

Gilligan, C. (1982). *In a Different Voice: Psychological Theory and Women's Development*. Cambridge, MA: Harvard University Press.

Goerner, S. (1994). *Chaos and the Evolving Ecological Universe*. Luxembourg: Gordon & Breach.

Goffman, E. (1959). *The Presentation of Self in Everyday Life*. Garden City, NY: Doubleday.

Gramsci, A. (1957). *The Modern Prince and Other Writings*. New York: International.

Habermas, J. (1984). *The Theory of Communicative Action*. Boston: Beacon.

Harvey, D. (1989). *The Condition of Postmodernity*. Oxford, UK: Blackwell.

Hebdige, D. (1979). *Subculture: The Meaning of Style*. London: Routledge.

Heidegger, M. (1927, translated 1962). *Being and Time*. New York: Harper & Row.

Henriques, J., Hollway, W., Urwin, C., Venn, C., and Walkerdine, V. (1984). *Changing the Subject: Psychology, Social Regulation and Subjectivity*. London: Methuen.

Hirschhorn, L., and Gilmore, T. (1992). The new boundaries of the "boundariless" company. *Harvard Business Review*, May–June, pp. 104–15.

Hochschild, A. R. (1983). *The Managed Heart: Commercialization of Human Feeling*. Berkeley: University of California Press.

Hock, D. W. (1995). The chaordic century: the rise of enabling organizations. Governors State University Consortium and The South Metropolitan College/University Consortium, University Park, IL.

Holmes, S. (1993). *The Anatomy of Antiliberalism*. Cambridge, MA: Harvard University Press.

Holzkamp, K. (1983). *Grundlegung der Psychologie*. Frankfurt: Campus.

Holzkamp, K. (1987). Critical psychology and overcoming of scientific indeterminacy in psychological theorizing. In R. Hogan and W. H. Jones (eds.), *Perspectives in Personality*. Greenwich, CT: JAI Press.

Hutchins, E. (1995). *Cognition in the Wild*. Cambridge, MA: MIT Press.

Jackall, R. (1988). *Moral Mazes: The World of Corporate Managers*. Oxford University Press.

Jacobs, J. (1992). *Systems of Survival: A Dialogue on the Moral Foundations of Commerce and Politics*. New York: Random House.

Johnson, M. (1987). *The Body in the Mind: The Bodily Basis of Meaning, Imagination, and Reason*. Chicago University Press.

Jordan, B. (1989). Cosmopolitan obstetrics: some insights from the training of traditional midwives. *Social Science and Medicine* 28: 925–44.

Kanter, R. M. (1977). *Men and Women of the Corporation*. New York: Basic Books.

Kauffman, S. (1993). *The Origins of Order: Self-Organization and Selection in Evolution*. Oxford University Press.

Latour, B. (1986). Visualization and cognition: thinking with eyes and hands. *Knowledge and Society* 6: 1–40.

Latour, B., and Woolgar, S. (1979). *Laboratory Life: The Social Construction of Scientific Facts*. Beverly Hills, CA: Sage.

Lave, J. (1988). *Cognition in Practice*. Cambridge University Press.

Lave, J. (in preparation). *Tailors Apprenticeship: The Political Relations of Everyday Life and Learning*. Cambridge University Press.

Lave, J., and Wenger, E. (1991). *Situated Learning: Legitimate Peripheral Participation*. Cambridge University Press.

Lave, J., Duguid, P., Fernandez, N., and Axel, E. (1992). Coming of age in Birmingham: cultural studies and conceptions of subjectivity. *Annual Reviews in Anthropology* 21: 257–82.

Leonard-Barton, D. (1995). *Wellsprings of Knowledge: Building and Sustaining the Sources of Innovation*. Boston: Harvard Business School Press.

Leont'ev, A. N. (1981). The problem of activity in psychology. In J. Wertsch (ed.), *The Concept of Activity in Soviet Psychology*. Armonk, NY: M. E. Sharpe.

Lévi-Strauss, C. (1958, translated 1963). *Structural Anthropology*. New York: Basic Books.

Linde, C. (1993). *Life Stories: The Creation of Coherence*. New York: Oxford University Press.

Lukács, G. (1922, translated 1971). *History and Class Consciousness: Studies in Marxist Dialectics*. Cambridge, MA: MIT Press.

Lyotard, J.-F. (1984). *The Postmodern Condition: A Report on Knowledge*. Minneapolis: University of Minnesota Press.

Martin, J. (1992). *Cultures in Organizations: Three Perspectives*. Stanford University Press.

Marx, K. (1844). *The Economic and Philosophic Manuscripts of 1844*. New York: International.

Marx, K. (1967). *Capital: A Critique of Political Economy*. New York: International.

Maturana, H. R., and Varela, F. (1980). *Autopoiesis and Cognition: The Realization of the Living*. Dordrecht: Reidel.

Mead, G. H. (1934). *Mind, Self and Society*. University of Chicago Press.

Mendoza-Denton, N. (1997). Chicana/Mexicana: identity and linguistic variation. Doctoral dissertation, Department of Linguistics, Stanford University.

Moore, D. (1994). On the idea of community of practice. Working paper, Nynex Science and Technology, White Plains, NY.

Nonaka, I., and Takeuchi, H. (1995). *The Knowledge-Creating Company*. New York: Oxford University Press.

Oakeshott, M. (1933, reprinted 1971). *Experience and Its Modes*. Oxford, UK: Blackwell.

Ong, A. (1987). *Spirits of Resistance and Capitalist Discipline: Factory Women in Malaysia*. Albany: State University of New York Press.

Orr, J. (1996). *Talking about Machines: An Ethnography of a Modern Job*. Ithaca, NY: Cornell University Press.

Ortner, S. B. (1984). Theory in anthropology since the sixties. *Comparative Studies in Society and History* 26: 126–66.

Packer, M. (1985). Hermeneutic inquiry into the study of human conduct. *American Psychologist* 40: 1081–93.

Papert, S. (1980). *Mindstorm*. New York: Basic Books.

Parsons, T. (1962). *The Structure of Social Action*. New York: Free Press.

Piaget, J. (1954). *The Construction of Reality in the Child*. New York: Basic Books.

Polanyi, M. (1983). *The Tacit Dimension.* Magnolia, MA: Peter Smith.

Prahalad, C. K., and Hamel, G. (1990). The core competencies of the corporation. *Harvard Business Review* 68: 79–91.

Rheingold, H. (1993). *The Virtual Community: Homesteading on the Electronic Frontier.* New York: Harper Perennial.

Rousseau, J.-J. (1762, reprinted 1964). *Emile, ou, de l'éducation.* Paris: Garnier Freres.

Schön, D. A. (1983). *The Reflective Practitioner: How Professionals Think in Action.* New York: Basic Books.

Senge, P. M. (1990). *The Fifth Discipline: The Art and Practice of the Learning Organization.* New York: Doubleday.

Skinner, B. F. (1974). *About Behaviorism.* New York: Knopf.

Snyder, W. (1996). Organization, learning and performance: an exploration of the linkages between organization learning, knowledge, and performance. Doctoral dissertation, University of Southern California, Los Angeles.

Star, S. L. (1989). The structure of ill-structured solutions: boundary objects and heterogeneous distributed problem solving. Working paper, Department of Information and Computer Science, University of California, Irvine.

Star, S. L. (1990a). Layered space, formal representations and long-distance control: the politics of information. Working paper, Department of Information and Computer Science, University of California, Irvine.

Star, S. L. (1990b). The sociology of the invisible: the primacy of work in the writing of Anselm Strauss. Working paper, Department of Information and Computer Science, University of California, Irvine.

Star, S. L., and Griesemer, J. (1989). Institutional ecology, "translations" and boundary objects: amateurs and professionals in Berkeley's museum of vertebrate zoology, 1907–1939. In *Social Studies of Science,* vol. 19. London: Sage, pp. 387–420.

Starr, P. (1982). *The Social Transformation of American Medicine: The Rise of a Sovereign Profession and the Making of a Vast Industry.* New York: Basic Books.

Strauss, A. (1959). *Mirrors and Masks: The Search for Identity.* Glencoe, IL: Free Press.

Strauss, A. (1978). A social world perspective. *Studies in Symbolic Interaction* 1: 119–28.

Suchman, L. (1987). *Plans and Situated Actions: The Problem of Human–Machine Interaction.* Cambridge University Press.

Sullivan, L. (1993). Imagining communities, imagining selves: constructing Japanese Americanness in a San Joaquin Valley city. Doctoral dissertation, University of California, Irvine.

Sylwester, R. (1995). A celebration of neurons: an educator's guide to the human brain. Association for Supervision and Curriculum Development, Alexandria, VA.

Tönnies, F. (1887, translated 1957). *Gemeinschaft und Gesellschaft* [*Community and Society*]. East Lansing: Michigan State University Press.

Turner, S. (1994). *The Social Theory of Practices: Tradition, Tacit Knowledge, and Presuppositions.* University of Chicago Press.

Valli, L. (1985). Becoming clerical workers: business education and the culture of femininity. In M. Apple and L. Weis (eds.), *Ideology and Practice in Schooling.* Philadelphia: Temple University Press.

Van Maanen, J. (1991). The smile factory: work at Disneyland. In P. Frost, L. Moore, M. Louis, C. Lundberg, and J. Martin (eds.), *Reframing Organizational Culture.* Newbury Park, CA: Sage.

Van Maanen, J., and Barley, S. (1984). Occupational communities: culture and control in organizations. *Research in Organizational Behavior* 6: 287–365.

Vygotsky, L. S. (1934). *Thought and Language.* Cambridge, MA: MIT Press.

Vygotsky, L. S. (1978). *Mind and Society: The Development of Higher Psychological Processes.* Cambridge, MA: Harvard University Press.

Waterman, R., Waterman, J., and Collard, B. (1994). Toward a career-resilient workforce. *Harvard Business Review* 72: 87–95.

Weber, M. (1922, translated 1978). *Wirtschaft und Gesellschaft* [*Economy and Society*]. Berkeley: University of California Press.

Weick, K. (1995). *Sensemaking in Organizations.* Thousand Oaks, CA: Sage.

Wellman, B., and Berkowitz, S. D. (1988). *Social Structures: A Network Approach.* Cambridge University Press.

Wenger, E. (1987). *Artificial Intelligence and Tutoring Systems: Computational and Cognitive Approaches to the Communication of Knowledge.* San Francisco: Morgan Kaufmann.

Wenger, E. (1990). Toward a theory of cultural transparency: elements of a discourse of the visible and the invisible. Doctoral dissertation, Information and Computer Science, University of California, Irvine.

Wertsch, J. (1981). *The Concept of Activity in Soviet Psychology.* Armonk, NY: M. E. Sharpe.

Wertsch, J. (1985). *Vygotsky and the Social Formation of Mind.* Cambridge, MA: Harvard University Press.

Whalen, J. (1992). Conversation analysis. In E. F. Borgatta and M. L. Borgatta (eds.), *The Encyclopedia of Sociology.* New York: Macmillan, pp. 303–10.

Wheatley, M. (1995). *Leadership and the New Science: Learning about Organization from an Orderly Universe.* San Francisco: Berrett-Koehler.

Whyte, W. (1943). *Street Corner Society: The Social Structure of an Italian Slum.* University of Chicago Press.

Williams, R. (1976). *Keywords: A Vocabulary of Culture and Society.* New York: Oxford University Press.

Willis, P. (1977). *Learning to Labor: How Working Class Kids Get Working Class Jobs.* New York: Columbia University Press.

Willis, P. (1981). Cultural production is different from cultural reproduction is different from social reproduction is different from reproduction. *Interchange* 12: 48–67.

Willis, P. (1990). *Common Culture.* Boulder, CO: Westview.

Winograd, T., and Flores, F. (1986). *Understanding Computers and Cognition: A New Foundation for Design.* Norwood, NJ: Ablex.

Wittgenstein, L. (1953). *Philosophical Investigations.* Oxford, UK: Blackwell.

Zuboff, S. (1984). *In the Age of the Smart Machine: The Future of Work and Power.* New York: Basic Books.

Index

abstraction, 107
versus concrete, 47–8
institutional, 247, 256, 262
versus practice, 73, 124, 136, 145
as reification, 58, 59, 67, 132
see also generality
access
to information, 166, 175, 200, 204, 206, 210, 220
to practice, **100–1**, 117, 120, 157, 173, 184, 185, 237
see also peripherality
accountability
to discourses, 57, 141
institutional, 229, 245
in practice, **81**, 137, 152, 160, 185, 232, 238, 252, 254, **288**
regime of, **115–16**, 175, 240, 275, 288
see also negotiability
action
as level of analysis, 13, 125
as negotiation of meaning, **53–4**, 59
see also negotiation of meaning
activity theory, 280, 282, 286, 288
adolescence, 163, 275–6, 290, 293, 296
adoption of meaning, 202–3, 210
adults as models, 276–7
affiliation, 162, 242, 253, 283
affinity, 14, 195, 210
affordance, 229, 231–2, 298
agency, 12, 13, 15, 284
aggregation, level of, 208–9, 211
Alcoholics Anonymous, 295
alienation, 201–2, 204–5, 220, 243
see also non-participation
alignment, **178–81**, 186–7, 189, 209
and design, 238–9, 240, 260–2, 273–5
and identity, 195–7, 205–6
and learning, 217–18, 228
see also discourse; energy, social

Alinsu, **16**, 45, 55, 79, 98, 124, 241
allegiance, 181, 191, 216, 229, 248
versus compliance, 196–7, 235, 253
Althusser, Louis, 284
ambiguity, **83–4**, 218
of reification, 64, 110–12, 232
analysis (*see* level of analysis)
Anderson, Benedict, 294
Anderson, John R., 279, 287
anthropology, 12, 204, 280, 284, 291
apprenticeship, 11, **100–2**, 238, 274, 277
appropriation, **201–2**, 203, 204, 205, 208, 210
architecture, conceptual, 230–1
see also learning
Argyris, Chris, 280, 298
Ariel, **16**, 18–34
Armstrong, Arthur, 295
artifact (*see* reification)
assumption of meaningfulness, 185, **204–5**
Attewell, Paul, 295
authority, 239, 240, 261
see also negotiability

Bach, Johann Sebastian, 67
Bandura, Albert, 280, 290
Barley, Steve, 283, 295
Bateson, Gregory, 296
behaviorist theories, 279
belief, shared, 84, **289**
see also perspective
belonging, 208–9
modes of, **173–81**, 209, 217–18, 236–240, 283
Benhabib, Seyla, 284, 292, 297
Berger, Peter, 284
Berkowitz, Stephen, 283, 287, 298
bicycle riding, 69, 140
Blau, Peter, 281
Blumer, Herbert, 281

309